Fields of Battle

Fields of Battle

Retracing Ancient Battlefields

Richard Evans

Pen & Sword
MILITARY

First published in Great Britain in 2015 by
Pen & Sword Military
an imprint of
Pen & Sword Books Ltd
47 Church Street
Barnsley
South Yorkshire
S70 2AS

ISBN 978 1 84884 796 5

A CIP catalogue record for this book is available from the British
Library

Typeset in Ehrhardt by
Mac Style Ltd, Bridlington, East Yorkshire
Printed and bound in the UK by CPI Group (UK) Ltd,
Croydon, CRO 4YY

Pen & Sword Books Ltd incorporates the imprints of Pen & Sword
Archaeology, Atlas, Aviation, Battleground, Discovery, Family
History, History, Maritime, Military, Naval, Politics, Railways,
Select, Social History, Transport, True Crime, and Claymore Press,
Frontline Books, Leo Cooper, Praetorian Press, Remember When,
Seaforth Publishing and Wharncliffe.

For a complete list of Pen & Sword titles please contact
PEN & SWORD BOOKS LIMITED
47 Church Street, Barnsley, South Yorkshire, S70 2AS, England
E-mail: enquiries@pen-and-sword.co.uk
Website: www.pen-and-sword.co.uk

Contents

Acknowledgements

Ishould like to thank Dr Martine de Marre, Professor Philip Bosman and Professor Rosemary Moeketsi (Executive Dean of the College of Humanities, UNISA) who have all been colleagues and friends for many years for their kindness, support and valuable encouragement in making this volume possible. Through their efforts and support I was able to obtain a research grant from the University of South Africa, Pretoria, which has allowed the time to engage fully with the topics dealt with in the following pages and so considerably eased the process of completion of the project.

I should also like to record a special word of thanks to the team at Pen & Sword: Matt Jones, Ting Baker, and Phil Sidnell for their constant professional advice and acute insights, which have proved invaluable in bringing this project to a successful conclusion.

Abbreviations

Standard abbreviations are applied throughout this work for ancient authors cited in the text and in the footnotes. Modern works are referenced by surname and date alone but are fully referenced in the bibliography at the end of the volume.

The translations of the ancient texts and any inaccuracies in these or indeed elsewhere in the following pages are solely my responsibility.

Maps

Plates

1. Halicarnassus (modern Bodrum) birthplace of Herodotus
2. The Temple of Apollo at Didyma
3. The River Meander below Miletus (centre distance)
4. View of the acropolis at Miletus from the Meander River
5. Theatre at Miletus from the harbour, now silted up
6. View from the theatre at Miletus towards Lade (top right)
7. View from Miletus looking north across the Gulf of Latmos
8. View from Priene south across the Latmian Gulf, now silted up
9. Acropolis of Sardis from the Temple of Artemis outside the city walls
10. The fortifications at Eretria
11. View of southern Euboea from Rhamnous
12. View of the plain of Marathon from Rhamnous
13. The tumulus at Marathon in honour of the 192 Athenian dead
14. The plain of Marathon today
15. Plataea with Mount Parnassus in the background
16. Thermoplyae and the Gulf of Lamia today
17. General view of Delphi with the valley of the Pleistos River in the background
18. The Temple of Apollo at Delphi
19. Fissures in the rocks above the stadium at Delphi
20. Shrine of Athena Pronaia ('Athena before the sanctuary [of Apollo]')
21. Crossing from Oropus to Eretria
22. View north along the Gulf of Leon from above Collioure
23. Pyrenees from Agèle sur Mer (Caesar's route to Ilerda)
24. The River Segre (Sicoris) at Ilerda (Lleida) in spate (June 2013)
25. River crossing on the Segre submerged (June 2013). Caesar's camp lay in this vicinity on the north bank of the river.
26. The acropolis at Ilerda (Lleida) from the hills beyond the south bank of the Segre (Caesar *BC* 1.65)
27. Dry farming land on the south bank of the Segre (June 2013)
28. Tarraco (Cathedral of Tarragona)
29. The aqueduct at Tarraco (Tarragona)

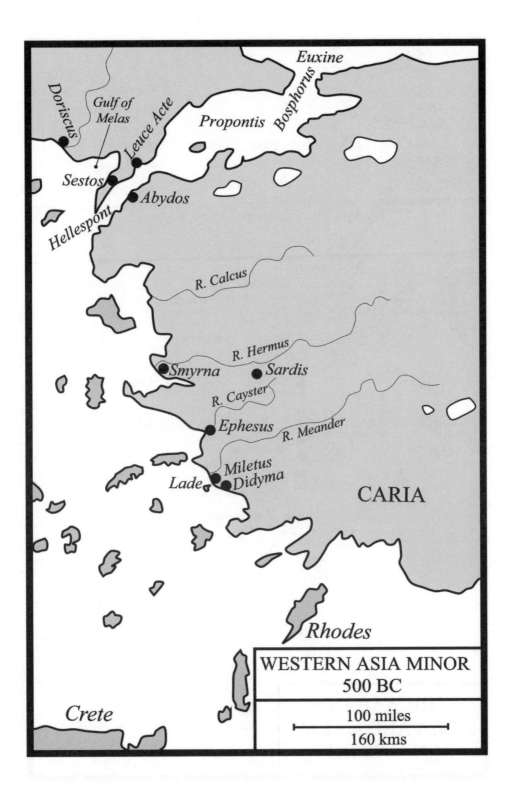

Doriscus

Gulf of Melas

Leuce Acte

Euxine

Bosphorus

Propontis

Sestos

Abydos

Hellespont

R. Calcus

R. Hermus

Smyrna

Sardis

R. Cayster

Ephesus

R. Meander

Miletus

Lade

Didyma

CARIA

Rhodes

Crete

WESTERN ASIA MINOR
500 BC

100 miles

160 kms

● Troy

LESBOS

Mytilene

● Phocaea

R. Hermus

● Sardis

CHIOS

Smyrna

● Hypaepa

R. Cayster

ICARIAN SEA

SAMOS

Ephesus

R. Meander

● Alabanda

Mt. Mycale

Priene

ICARUS

LADE ○

● Myus

Miletus

Alinda

Didyma

● Mylasa

● Cindya

● Pedasa

Halicarnassus

RHODES

THE WAR IN
IONIA AND CARIA
499 - 493 BC

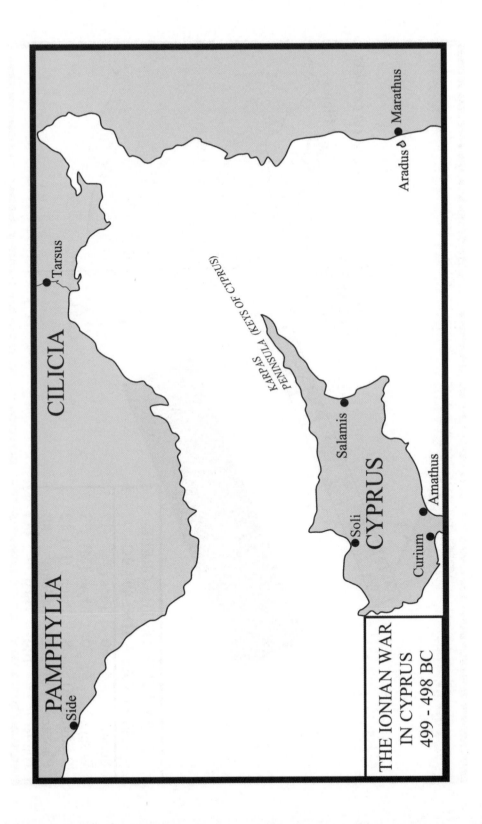

PAMPHYLIA

Side

CILICIA

Tarsus

Marathus

Aradus

KARPAS (KEYS OF CYPRUS)
PENINSULA

Salamis

Amathus

CYPRUS

Soli

Curium

THE IONIAN WAR
IN CYPRUS
499 - 498 BC

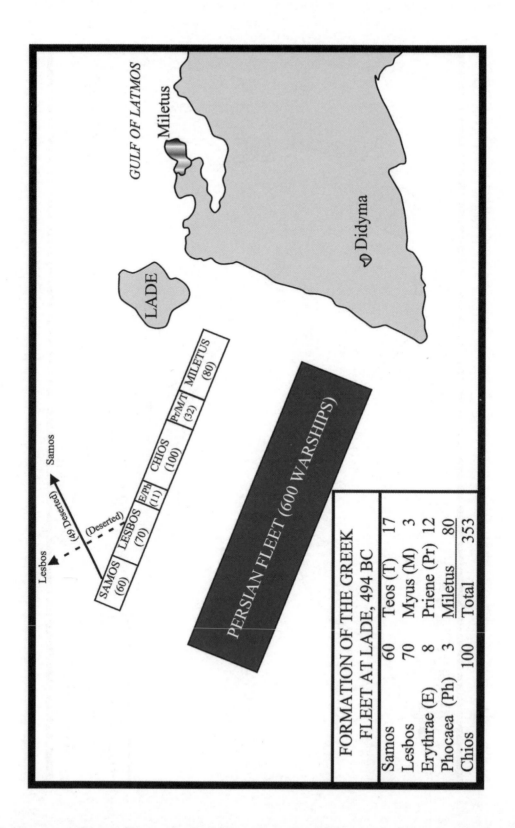

GULF OF LATMOS

Miletus

Didyma

LADE

Samos

Lesbos

(49 Deserted)

(Deserted)

| SAMOS (60) | LESBOS (70) | E/Ph (11) | CHIOS (100) | Pr/M/T (32) | MILETUS (80) |

PERSIAN FLEET (600 WARSHIPS)

FORMATION OF THE GREEK
FLEET AT LADE, 494 BC

Samos	60	Teos (T)	17
Lesbos	70	Myus (M)	3
Erythrae (E)	8	Priene (Pr)	12
Phocaea (Ph)	3	Miletus	80
Chios	100	Total	353

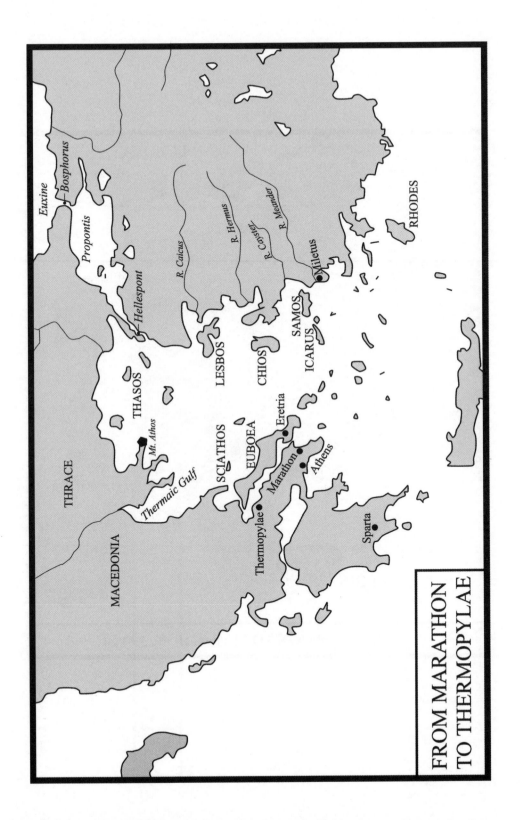

FROM MARATHON
TO THERMOPYLAE

EUBOEA

Chalcis   Eretria

BOEOTIA

Delium

● Thebes

Oropus

Rhamnous

Mt. Parnes

Aphidnae

Mt. Pentelicon

Marathon

MEGARID

Megara

Athens

Piraeus

Salamis

Phaleron

Mt. Hymettus

Brauron

AEGINA

LAURION

Sounion

THE CAMPAIGN TO MARATHON, 490 BC

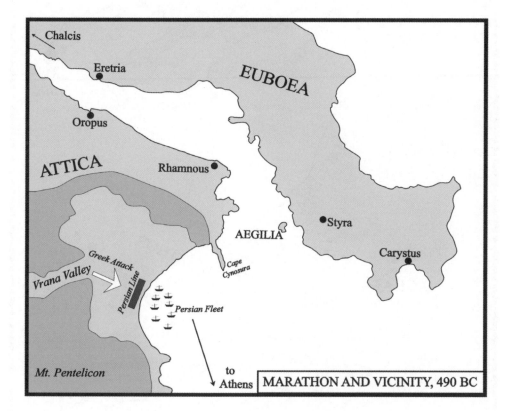

Chalcis

Eretria

EUBOEA

Oropus

ATTICA

Rhamnous

Styra

AEGILIA

Carystus

Greek Attack

Cape
Cynosura

Vrana Valley

Persian Line

Persian Fleet

Mt. Pentelicon

to
Athens

MARATHON AND VICINITY, 490 BC

MACEDONIA

THRACE

R. Strymon

Eion

Therme

R. Haliacmon

canal

Olynthus

Thermaic Gulf

Mt. Athos

Mt Olympus

R. Pineus

Tempe

THESSALY

MAGNESIA

SEPIAS

SCIATHOS

Pherae

Pharsalus

ACHAEA

Halus

Artemesium

Thermopylae

Chalcis Eretria

BOEOTIA

Delium

Oropus

Delphi

XERXES' ADVANCE TO THERMOPYLAE, 480 BC

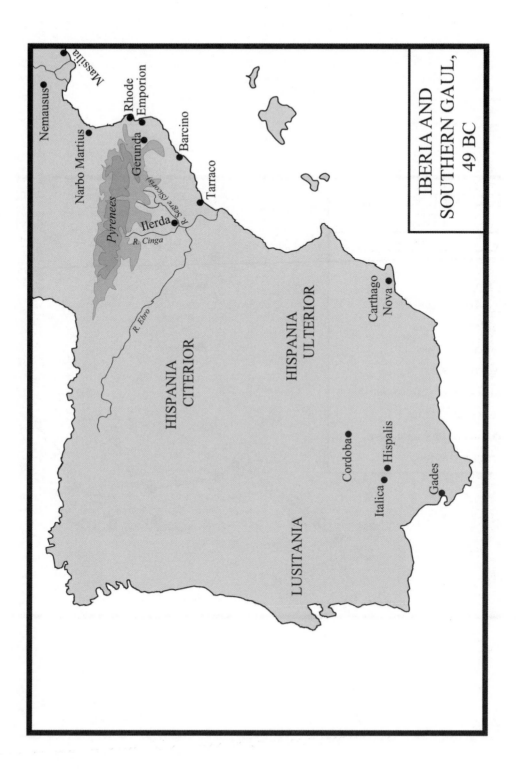

IBERIA AND
SOUTHERN GAUL,
49 BC

Massilia

Nemausus

Rhode
Emporion

Narbo Martius

Gerunda

Barcino

Pyrenees

R. Segre (Sicoris)

Tarraco

Ilerda

R. Cinga

R. Ebro

HISPANIA
CITERIOR

HISPANIA
ULTERIOR

Carthago
Nova

Cordoba

Italica ● Hispalis

Gades

LUSITANIA

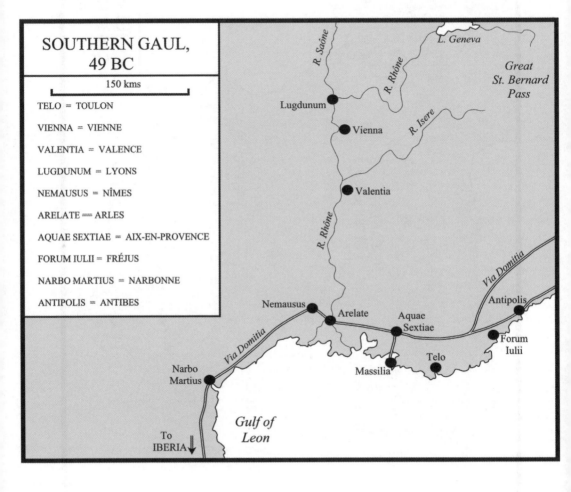

SOUTHERN GAUL, 49 BC

150 kms

TELO = TOULON

VIENNA = VIENNE

VALENTIA = VALENCE

LUGDUNUM = LYONS

NEMAUSUS = NÎMES

ARELATE = ARLES

AQUAE SEXTIAE = AIX-EN-PROVENCE

FORUM IULII = FRÉJUS

NARBO MARTIUS = NARBONNE

ANTIPOLIS = ANTIBES

R. Saône

L. Geneva

Great
St. Bernard
Pass

R. Rhône

Lugdunum

R. Isere

Vienna

Valentia

R. Rhône

Via Domitia

Antipolis

Nemausus

Arelate

Aquae
Sextiae

Forum
Iulii

Via Domitia

Narbo
Martius

Telo

Massilia

To
IBERIA

Gulf of
Leon

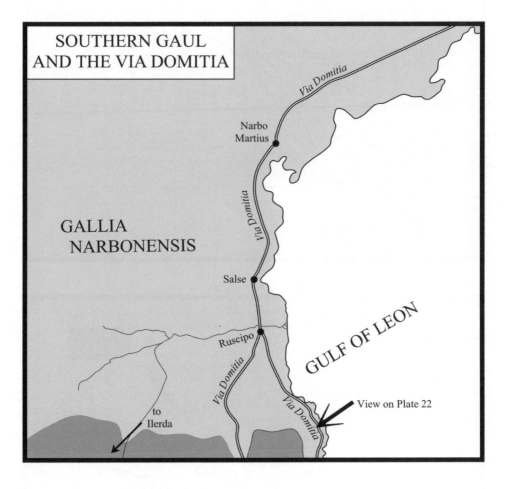

SOUTHERN GAUL
AND THE VIA DOMITIA

Via Domitia

GALLIA
NARBONENSIS

Narbo
Martius

Via Domitia

Salse

Ruscipo

Via Domitia

GULF OF LEON

Via Domitia

View on Plate 22

to
Ilerda

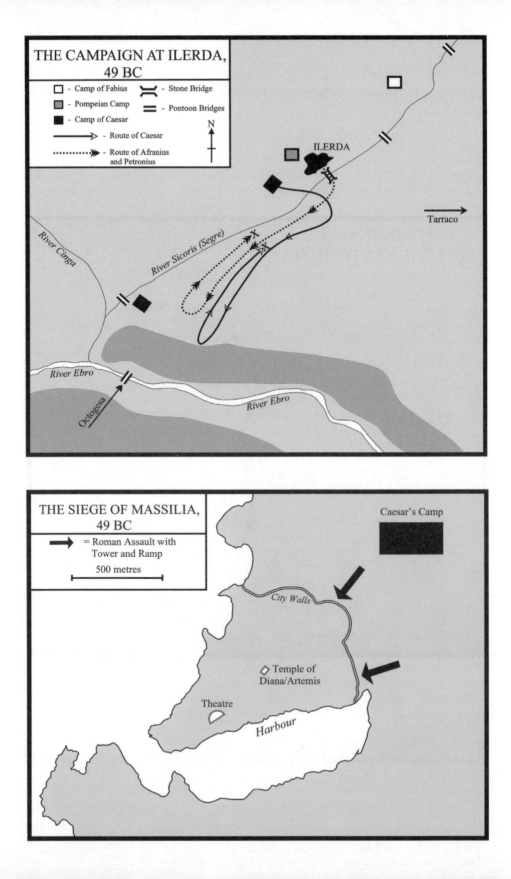

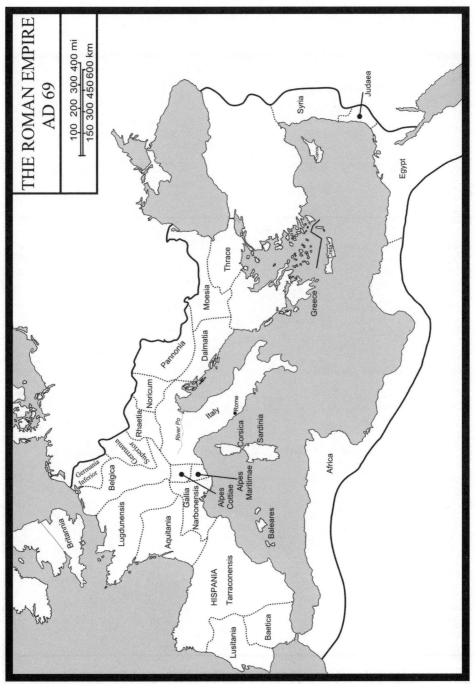

THE ROMAN EMPIRE
AD 69

100 200 300 400 mi
150 300 450 600 km

Judaea

Syria

Egypt

Cyprus

Thrace

Greece

Crete

Moesia

Pannonia

Dalmatia

Noricum

Rhaetia

Germania
Superior

Germania
Inferior

Belgica

Lugdunensis

Aquitania

Gallia
Narbonensis

Alpes
Cottiae

Alpes
Maritimae

Italy

River Po

Rome

Corsica

Sardinia

Africa

Baleares

HISPANIA

Tarraconensis

Lusitania

Baetica

Britannia

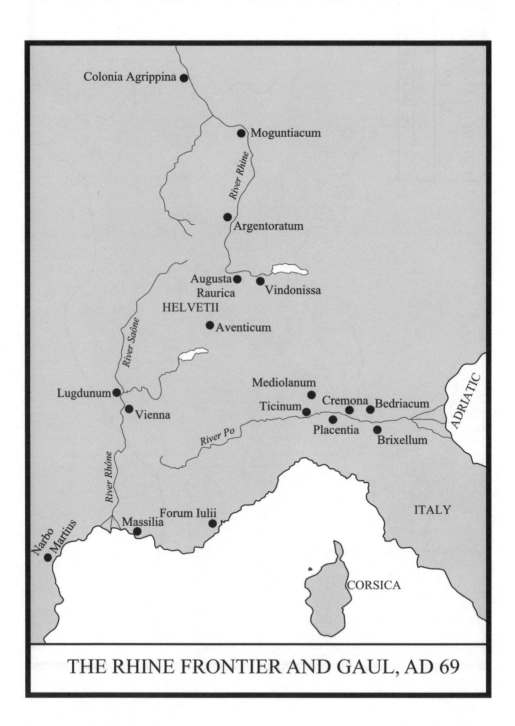

Colonia Agrippina

Moguntiacum

River Rhine

Argentoratum

Augusta Raurica

Vindonissa

HELVETII

Aventicum

River Saône

Mediolanum

Lugdunum

Ticinum

Cremona

Bedriacum

Vienna

Placentia

River Po

Brixellum

ADRIATIC

River Rhône

ITALY

Narbo Martius

Massilia

Forum Iulii

CORSICA

THE RHINE FRONTIER AND GAUL, AD 69

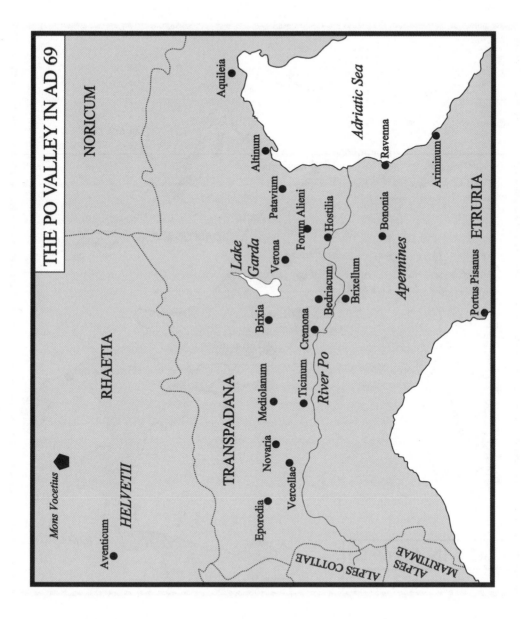

THE PO VALLEY IN AD 69

Mons Vocetius

HELVETII

Aventicum

RHAETIA

NORICUM

Aquileia

Altinum

Adriatic Sea

Patavium

Verona

Forum Alieni

Lake Garda

Hostilia

Ravenna

Brixia

Bononia

Ariminum

Cremona

Bedriacum

Brixellum

Apennines

Ticinum

ETRURIA

Mediolanum

River Po

TRANSPADANA

Novaria

Vercellae

Eporedia

Portus Pisanus

ALPES COTTIAE

ALPES MARITIMAE

ITALY IN AD 69 (I)

ITALY IN AD 69 (II)

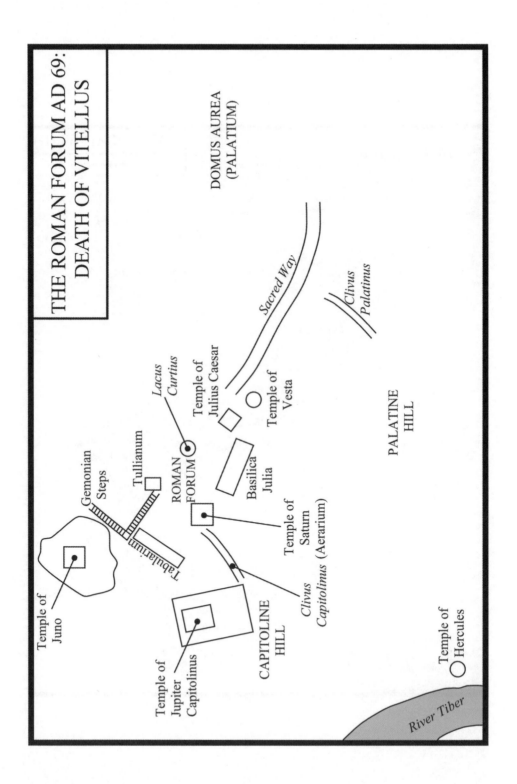

THE ROMAN FORUM AD 69: DEATH OF VITELLUS

DOMUS AUREA (PALATIUM)

Sacred Way

Clivus Palatinus

Lacus Curtius

Temple of Julius Caesar

Temple of Vesta

Tullianum

Gemonian Steps

ROMAN FORUM

Basilica Julia

PALATINE HILL

Temple of Juno

Tabularium

Temple of Saturn (Aerarium)

Temple of Jupiter Capitolinus

CAPITOLINE HILL

Clivus Capitolinus

Temple of Hercules

River Tiber

Introduction

Whereas in the volume *Fields of Death* (2013) I focussed on the sieges of the cities of Sybaris (510 BC), Syracuse (414–413 BC), Motya (397 BC), and Alexandria (48–47 BC), in the following pages the discussion concentrates on how logistics, geography and weather all affected the military campaigns of the Ionian War (500–493 BC), the battles at Marathon and Thermopylae (490–480 BC), the battle of Ilerda and the siege of Massilia (49 BC) and finally the two battles that occurred near Cremona in AD 69.

No battlefield is a static place because of the constant movement of the opposing sides, but it is not just the personnel on the ground who have a role to play. The logistics of moving an army or fleet or both, as is often a feature of this discussion, to the battlefield plays a fundamental role in the outcome. It was poor logistics that arguably cost Darius a triumph north of the Danube or Xerxes his victory in Greece, while Otho lost his war and life at Brixellum because his legions were late arriving to do battle with his opponent Vitellius. The problem of supplying an army is continually apparent in Caesar's account of the campaign around Ilerda. But it is not simply logistical problems that can affect the result of military campaigns; there is also the weather, about which ancient writers and their audiences were clearly as concerned as they are today. Unusually early snow became a problem for the supporters of Vespasian after the second battle of Bedriacum in November 69, which slowed down their advance from the Po Valley because the Apennine passes were almost impassable. The worst storms in anyone's memory adversely affected the lines of communication and caused severe shortages in supplies for the protagonists in the fighting around Ilerda. Flash flooding and high water levels in the rivers destroyed bridges and isolated both Caesarian and Pomepeian armies until repairs could be made. On the other hand, high winds caused problems for the besiegers and defenders at Massilia at the same time as the floods in Iberia. The landscape of the Po Valley, with its multiplicity of streams and rivers, and its unique system of dykes and drainage channels over a very extensive area of cultivatable land, became both an obstacle and a much sought after advantage in the bitter conflicts played out in AD 69. Finally there are the geographical factors such as mountains, valleys, rivers and coastal waters, all of which affected the strategies employed by the commanders in the field. Arguably much of the combat that took place on land in the Ionian War (499–493 BC) lay along river valleys which gave access either to the interior of Asia Minor or to the coast where the Greek cities were situated. The inability of the Pompeians to reach the safety of the hills above the Ebro Valley was their undoing in 49 BC. Storms in the Aegean caused severe damage to the Persian fleets in both 492 and 480 BC and no forward planning could take account of this factor, which caused Mardonius to fail in Thrace and Xerxes' ambitions to occupy Greece to be wrecked. Storms disrupted the bridging and the crossing of the Hellespont in 480 and ultimately destroyed Persian pride in their great undertaking. 'Secret' tracks in the mountains gave the Persians the advantage they needed to inflict their famous victory over the Spartans at Thermopylae in 480. Columns of Athenian troops hidden in the Vrana Valley took the Persians by surprise on the plain of Marathon in 490. The military tacticians might plan their strategies but there were a plethora of reasons for success or failure.

Together with as detailed an analysis of the battlefields concerned as possible the intention has been moreover to provide a detailed chronology of the events in order that the temporal context can be fully appreciated. Finally, an observation not for the first time voiced here is the fact that the details of the battle or battles that are found in the ancient sources, whether it is Herodotus, Caesar or Tacitus, are usually surprisingly brief, while the circumstances that led to these encounters occupy far more space. Modern interest often dwells on just the battlefields and the combatants, but it is as much retracing the events that led to armies facing one another across some level space that provides the fullest understanding of these intriguing episodes in antiquity.

Chapter One

New Perspectives on the War in Ionia (499–493 BC)

The distance sailing along the coast around Ionia is roughly three thousand
four hundred and thirty stadia. The distance is so great because of the bays
and peninsulas which characterize this region although the length as the
crow flies is much less. For example, the distance from Ephesus to Smyrna
in a straight line is just a journey of three hundred and twenty stadia, from
Ephesus to Metropolis one hundred and twenty and from there to Smyrna
another two hundred. However, the distance by sea is hardly less than two
thousand two hundred stadia.[1]

(Strabo, 14.1.2)

Ancient Ionia comprised the heavily indented coastal strip of land on a
section of the western coast of Asia Minor. This littoral zone extended
barely more than forty kilometres (25 miles) inland and was identified
in Antiquity as Ionia stretching from the city of Phocaea in the north to the
city of Miletus in the south.[2] To the north of Phocaea lay Mysia, Aeolis and the
Troad, while the cult centre at Apollo at Didyma marked the boundary between
southern Ionia and adjacent Caria. The rivers of Ionia drain east to west rising
in the heights of the Anatolian plateau and emerge from the hills crossing this
broad flat plain before joining the sea. The valleys are separated from one
another by these hills, which are steep sided and generally impassable, although
there are some routes through, most notably that which joins the Hermus with
the Caicus Valley via Thyateira. There are four major rivers of Ionia: the Caicus,
Hermus, Cayster and Meander. Understanding the geography of the region,
its specific coastal features, and in particular its river systems and the lines of
communication that these governed are all important for an understanding of
the course of this war and the battlefields traced in this discussion.

At the start of the fifth century BC this region was engulfed in warfare, and
this conflict soon affected much of western Asia Minor. The usual view about
the causes for this Ionian Greek revolt again Persian rule is twofold: that
Persian rule was regarded as oppressive both in terms of tribute expected from
the cities coupled with a system of government encouraged and supported by
the Persians, namely tyranny or rule by a single individual.[3] Besides these

factors could be added the personal ambitions of certain of the leading figures of the political elite at Miletus especially its tyrant Histiaeus and his son-in-law Aristagoras. It is argued that these personal intrigues so inflamed a current disquiet with Persian rule that a widespread, popular and protracted rebellion broke out. This lengthy and ultimately desperate struggle has occasioned far less interest than the two later invasions of mainland Greece, and yet occurring within the Persian Empire it was costly in terms of lives and materials involving many thousands of combatants and civilians. This was no minor prelude to a later great struggle but arguably a Herculean struggle followed by a relatively straightforward and quiet coda.[4]

The first question to address was whether or not Persian rule was oppressive enough to cause this conflagration. There have been arguments for and against this issue and it is possibly true that for the Ionian cities indirect rule, since they did not fall within one of the three western Asia satrapies, was not as tightly administered as if these were under the direct supervision of a governor as in Lydia, Caria or Hellespontine Phrygia (Dascyllium). However, the presence of the Persian monarch and his recent campaigns in Thrace and as far north as the Danube will have imposed heavy financial burdens on all the cities of Asia Minor. Those closest to the centre of military operations among which were the wealthy Ionian cities would have been liable for contributions. Miletus, Ephesus and Smyrna were all large cities with extensive trading links, busy ports and sophisticated infrastructure, and these would undoubtedly have been called upon to contribute to Darius' ambitious plans to extend his empire westwards. Darius usurped the Persian throne in 522/1 and having secured the centre of his rule within a year then campaigned in his eastern provinces before turning his attention to the west.[5] The fact that he was present in Asia Minor in 513/12 having levied and led an army from Susa also suggests some years of planning beforehand. He was plainly intent on making a name for himself in the one area where the Persians had not made their presence felt before (Diod. 10.19.5), but not at that stage a desire to bring Greece under his control. Herodotus who covers Darius' Danubian campaign shows that the king was unfamiliar with the territory.

> Darius marched from Susa and arrived in the vicinity of Chalcedon where the Bosphorus had been bridged. He sat on a promontory there and looked at the Euxine which is indeed a sight worth seeing since this is the most marvellous of all seas. (Herodt. 4.85)

After Darius had viewed the sea he sailed back to the bridge which had been built by Mandrocles of Samos and when he had looked at the

Bosphorus he ordered the construction of two white stone pillars and had engraved on them in Assyrian and in Greek a list of all the peoples he had led there. These numbering 700 000 were drawn from all his subjects including cavalry, but excluding the fleet which consisted of six hundred ships. (Herodt. 4.87)

The number of warships was probably the crux of the matter for the Ionian cities for it was surely in the numbers of Darius' fleet that the main cause for complaint is to be identified. Indeed if one reflects on the problem it is easy to see why this could have become a sufficiently serious issue and be the cause of such discontent that could have led to an uprising. Herodotus does not describe the nature of these warships, but a word of caution might be useful here since the historian was writing after 450 BC when Greek shipping had become almost exclusively based on the construction of the trireme, which depending on the age of the vessel passed from being a warship with three banks of oars, a military transport with two banks and a supply ship with a single bank. In the decade before the Ionian revolt began such ships were a very recent innovation and most shipping still probably comprised pentekonters or fifty-oared galleys and biremes, which were vessels with a double bank of oars. Both were considerably smaller than the trireme, which had a crew of about two hundred. The bireme contained a crew of perhaps one hundred and twenty, while the complement of a pentekonter was as few as sixty.

Still, the numbers involved in the fleet will have been immense if Herodotus is even reasonably accurate in the figures he gives. Six hundred warships each with roughly a crew of a hundred would have involved no fewer than sixty thousand men and from where did these crews come from and where were they stationed during this campaign? The Persian king levied his troops from all his satrapies, but his fleet was summoned from just a few places in his realm. Egypt and Phoenician cities such as Sidon and Tyre are known to have made a major contribution to Persian sea power,[6] but so did the communities of Asia Minor and the eastern Aegean.[7] The Milesians were in possession of a powerful fleet in their own right and had long been active in trade around the Aegean and especially around the Euxine where the Persians hoped to acquire new territories.[8] Darius would have expected generous help from Miletus in his expedition but all cities would have been expected to deliver aid. Moreover, this was simply in terms of ships and men but in supplies for which there may have been payment but still the additional costs of supporting a war would have fallen heavily on this sector of Darius' empire. He may have believed that there was profit to be made from new territorial acquisitions but this expectation may not have been shared by his Greek subjects who because of their knowledge of the Euxine and their expertise in shipbuilding and maintenance would have been hard pressed to provide resources, especially over a protracted period of time. Darius campaigned some distance to the north of the (Ister) Danube (Strabo, 7.3.14) but probably did not reach as far north as the Dniester River before retreating because of a shortage of supplies.[9] He clearly did not make full use of his huge fleet in a support capacity in waters well known to at least his Greek levies. Herodotus also states (4.89) that Darius had a bridge over the Danube constructed from some of the ships in his fleet and that these were guarded by the Greeks and that it was situated at the point where the Danube's delta begins and about two days' sailing from its mouth. Herodotus (4.98) also claims that Darius said that he would return to that bridge within sixty days. He was late in returning and in some disorder having deserted a large number of his troops. The Greek leaders debated among themselves whether or not to break up the bridge and return to their homes and indeed Miltiades, the Athenian ruler of the Chersonese, is said to have argued that it would be a good time to free Ionia and reassert its independence from Persian rule. Histiaeus the tyrant of Miletus, however, argued against this move and won the debate by urging loyalty to the Persian king to whom they owed their positions of power and whose own positions would become extremely vulnerable without this support.[10] So Darius was able to safely regain the southern bank of the Danube and he re-crossed the Bosphorus but remained in Sardis for some time after, although he delegated further operations to a trusted subordinate Megabazus (Herodt. 4.143).[11] This means that while Darius' personal intervention may have lasted for just a single campaign in 513/2 the Persians remained highly active in the region afterwards. As a result there was a constant demand for supplies for an army that Herodotus claims (4.143) numbered eighty thousand from the local communities, an additional burden to their tribute and surely cause for grumbling complaints, but perhaps not outright rebellion when there was clearly a formidable army and fleet at hand to quell any disturbance to Persian rule.

There was a further concatenation of events, which almost certainly contributed to the surprising enthusiasm for an uprising. For example, the Persians were clearly intent on taking direct control over their newly acquired lands in Europe and Megabazus was given instructions by Darius, although Miltiades, whose position might have been considered unsafe following his supposed call for insurrection, was left in control of the Chersonese and Cardia. A word of caution needs to be sounded since Miltiades went on to be victorious general at Marathon hence Herodotus would want future generations to regard him as outspoken in his loyalty to the Greeks. He may well have been far less disloyal than was later portrayed and lost his lands in the Chersonese because of a more general tightening of control by the Persians over this region. Note that Ionia is specified by Herodotus not Greece, which does look as if there is some construction at work in the narrative. While the Persians campaigned in Thrace and Darius was in residence in Sardis additional financial burdens must have been imposed on all the cities in Asia Minor and this would have been resented. It was these additional financial demands rather than antagonism towards the general system of tribute that may therefore have been the underlying reason for unrest.

Pitched into this potentially explosive situation was the second ostensible cause for war, namely the personal ambitions of Histiaeus of Miletus and his son-in-law Aristagoras. Histiaeus did well out of his loyalty to Darius who, once returned from Thrace, wished to grant him any request he might make. Histiaeus asked for the town of Myrcinus, on the left bank of the River Strymon close to where the Athenian town of Amphipolis would be established by Pericles in about 461 BC. The area was to be much sought after because it had excellent supplies of timber and was clearly chosen by Histiaeus precisely for this resource, which would allow Miletus to greatly increase its naval power. But it also lay close to Mount Pangaeus, which was known for its gold and silver deposits, which would make Miletus even more wealthy and powerful (Herodt. 7.23). For Darius of course this place was of no consequence and so he had no reservations about granting this favour (Herodt. 5.11–12). However, Megabazus who had been campaigning in Paeonia very close to the Strymon and Mount Pangaeus, perhaps from personal enmity or, as Herodotus claims (Herodt. 5.23), from some profound foresight, when he returned to Sardis argued that Histiaeus' new acquisition allowed him to indulge his own ambitions, which would threaten the security of Persia.[12] Darius perceived the wisdom of this point of view and he also followed his satrap's advice of how to deal with Histiaeus. The Milesian was invited to come to Sardis but far from being accused of treacherous behaviour Darius instead declared that he wished to give Histiaeus further and higher honours for his loyalty and so instructed him to accompany the king to Susa and become one of his closest advisers. Histiaeus could hardly refuse this honour even if for the time being his ambition was thwarted. Darius appointed his brother Artaphernes satrap of Lydia and Otanes to replace Megabazus in Hellespontine Phrygia and Thrace. The latter was quickly active in the northern Aegean, capturing Imbros and Lemnos, and around the Propontis taking Byzantium and Chalcedon, and also Antandrus and Lamponium in the southern Troad. The occupation of the islands is probably indicative of an intention by Darius to follow up Megabazus' conquests in Thrace and extend the western frontier of his kingdom at least to the Strymon or beyond.

Megabazus' successor may have been freed from an anxiety about Histiaeus' aims and had had a potential troublemaker removed from his satrapy. Still Myrcinus remained a Milesian town with all its resources a fine asset for this Ionian city to possess, and which it evidently was able to exploit later. In Miletus, Aristagoras was chosen to act in Histiaeus' name and he was equally quick to pursue his own ambitions when the opportunity arose. Some exiles from Naxos arrived in Miletus driven out as a result of stasis or civil unrest between certain wealthy families and the general citizen body, a situation usually exploited by political figures using the situation as means to obtain power for themselves rather than solving ongoing socio–political problems. These wealthy Naxians came to Miletus because of past links between the two *poleis* and they asked for help so that they might return. Aristagoras rather than agree immediately to this request, like Histiaeus, saw the possibility of far greater gains if he played his cards cleverly. He thought that if indeed he led a successful expedition to Naxos then he might well make the island his personal domain, and the prospect of further conquest of the Cyclades islands was too attractive to let pass. Nonetheless Aristagoras clearly had some logistical problems with such a major expedition. First of all it is very unlikely that he would have been able to act without first referring the matter to the satrap of Lydia Artaphernes. Miletus politically was self-governing but in military affairs beyond its territory the Milesians would have needed Persian approval. Therefore, Aristagoras informed the Naxian exiles that while he was very much in favour of helping them he claimed that he lacked the military capability to do so. This is perhaps surprising since Herodotus says (5.30) that the faction in power on Naxos possessed eight thousand heavy infantry and 'many warships'. Miletus must have possessed stronger military resources than Naxos and the Milesians must have had many more ships at their disposal than the Naxians. However, it seems likely that Aristagoras was playing according to the unwritten rules of his appointment. He extracted from the Naxians a promise that they would finance any expedition to place them back in power and suggested that he would go on their behalf to Artaphernes who had many times the military strength of either Miletus or Naxos and that he would easily be able to place at the exiles' disposal a fleet of two hundred warships. The Naxians agreed and Aristagoras went up to Sardis. There Aristagoras presented his case: return of the Naxian exiles with Persian help and the island would then become another gain for Darius' rule, but more than that since Naxos was the most wealthy and powerful of the Cyclades so if Naxos was to be taken then Andros and Paros and the remaining island states would follow. With the Cyclades under Persian control Euboea was within easy reach and from there the Greek mainland. Artaphernes plainly found the proposal irresistible as indeed did Darius when he was informed by his satrap. Darius ordered an army and fleet to be gathered, which was to be commanded not by Aristagoras but by a Persian named Megabates. The relationship between the Persian general and the Milesian Aristagoras became strained when the former tried to instil discipline among the various contingents in the fleet. The fleet had sailed probably from Miletus north to Chios before heading towards the Cyclades. At some point during an inspection of the ships Megabates is said to have found left unguarded a warship from Myndos in Caria. The captain of this vessel, a certain Scylax, was promptly punished, according to Herodotus (5.33), by being bound and having his head thrust through one of his own ship's oar holes. Scylax also happened to be a friend of Aristagoras. When he heard of the undignified punishment meted out to the Carian captain he immediately took issue with Megabates. The Persian was not impressed and Aristagoras simply went away and released Scylax. Megabates obviously felt his position had been undermined and a furious confrontation ensued in which Aristagoras is said to have claimed that the Persian was his subordinate, not the overall commander of the expedition.[13] That night Megabates sent word to the Naxians that the Persian forces would soon arrive at their island and so removed any chance of a swift victory by making an unexpected landing. The Naxians seem to have had plenty of time in which to fortify their defences and bring in their harvest and other vital supplies to withstand a siege. It does seem remarkable that a Persian fleet numbering two hundred warships with the capability for transporting either siege machines or the technical knowhow to construct these in situ had no effect. The siege dragged on for four months and must have extended into the winter. The Persians and their allies ran short of materials and probably food, which is yet again remarkable when they commanded the sea lanes and could have brought in reinforcements and supplies from the Ionian ports. It looks as if Megabates wanted the siege to fail and that Aristagoras had neither the power nor the presence to be able to pursue the goal. The funds provided by the Naxian exiles were soon exhausted and very plainly Artaphernes was not prepared to step in with further aid. Again this should strike one as odd since the conquest of Naxos certainly opened up the western Aegean to Persian conquest considering Darius' expressed interest in expanding his kingdom westwards. It is possible that there were internal problems elsewhere that drew Darius' attention and perhaps Artaphernes had never been as enthusiastic as Herodotus claims. Whatever the precise causes for what became little less than a debacle the Persians and their allies retreated in some disorder.

The size of the attacking force may well have been the cause of its undoing since there were insufficient resources on the ground to be drawn on to prolong the siege through the winter months. The fate of the Naxian exiles stranded in their fort and abandoned by the Persians is left unrecorded. The date of the expedition against Naxos is usually placed chronologically close to the general uprising in Ionia by Herodotus, although some longer lapse in time must have occurred. It is likely that the arrival of the Naxian exiles in Miletus and Aristagoras' appeal to Artaphernes may be assigned to one year, the assembling of a composite infantry, fleet and any necessary transport vessels from various quarters of the empire would have taken at least another winter if not the entire next year, and the expedition itself clearly consumed an entire campaigning season with the withdrawal of the Persian forces coming only very late in the autumn. Herodotus is quite specific that the journey time from Sardis to Susa could take three months (Herodt. 5.50 and 5.54) and even by special messenger perhaps half that length of time. Therefore, the date of the Naxos episode is most likely to cover a number of years from about 505/4 to 501/0 BC.[14]

When Aristagoras returned to Miletus he was afraid that he would be relieved of his position not so much because of the failure at Naxos but because of the well-publicized enmity with Megabates who might use his influence with Artaphernes and Darius to secure his fall. His thoughts had evidently turned to rebellion (Herodt. 5.35) when at that precise moment a messenger came from Histiaeus. This is the famous episode of the slave belonging to Histiaeus on whose shaved head a message urging Aristagoras to rebel had been tattooed. Histiaeus had thought this was the only way that he could send such a sensitive message to Miletus without being discovered. The slave had only been allowed to depart on his errand when his hair had grown back sufficiently only to be shaved again on his arrival in Ionia. The tale is entertaining and amusing and not feasible of course, for not only did it become so famous, when it is supposed to have been conducted in the greatest secrecy since Histiaeus believed that he was being watched and that the roads by which any messenger might go were also heavily monitored, but that the message itself seems so nonsensical. Aristagoras had just returned from Naxos in disgrace, also having quarrelled with an influential Persian general, then a message arrived, fortuitously Herodotus had his audience believe, from the ever ambitious Histiaeus. Histiaeus must surely have already known of the withdrawal from Naxos before he sent his message for it to have any impact. Aristagoras was not likely to have wanted to rebel a matter of four months earlier when he had hoped to rule Naxos. Therefore the chronology needs some adjustment as do the circumstances leading up to the general uprising.

Darius must have been informed of the failure of the Naxian expedition and voiced his concern to Histiaeus who perhaps only then seized the opportunity of urging a rebellion. Herodotus thought that Histiaeus' sole chance of ever returning to Miletus was as a peacemaker in the event of a serious rebellion, but the course of that revolt had to be left to Aristagoras' planning and organization. But if Aristagoras did not possess the resources to make an attack on Naxos without substantial Persian aid – indeed it was almost entirely a Persian undertaking in the end – how on earth could Histiaeus have expected Miletus to rebel against the might of the occupying power? This must indicate that Histiaeus 'sent his message' only after the revolt had broken out, which reduces its dramatic effect for anyone but an inattentive audience.

Aristagoras may have thought that he was in a tight corner, and whether he had received encouragement from Histiaeus or not, he consulted with his friends and supporters who not surprisingly agreed with his plan to launch a rebellion. Yet some skilful diplomacy was needed to secure allies of sufficient stature and resources to counteract Persian power if that uprising was not to be stillborn. Among those in discussion with Aristagoras was Hecataeus, the Milesian philosopher and widely regarded today as among the very the first to begin to record historical events and the creation of history as a discipline and literary pursuit. Hecataeus argued that a war against Persia was doomed to fail but as he could not convince any of those with Aristagoras of the validity of his case he said instead that if Miletus should revolt then the rebels must first seize the treasures contained in the shrine of Apollo at Didyma. The sanctuary was wealthy, containing many gifts given by the Lydian king Croesus (Herodt. 5.36) and with these funds they would be able to build enough ships to command the sea, a vital prerequisite for victory, and would also deprive their enemy of this potential plunder. With Myrcinus already under Milesian control the argument was sound since it was not so much the building of a fleet that would drain their financial reserves but the cost of maintaining it on the sea for the duration for what was likely to be a lengthy period of warfare. Hecataeus' advice was ignored;[15] and instead it was decided to attempt to win over the troops that had recently returned from Naxos and were still at Myus. If that attempt was successful the Greek troops were also to be persuaded to arrest their current generals, most of whom were pro-Persian. A Milesian named Iatragoras (Herodt. 5.37) was chosen for this difficult task,[16] but he accomplished everything and more by evidently winning over the Greek rank and file who immediately arrested their leaders who included those from Mylasa, Termera, Mytilene and Cyme.[17] Moreover, the fleet that was also beached at Myus was also secured.[18] When this mutiny against Persian authority and the rulers who had been chosen by them occurred the rebellion became common knowledge and the war began. And any Persians who were with the assembled local forces must either have fled or been killed. The narrative suggests that these troops dispersed to their own cities (Herodt. 5.37), although there have been some modern suggestions that these remained at Myus and were the same troops used for the Sardis attack.

Some points need clarification here since they seem to complicate what is Herodotus' otherwise neat and tidy tale. First of all the general use of 'The Ionian Revolt' will clearly not do if Carian Mylasa, Lesbos and Aeolian Cyme were keen supporters of the rebellion from its inception.[19] It is an interesting glimpse of the question of ethnicity in antiquity in that some of the inhabitants of Asia Minor were clearly perceived by an audience of Herodotus to have less significance than others. The people of Lesbos were to play a major role, not entirely positive as we shall see in the entire war while fighting in Caria was probably more severe and lengthy than in Ionia and the Carians were able to extract more favourable terms from the Persians at the conclusion of the hostilities in 494/3. It seems likely that Herodotus saw the war as one led by Ionian Miletus and then simplified a rather more complex picture.

Furthermore, how was Aristagoras able to leave Ionia for mainland Greece if he was the supposed leader of the rebellion? Herodotus states quite plainly that the leader of the rebellion departed for Sparta in a trireme. The express purpose of this mission was the now desperate search for allies without whom the Asia Minor Greeks would be lost or as Herodotus puts it 'for he wanted to find some great alliance' (Herodt. 5.38). Why did Aristagoras go to Sparta when there were other possible alliances to be sought? In fact, Aristagoras may well have gone to Argos and although Herodotus does not describe a visit here he does relate that the Argives sought oracular advice about involvement in the war (Herodt. 6.19). The Argives, unlike the Carians however, were deterred from participation since the oracle they received foretold the destruction of Miletus, which gave them enough reason to remain cautious about any undertaking that might have only negative results.[20] Was this in the air when Aristagoras went to Sparta? Aristagoras' route from Miletus to Sparta would have made a stop at Argos easy enough. Having gained no support there the Milesian had an interview with the Spartan king. Herodotus devotes more detail to his visit to Cleomenes the Spartan king than to any other stop in his search for allies. It is claimed that Aristagoras attempted to win over Cleomenes by offering a bribe in order to win his support. This is credible given Spartan apparent susceptibility to corruption in later times at least.[21]

Sparta had been active in the preceding decade in lending aid to the Athenians in expelling their tyrant Hippias and although the Spartans would have preferred his replacement to have been an oligarchic government they had acquiesced in the emergence of broader participative rule or democracy. Before that the Spartans had not been averse to intervening in affairs on the Asia Minor side of the Aegean and had launched a naval attack on Samos in the 520s, nor indeed in sending Spartans as far afield as Cyrene, southern Italy and Sicily between 520 and 510.[22] Therefore, there was a recent history of vigorous and interventionist foreign policy and the Milesians, at least Aristagoras, probably hoped that a war with the Persians and the prospect of lucrative plunder would be enough to enlist Spartan help. He was sadly mistaken for not even bribery was sufficient to entice Spartan involvement not because the Spartans felt compelled to protect their lands in the Peloponnese from attackers or Helot rebellion but because the chances of permanent success against Persia at that moment seemed quite remote and a drain on resources rather than a source for new revenues.[23]

It is interesting that Aristagoras was not the sole distinguished visitor to the Peloponnese in the early summer of 499. Herodotus (5.91) states that Hippias, former tyrant of Athens, came to Sparta in response to an invitation because the Spartans had become aware of the increasing power and influence exercised by the Athenians. They seemed to be about to offer Hippias help in regaining his position in that city. In the event, the allies of Sparta in the Peloponnesian League who were also summoned for discussion about this matter persuaded the Spartan leadership not to support the proposal notably by a speech delivered by the Corinthian delegate, and the move came to nothing. Hippias returned to his place of exile at Sigeum (Herodot. 5.96). The entire affair is a digression in Herodotus' narrative just before he begins his coverage of the war in Asia Minor, but it is curious for the details it possibly exposes about the political climate in Ionia and the other western areas of the Persian Empire. Hippias clearly hoped to regain his place as tyrant in Athens and did not regard his stay at Sigeum on the Hellespont as necessarily permanent.[24] When he perceived an opportunity of gaining external support for retaking Athens he did not delay.[25] Hippias' whereabouts after his failed mission to Sparta is not disclosed but it is certainly possible given the general instability throughout Asia Minor that he was not immune to this in Sigeum. He and other members of the Pisistratid clan who were living on Hellespont may, like many of the other pro-Persian rulers of the Greek and Hellenized cities fled for safety at Sardis or to Susa. It is also possible that his eagerness to attempt a return to Athens was actually spurred on by the growing uncertainty around him. Agitation among the Greek cities of Asia Minor seems to have been widespread and may already have been affecting Sigeum and Hippias may even have found himself under considerable pressure and came to Sparta partly in the hope of avoiding expulsion from his place of exile. Still, like many of the tyrants in these parts Hippias survived and Sigeum was presumably restored to his rule once the war ended.[26] It is a curious incident, which Herodotus uses to digress about the end of tyranny at Athens and the introduction of democracy by Cleisthenes the Alcmaeonid,[27] but his source may have linked the missions of Aristagoras and Hippias more closely especially since they were diametrically opposed, with the former a tyrant acting against tyranny and the latter another ex-tyrant in support of it. This dichotomy of governance and the constant search for an ideal form of government, which results almost in a conundrum, became a topical element in much of Greek philosophical discourse during the Classical period of Greece and it was one that Herodotus himself visited in his discussion of the ideal constitution in the third book (3.80–83) of his history. Therefore, aside from the military history contained in his work interspersed with entertaining anecdotes is a deeper philosophical subtext that cannot be ignored.

Thus for the Athenians the arrival of Aristagoras coincided with a decade of rule without tyrants, but they will have known that Hippias had been in evidence again in the vicinity (Herodt. 5.97). Therefore its citizens perhaps saw this opportunity as a time to assume a wider role in military affairs in the Aegean. Moreover, the Athenians cannot possibly have been unaware that the Spartans had not agreed to help Aristagoras and at the same time had played with the idea of giving military aid to Hippias. Athenian support for the Ionians would show Sparta that the Athenians would be too formidable for further interference and perhaps there were some who thought that an Ionian victory would see the removal of Hippias from Sigeum as well. There may already have been fears of Persian encroachment in the Aegean and that the conquest of Naxos had simply been deferred or delayed rather than abandoned altogether, so that an Athenian intervention in Ionia might be used to divert Persian attention elsewhere.[28] Aristagoras is said to have addressed an assembly of thirty thousand Athenian citizens (Herodt. 5.97), offering many of the same arguments that he had presented to the Spartans but these drew immediate popular support. Although there were ethnic ties between the Ionians and the Athenians, and there was also the prospect of plunder it was the negative attitude of the Spartans that no doubt influenced the thoughts of Aristagoras' audience.[29] A positive reaction from Sparta would have drawn the opposite from Athens simply because at this time the two states had drawn apart, especially with regard to the former's support for Hippias. Herodotus, rather uncharacteristically for him, is critical of Athenian thinking and considered that the *demos* was duped by Aristagoras. In this he perhaps gives an inkling of his own attitude towards the sort of government he believed in when he says that 'it was easier to persuade a crowd than a single man, for Aristagoras was not able convince Cleomenes but he was successful with thirty thousand' (Herodt. 5.97). The Athenians enthusiastically decreed that twenty warships be sent to help Miletus and appointed Melanthius to command this force.

There is yet another unusual undercurrent in the narrative of this war. It is the very curious omission in Herodotus' history, our main and almost sole source for the revolt of the Ionian cities against Persia,[30] of any notice about oracular advice sought or given by the participants in this conflagration of Asia Minor, which lasted for nearly a decade at the start of the fifth century BC. On the other hand, there are numerous oracles preserved throughout Herodotus' account and many episodes of individuals and states seeking advice from cult centres such as Delphi and Didyma. His information illustrates the importance, albeit perhaps of fairly recent significance,[31] of the oracles in everyday life among the Greeks. This is surely of some significance in an analysis of the record of this affair for there is hardly a mention whatsoever of an oracle in connection with this rebellion. Thus it would not have been out of place for Aristagoras to seek the advice of an oracle before he committed himself and Miletus to the rebellion. The absence of such an episode is striking considering the importance of the oracles delivered by the priestess at Delphi in, for example, the story of Croseus' fall from power in Lydia in 545 BC or indeed the stark warnings to the Athenians about their future when faced with invasion by Xerxes.[32] Finally, on this question it should be noted that the section of Herodotus' history devoted to the visit of Aristagoras and Hippias to Sparta in 500 BC is particularly rich in oracular material of warnings to the Spartans (5.90) and to the Corinthians (5.92), but there is nothing at all regarding the revolt of the Ionians. The omission is startling and must surely have struck the audience as extremely menacing. In the few fragments we possess of Diodorus' account of the war significantly one relates to the Carians (10.25.2) seeking an oracle for advice about whom they should ally themselves in their fight with the Persians. The oracle is said to have been: 'The Milesians of old once were brave.' This is typically ambiguous since it might simply imply that the Milesians were great warriors or, less charitably, that they had been in the past but were no longer. The Carians chose to ally themselves with the Greeks. If the Carians who were not Greeks, although their cities, including Halicarnassus, were very close to Ionia sought an oracle why indeed does Herodotus not recount a similar action for any of the Greek cities, and why should he also omit to mention the information that Diodorus provides and which the much later historian probably obtained from the Athenian historian Ephorus? Furthermore, Herodotus actually mentioned the oracle at Didyma near the beginning of his history (1.157) where he says that: 'There was an oracle established there from long ago.' And that 'this place belongs to the Milesians and is above the harbour at Panormus.' So famous was the oracular site at Miletus that failure to consult it before embarking on such a dangerous course seems almost too incredible to contemplate. Herodotus either really did not think it worthwhile relating or that Aristagoras chose to ignore a normal and almost obligatory habit or was it that it meant to the audience that failure was inevitable from the outset? This may in part be related to the fact that Aristagoras who was regent for Histiaeus evidently turned demagogue and while he had himself elected general of the Milesians left the running of the government to some other form of representative or participative body, which means that a democracy could well have been established.[33] His argument for a revolt was not greeted with universal enthusiasm and was strongly countered by Hecataeus (Hdt. 5.35) who must have represented some influential opinion in Miletus but on whose behalf did he speak? Herodotus sadly gives no indication but it is very likely that there was a strong sentiment against rebellion even if this was silenced in the face of enthusiasm for a war against the dominant power in the region.

The role of Miletus is highlighted by Herodotus but he also indicates that the cities of Ionia acted together as a league or confederacy with some form of governing council that could organize the rebellion, seek out new allies by whom it was also approached when ties were sought against Persia. There has been some argument to the effect that such a council was able to manage the campaign in the same way that as the later campaign against Persia were coordinated by the Hellenic League under Spartan leadership or the Delian League under Athenian leadership. Representatives of the cities of Ionia and some of the islands probably met from time to time but there does not appear to have been a high level of cooperation between them and Aristagoras seems to have maintained a major role at least in the first three to four years of the war. He was the person to win over the Athenians and Eretrians who dealt exclusively with Miletus and came to the aid of this city and not to a broader community. Their presence allowed the rebels to contemplate the attack on Sardis, which began as soon as the mainland Greeks arrived in Ionia. What was the purpose of the Ionian-led invasion of Lydia other than the capture and sack of Sardis, the residence of the satrap Artaphernes? Was the campaign simply meant to provide the Greeks with a propaganda coup or was something more tangible at stake such as plunder to finance the revolt? What made the Greeks believe that this expedition could be successful and that they would not fall foul of Persian troops? Herodotus offers a creditable reason for an attack on Sardis, which was probably meant to be for its moveable resources rather than an occupation (Herodt. 5.101). However, the Greeks probably had little in the way of siege equipment or a baggage train so how did they intend to take such a well-fortified city, which could easily endure a siege of many weeks if not months?

The Athenians and Eretrians and some other unspecified allies, probably islanders, came to Aristagoras, but Herodotus is actually rather vague and it looks as if there was little contact between the former and the Milesians before they arrived. The Greeks will probably have made for Miletus since they were asked to help this city by its most prominent citizen. But this implies that little planning had yet been considered by the rebels whose forces were scattered among the various cities and clearly there had yet to be a central rendezvous point and some plan for future warfare. Whatever forces the Milesians possessed, and they were probably not that strong, perhaps about five thousand hoplites, possibly less, they were joined by the Athenians and Eretrians, numbering not many more than about two thousand, which represents the crew of twenty biremes or pentekonters from Athens and five from Eretria.[34] Rowers might be armed but, in later times at least, these constituted light armed troops and were certainly not hoplite heavy infantry since these would have been carried in transport ships and there is no mention of such vessels in addition to the twenty voted under the command of Melanthius. Herodotus is quite specific here in claiming that it was the twenty warships, which probably represent a half the Athenian war fleet that was the cause of all the later warfare between the Greeks and the Persians. At Marathon a decade later the Athenians could field ten thousand hoplites and it is highly unlikely that any were despatched to Ionia. The combined army that left Miletus was therefore somewhere between six and ten thousand infantry or various sorts, some hoplites some light armed troops. There may also have been some cavalry numbered in hundreds rather than thousands.

Considering its composition therefore this was no army intent on a pitched battle but a raiding party. It cannot have constituted the entire armed forces available to the Ionian cities moreover and, although it is not stated by Herodotus, further troops must have joined the expedition from Ephesus and the other centres. He also states that although it was Aristagoras who initiated the campaign he did not command in person, but had appointed two other Milesians, Charopinus and Hermophantus, as generals.[35] These evidently then proceeded north to Ephesus where they were met by other Ionians who had come by sea and who had brought their ships ashore at Coresus (Herodt. 5.100). Ephesus was not, however, the most obvious starting place for this attack since the easiest and most direct route for any invading force coming from the coastal fringe into the interior is by the Hermus Valley, starting at Phocaea past Magnesia ad Sipylum and then to Sardis. This was a well-established line of communication, and remains so today, and a distance of one hundred and fifty kilometres (90 miles) would have taken a largely infantry force a little less than a week's march. Herodotus' account of the attack on Sardis (5.100) shows that the Ionian Greeks chose instead to march up the valley of the Cayster and approach Sardis from the south, which also meant that they would have to cross Mount Tmolus perhaps via the town of Hypaepa. The distance involved is a great deal less than the more northerly route and only approximately one hundred kilometres (62 miles). It was, however, more difficult for an armed force to cross the mountain and probably meant that any thought of conveying a siege train was abandoned for the element of surprise. The tactic certainly paid off because the authorities in Sardis were so nonplussed that the Greeks were able to gain entrance without much fighting. Yet how were the Ionians able to enter Sardis, which resulted in the accidental burning of the city? Sardis surely possessed extensive and formidable fortifications, as the later city certainly possessed (see plate), but the ease with which the Greeks obtained entry suggests either that after the fall of Croesus in 545 when there had been a siege of Sardis and the city had been captured by the Persian army with Cyrus in attendance, that the walls had been dismantled or that in some way the city had been left weakened against possible uprising,[36] or that there had been a traitor inside the garrison who had allowed the enemy to gain entrance. The citadel remained in Persian hands because Artaphernes was in residence with sufficiently strong forces to withstand an attack but evidently not enough to defend the whole city. The coverage is rather confused here for it has also been claimed that the Greeks were not prepared to remain since a Persian relief column was expected. At the same time, while the Greeks seemed about to succeed in at least one objective by securing rich plunder to fund their rebellion they apparently had no time to ransack the city. This was because the private dwellings in the city so Herodotus tells us (5.101) were either made of wattle and daub or had thatched roofs, and when one of these was mistakenly set alight the fire rapidly took hold because the civilian population had fled. However, Herodotus also says that the population had not entirely quit the city but together with Persian armed forces that had not retired to the citadel had congregated beside the Pactolus River that flows down from Mount Tmolus and through the city before it joined the Hermus. There they put up such a spirited defence that the Greeks, with fire on the one hand and a determined fight on the other and wary no doubt of a possible sortie from Artaphernes' troops decided to effect an immediate withdrawal.

How long could the Ionians have fielded his expedition? It was clearly not a campaign that occurred over longer than two to three weeks in the summer months. Indeed, Herodotus' account of the brief presence of the Greeks inside Sardis appears to indicate that they were there for no longer than a single day. But is this campaign to be dated to the summer of 499 or 498? While considerable haste is implied it is highly unlikely that Aristagoras can conceivably have visited Sparta, Athens, Eretria and other putative allies early enough in 499 in order to return to Miletus to raise the banner of revolt, receive the promised aid from the Athenians and Eretrians and move to sack Sardis and be defeated outside Ephesus, all within the space of one summer. Furthermore, an assessment of the entire regional situation indicates that contacts between various cities across Asia Minor had been taking place and some planning for a revolt seems at least plausible. Therefore, it is probably more likely that Aristagoras was in mainland Greece searching for allies either in the course of 500 or in 499 and the Sardis campaign probably belongs to the next year, either 499 or 498. The expedition to Naxos is usually dated to shortly before the start of the Ionian War thus either to the campaigning season before 500 or 499 since a causal connection is advanced between Aristagoras' failure and his artifice in persuading the Greeks to rise against Persia. But Aristagoras' position was not so precarious and it is by no means certain that his role in the Naxian affair would have resulted in his demotion or replacement. His place as ruler of Miletus was clearly not Artaphernes' gift so consultation with Darius would have had to take place before any action could have been taken and this again was not likely to occur seeing the continued favour shown to Histiaeus. The chronology of events before the banner of revolution was raised might indeed be less closely connected with the date of Aristagoras' participation in an attack on Naxos. When the temporal relationship between the earlier events is loosened then the chronology of the events in 499/8 also has more sense. The course of events then covers the whole of the summer months of the year probably following the one in which Aristagoras went to Greece since the logistics of providing support to the Ionians would have taken time to organize. The campaign of probably 498 then hinges on the routes of two armies, their origins of departure and the objectives of each and the three valleys involved: Sardis in the Valley of the Hermus with Phocaea at its mouth, Ephesus at the mouth of the Cayster, Miletus on the southern shore of the Gulf of Latmos on the estuary of the Meander River. It has been argued that the Greeks were able to destroy Sardis because it had been left with insufficient garrison because Artaphernes had ordered an attack on Miletus.[37] If that was the case then the two armies had passed by one another, the Greeks advancing up the Cayster, the Persians moving down the Meander. But is this feasible? It was certainly not unique for armies in antiquity to miss one another even if in close proximity of one another because the practice of scouts and reconnaissance was haphazard. Alexander the Great and Darius III lost one another on the Taurus Mountains in 331 before they eventually fought as Issus, while Philip V of Macedonia was not aware that a Roman army was marching alongside his army separated by a line of low hills at Cynoscephalae in 197 BC. Nonetheless, it is plausible to argue that the Persians attacked Miletus in 499 while Aristagoras was in Greece and that the counterattack with mainland Greek support belongs to possibly late 499 or the summer of 498. This drew the Persians north where they intercepted the Greeks on their return down the Cayster Valley and unluckily for the rebels they were defeated outside Ephesus and safety.[38] There were severe losses including the Eretrian commander. At this point the Athenians returned to their ships and departed and later when requested by the Ionians refused further aid. Did they perhaps blame the Ionians for the defeat or was this change of sentiment meant to illustrate the quixotic nature of Athenian democracy in this period? Herodotus possibly out of loyalty towards the Ionian Greeks leaves unclear just why the Persians appear to have been unable to make the most of their victory and extinguish the rebellion in its early stages. They had defeated the combined Greek and Ionian forces and appear to have had Miletus under siege yet there was no forceful move to stamp out the rebellion. This suggests that the defeat at Ephesus was not comprehensive and that the Ionian cities had the resources to move forward with their war.[39]

Did the campaign to Sardis occur simultaneously with a Persian attack on Miletus or was it a counterattack? In Plutarch's *de Herodoti Malignitate* (24) he notes that according to Lysanius of Mallus Herodotus was economical with the truth when he assigned so much significance to the presence of the Athenians in Ionia. We might infer from this comment that Plutarch wanted to draw attention to the Atheno–centric nature of Herodotus' history and that here the Eretrian contingent deserved at least as much notice for he says that it had contributed greatly to a defeat of Persian fleet somewhere along the coast of Pamphylia before it arrived at Ephesus. Herodotus clearly conflates the information giving out that all the allies gathered by Aristagoras went initially to Miletus. However, this may be improbable if the city was already under siege from a Persian army sent by Artaphernes from Sardis to quell the first signs of rebellion in Ionia. If Miletus was already under siege then it is unlikely that the Milesians will have been able to spare any large number of troops for a diversionary attack on Sardis but would explain why Aristagoras did not take personal command of the expedition. It would also mean that the newly arrived allies if they went to Miletus at all soon went on to Ephesus by sea.

The attack on Sardis therefore must have appeared to have been a successful venture in that it caused the Persian force if indeed outside Miletus to break the siege and move to intercept the Greeks. It was therefore a high risk strategy that ultimately failed since the Persians probably had superior forces in the field and may indeed have forced the Greeks to fight their way into Ephesus and not have the city behind them and facing the enemy coming from the west rather than from the east. This is of interest especially since Plutarch says that another early writer, in this case Charon of Lampsacus, indicated that the Athenians returned to Miletus after the attack on Sardis. The Greeks may have had no option after their defeat if they had been caught not only by the Persians from Sardis but also those coming from the south. Yet Herodotus claims (5.103) that far from being disheartened by this withdrawal the Ionian cities went on the offensive and sent a fleet through the Hellespont bringing over to them all the cities in the vicinity and capturing Byzantium. He then notes that the cities of Caria also joined the rebellion and specifically mentions Caunus, which had been reluctant beforehand, now as a result of the partial sack of Sardis, became an enthusiastic supporter of the revolt.[40]

The confusion in Herodotus' account is to some extent mitigated when he returns to affairs in Ionia but only after his lengthy discussion of the rebellion that occurred in Cyprus (5.103–115). He relates how the Persian generals Daurises, Hymaees and Otanes (5.116), all sons-in-law of the king, followed up their victory outside Ephesus by pursuing the Greeks – he probably means Athenians, Eretrians and other allies – to their ships.[41] Thereafter they divided their forces to attack the various cities and sacked them one by one. Yet, it is clear that this is very much a summary of the actual course of events since the historian concentrates albeit very briefly on the activities of Daurises. Moreover, this appears to have taken place at precisely the moment when the Ionian fleet was active in the same area winning over cities. So while this Persian general was clearly assigned the recapture of cities along the Hellespont and Propontis and seems quite rapidly to have regained control of Dardanus, Abydos, Percote, Lampsacus and Paesus this may not in fact have been the case at all. Besides all this military activity, as Daurises was advancing towards Parium, near the Granicus River, he heard that the Carians had joined the Ionians in rebellion and so turned south to deal with this latest crisis. And so the two threads in Herodotus' account come together again with events in Caria becoming the focus of the narrative. Following the battle at Ephesus in 499/8 Miletus was at least saved from a siege or the threat of a siege, but Ephesus may well have been invested by at least one of Darius' generals and had fallen to the Persians.[42] To draw off Persian forces away from Ionia and give some breathing space here the Ionians sent their fleet north and Daurises went after the Greeks. As the cities capitulated to the Greeks they were retaken by the Persians but the prize of Byzantium must have been a feather in the cap of the Greeks while efforts to persuade the Carians to rebel also forced Daurises to give up the chase in that sector.

Herodotus' focus suddenly changes from Ionia to Cyprus and Caria, and Ionia no longer features in the narrative until shortly before the entire war came to an end. The revolt in Cyprus, which was to involve a major sea and land battle followed by a number of sieges in mopping up operations, is enclosed between the Greek attack on Sardis and its immediate aftermath. Therefore if the chronological narrative of Herodotus is to be followed closely it suggests that the Cypriot cities also rose against the Persians at just about the same time as the Ionians and that there was an intention in this almost simultaneous action to cause maximum disruption as an aid to their eventual chance of success. However, Herodotus as usual in his approach places the blame for the rebellion on personal ambition. He claims that a certain Onesilas of Salamis was responsible for the starting the uprising in Cyprus. Onesilas had already attempted to persuade Gorgus, the king of Salamis, who was also his brother, to rebel but the latter would have none of it. Herodotus says that when Onesilas heard of the Ionian revolt he put the case again more forcibly but Gorgus was still not to be persuaded. When Gorgus left the city on some business Onesilas took power himself and barred his brother who fled into exile. Onesilas at once convinced the other Cypriot cities to join in a rebellion except for Amathus, which he began to besiege (Herodt. 5.108).

Herodotus claims that it was when the Cypriot cities first broke into rebellion that Darius learned of the sack of Sardis and the participation in this provocative act of the Athenians. Hence the timing must be tightly fixed to the summer of 499 or 498. Darius is said in anger to have fired off an arrow skywards and appealed to Zeus to allow him the opportunity to have his revenge on these Greeks of 'the other continent', and ordered, says Herodotus, a servant to always remind him of the Athenians' existence.[43] He was particularly concerned to hear that leadership among the Ionians seemed to have devolved on Aristagoras, kinsman of Histiaeus, who was present in the royal court. Histiaeus was summoned and asked to explain to a frankly sceptical Darius why these events at Miletus and elsewhere could have happened without the knowledge of this former dynast from Asia Minor. Histiaeus denied all knowledge of his son-in-law's actions, although Herodotus has already told of this man's encouragement of Aristagoras' plans and conniving in them. Instead Histieaus aiming to accomplish his subterfuge asked for permission to return to Ionia as a peacemaker. It seems unlikely that, for a king who was to reign for nearly thirty-five years, Darius can have been so naïve as to believe a character so obviously as wily as Histiaeus. Herodotus would have us believe that the Greek hoodwinked the Persian but it is far more probable that the astute Darius knew that by showing trust in the tyrant of Miletus and allowing him to return to Asia Minor a damaging conflict might be solved without further expense.[44]

Meanwhile, Darius had clearly given orders for the reconquest of Cyprus, and a general named Artybius (Herodt. 5.108) was appointed for this purpose. Onesilas was still held outside Amathus when he heard this news and convened a meeting of the leaders of the Cypriot cities who, realizing the need for allies in their war, applied to the Ionians for help. The Ionians did not hesitate, buoyed up by their recent victory at Sardis and not at all, it seems, depressed by their later defeat at Ephesus. It is likely that they expected the rapid spread in the revolt to lessen pressure on their own efforts, and despatched a large fleet. The Persians appear to have landed on the island near Salamis at about the same time as the Ionians, but had made their crossing from Cilicia, probably Tarsus, using Phoenician vessels as transports accompanied by a fleet of warships. This fleet, its defence of the land forces successfully completed now sailed north and rounded the long promontory that is known today as the Karpas Peninsula, but for Herodotus 'The Keys of Cyprus' (5.108) and headed along the north coast to offer battle to the Ionians. The Cypriot and Ionian Greeks are now supposed to have held a conference, and a rather odd debate is said to have taken place in which the former offered the latter a sort of carte blanche in the impending campaigns. Herodotus claims that the Cypriot leadership were happy to hand over the campaign on land to the Ionians if they preferred to leave their ships, which could be manned by their own local crews or they could fight on the sea in their own fleet. The reply was that the League of Ionians had sent them as a fleet and that therefore they would fight as such rather than as infantry on land. This matter was settled, and the land forces of both sides converged near Salamis. Onesilas drew up his forces for battle placing himself and the contingents from Salamis and Soli opposite Artybius and his Persians.[45] Quite obviously Herodotus had few if any details to draw on for this engagement so falls back instead on a lively but entertaining tale (Herodt. 5.111–112) about Artybius' warhorse, which had been trained to rear up against any enemy and kick and bite any potential attacker. Onesilas wanted to know whether an opponent in battle with Artybius should go for the rider or the horse and asked one of his soldiers, perhaps a Carian mercenary, for advice. This well respected and experienced soldier replied that he would attack either as his commanding officer chose but also suggested that a general should engage another general and that he as a subordinate should make for the horse. This agreed the battle began in earnest.

The Ionians are said to have engaged the Phoenician fleet and came off best with the ships of Samos showing particular bravery. On land the forces were more evenly matched. Artybius made for Onesilas and as they had planned beforehand the Cypriot general proceeded to engage his opposite number but the horse reared up and its hooves crashed against his shield. Meanwhile, the Carian infantryman came up behind and sliced off the horse's legs and with the horse went the Persian general, killed within a few minutes of the assault. The battle continued until the men of Curium broke rank and went over to enemy, and these were followed by the citizens of Salamis in their war chariots with the result that a rout began in which Onesilas was killed.[46] Salamis immediately surrendered to its former king, Gorgus, while Onesilas' head was impaled on a stake and set up on a gate at Amathus, although it was soon removed and buried with honours in a local shrine at which annual sacrifices were made for the prosperity of the city.[47] Soli was the sole city to be besieged and it fell after a being invested for five months when a part of its walls was undermined by the Persians (Herodt. 5.115).[48] The Ionians and their fleet returned home soon after the defeat of the Cypriots on land and no attempt was made to send help to the people of Soli. The revolt in Cyprus was therefore suppressed after just two military engagements, presumably within one campaigning season at the latest early in 498 or 497.

The revolt of Caria was much more serious, and its start is probably to be dated not much later than that of Cyprus. The timing shows not only the intensity of the local discontent with Persia, but that some skilful planning had taken place beforehand and that there were cool and calculating minds in the background who appear to have had a good grasp of strategy and had control over at least the initial phase of this rebellion. Sadly little information has survived about the leading figures in this dispute, except for Aristagoras. Herodotus our main source has little good to say about him (Herodt. 5.124) but that does not mean that he lacked ability. Some personal antagonism may lie at the root of the portrayal of this Milesian who was no friend of Hecataeus whose own record of events was employed by Herodotus. The fighting in Caria was also more intense and protracted and consisted of a larger number of land engagements than elsewhere. The Carian cities seem to have had more resources than their neighbours yet relatively little detail about the war and its protagonists exist in spite of the fact that Herodotus was a native of Caria. When the Carians heard that Daurises fresh from his re-establishment of Persian control of the Hellespont was moving south to meet them, they gathered at the Marsyas River (Herodt. 5.118) at a place called the 'White Pillars' or Λεύκαι στῆλαι to the south of the Meander River and a little to the north of the Carian cities of Alabanda and Alinda, although neither are mentioned by Herodotus. What he does relate is a discussion about strategy between the various Carian commanders who included a certain Pixodarus of Cindye, a town near to Miletus.[49] This general advocated an advance into Ionia and crossing the Meander River to face the Persian army, which was moving down from the north. His argument was that with the Meander behind them there was no easy refuge and that this fact would make the troops fight more keenly for a victory.[50] This was not accepted however, and the Carians allowed the Persian army to cross the Meander and into their own territory.[51] They hoped that the Carian troops would be able to push their enemy back to the river from where escape would be difficult. The engagement therefore began between the two rivers some distance inland from the Gulf of Latmos but still easy marching distance to Miletus. The Milesians must have watched with considerable anxiety the movement of Persian forces coming down the coastal plain either directly from Mysia and the Hellespont or via Sardis and the Hermus Valley. The siege of Miletus appears to have been lifted by the Persians just before they defeated the Greeks at Ephesus but a new assault was directly dependent on the performance in battle of the Ionians' latest allies. The battle was hard fought and the Carians were driven from the field with losses says Herodotus (5.119) amounting to ten thousand as opposed to Persian casualties numbering a fifth of that total. The high death rate among both sides indicates that the balance was fairly even before a rout began; and it is said that the surviving Carians fled first to Labraunda and were then besieged at the shrine of Zeus Stratios or 'Zeus of the Army', which was probably just outside this city.[52] Labraunda is situated close to Mylasa, then the chief city of Caria, and both of these cities are some distance to the south of Marsyas River, which indicates the extent of the retreat by Carian forces after their reverse at the Meander.

While they were near Labraunda the Carian leaders discussed whether they should come to terms with the Persians or leave Asia altogether. Before they reached a decision, however, relief arrived in the shape of Milesian and other Ionian forces, which promptly restored confidence. When the Persians launched another attack, rather than withdraw, the allies joined battle again in which they were even more comprehensively defeated than in the previous battle. The forces from Miletus were especially badly mauled in this fight. Persian superiority in numbers was clearly a decisive factor here and the army commanded by Daurises, which must have been around twenty thousand infantry, had a good advantage over the Greeks and Carians combined who may have totalled half this number after their recent losses. The Persians were confident now that they had gained so many victories while their opponents would have collected only a string of defeats. Nonetheless, the Greeks apparently left their defensive position inside the *temenos* of Zeus, which is said to have been unusual in that it was formed from a dense copse of plane trees. The Milesians may have been assigned the left wing, which then bore the brunt of the Persian right, which might explain why they received the most severe casualties in this encounter. Still, this second defeat did not bring about the capitulation of the Carians, far from it, since they seem to have made their escape and continued the fight. The Ionian Greeks perhaps withdrew after Labraunda to look after their own defences while the Persians decided to press on to Pedasa near Halicarnassus. The Persian strategy was probably to divide the coastal cities from the interior and so weaken resolve among the Carians. Fortunately for the Carians the Persians had become overconfident and when ambushed in a night attack the army of Daurises was routed and the general himself, with two of his senior commanders, Amorges and Sisimaces, was killed.[53] The details of this event are also scant, yet it was of immense importance since it more than compensated for all the previous Carian defeats.

This seems to have brought an end to the Persian offensive in Caria probably towards the end of the summer of 498, while in Ionia it appears as if there was also a lull in military activities. Herodotus (5.122) shifts his focus back to the Troad and the Hellespont where Hymaees, another of the Persian commanders, had clearly been working in tandem with Daurises. The latter had concentrated on the Hellespont where opposition to the Persians had been rapidly overcome, while Hymaees had marched further northwest and taken back the city of Cius.[54] When he heard that Daurises had turned south to face the revolt in Caria, Hymaees rather than proceeding along the southern shore of the Propontis towards the Bosphorus and thus placing himself at too great a distance from his fellow commander, also turned west to conduct a mopping up operation in the Troad and from there to link up with Daurises further south. Hymaees seems not to have encountered much opposition in the area but died suddenly of some illness (Herodt. 5.122). The loss of at least two experienced generals could have placed the Persian offensive in jeopardy but there was clearly no shortage of talent in this profession as the Lydian satrap Artaphernes now took direct control of military operations aided by Otanes, who had also been involved in the Ionian defeat at Ephesus. Between them they captured Cyme in Aeolia and then Clazomenae. The loss of this important city to the Ionian cause must have been viewed as ominous and grave. Indeed at Miletus there was a crisis of confidence among the leadership, especially the man whom Herodotus accuses (5.124) of full responsibility for the entire affair, namely Aristagoras.

Aristagoras was perhaps more astute than Herodotus gives him credit because he summoned his friends and advisers to discuss the deteriorating fortunes of the Ionian Greeks. He is said to have recognized that defeat of the Persians was now out of the question and flight from Asia was fast becoming the logical conclusion. The Carians had of course gone through a similar period of soul searching and had opted to carry on with the fight, but Aristagoras is portrayed as lacking that mettle. He advised that he and all his supporters might immigrate to Sardinia or failing that might occupy Myrcinus in the Chersonese, which had been granted to Histiaeus by Darius and which had been fortified by the former tyrant. Hecataeus, clearly still an influential figure in Miletus, argued that to go so far afield seemed unwise and would be a permanent move allowing no possibility of a return. He suggested instead that Aristagoras fortify the nearby Island of Leros – one of the Dodecanese – and keep a low profile until such time that he could return to Miletus. Notably Hecataeus did not appear to be about to follow Aristagoras, although he was present at the deliberations among the inner circle of the latter's friends.[55] Predictably, since this advice had come from Hecataeus, Aristagoras did not consider it sound and preferred instead to head to Thrace and Myrcinus. Clearly he was not in favour of skulking on some far off spot from which he could somehow regain his position at Miletus, and while there also ran the risk of capture. A prominent citizen named Pythagoras was given charge of the city while Aristagoras set sail with his friends for Myrcinus. How long he was in Thrace is not known and Herodotus merely says that he met his death fighting against a Thracian tribe whose city he was besieging.[56] A death in battle was not ignominious but Herodotus cannot resist stating that it was needless since the Thracians had offered to give up their city to the Milesians under a truce implying that Aristagoras was in some way being treacherous and paid the price for his intrigues (Herodt. 5.126). It is impossible to recover the reasons for Herodotus' relentlessly negative portrayal of Aristagoras who was probably a good deal more talented than is described.[57] The source may well have been Hecataeus who appears to have been largely at odds with Aristagoras over Miletus' policies in this period and who was held in some regard by Herodotus.[58]

Aristagoras' departure from Ionia might have signalled a good opportunity for coming to terms with the Persians, but clearly the Greeks were having none of that and warfare continued unabated. It was perhaps coincidental that it was precisely at this moment that Histiaeus should have reappeared in Asia Minor. He had made his way from Susa to Sardis where he met Artaphernes

(Herodt. 6.1) who questioned him closely about the causes of the rebellion and his own possible part in instigating the war.[59] Histiaeus again denied any involvement with his son–in–law's intrigues but Artaphernes was clearly not satisfied and the interview ended with the latter's retort: 'the entire affair is like this; Histiaeus it was you who planned it and Aristagoras who led it' (Herodt. 6.1).[60] Herodotus says that Histiaeus either lost his nerve or realized that he would soon be eliminated and so fled from Sardis to the coast and took a ship to Chios. However, no sooner had he arrived on the island that he was thrown into prison on suspicion of being a spy of the Persians. Yet when he told his story he was released. This is plausible enough but it seems at least as likely that Histiaeus and Artaphernes collaborated in this episode to have the former accepted back among the Ionians who can hardly have had friendly memories of this ex-tyrant, supporter and confident of Darius. Whatever the historical background to Histiaeus' arrival on Chios, his story was initially accepted but within a short time when he was questioned about why he had encouraged Aristagoras to organize a rebellion he spun another tale about mass removal of people from Ionia to Phoenicia and vice versa. This tale was meant to cause panic and seems to have had some impact on his audience for he was left in peace.[61] Still, his intrigues continued unabated with letters that he wrote to certain Persian friends and acquaintances in Sardis inciting them to rebel against Artaphernes. These letters were entrusted to a certain Hermippus who delivered them not to their recipients but to the satrap (Herodt. 6.4). Artaphernes took immediate action; he arrested and executed the conspirators so that Histiaeus' plotting was completely foiled. The Chians offered to intercede on his behalf with the Milesians and persuade them to take him back. The Milesians, says Herodotus, only recently relieved of Aristagoras and enjoying an unaccustomed freedom from autocratic rule, refused to consider the prospect of having their former ruler among them again. Histiaeus then made an attempt to enter the city by night and stage a coup, but he was driven out and wounded. The Chians may have transported him to Miletus and it was to the island he returned but they refused further military aid and so he departed for Lesbos. The citizens of Mytilene, surprisingly perhaps, offered to supply him with a flotilla of eight warships and with these he sailed to the Bosphorus. Herodotus says that Histiaeus established himself at Byzantium, which was presumably still in Greek not Persian hands, and indulged in some piracy by preventing any vessels from sailing out of the Euxine and into the Propontis unless their crews were prepared to serve under him.[62] Either that or Histiaeus exacted a tithe for ships passing through the Bosphorus with which he was able to maintained and strengthen his own position. His action may not have been without some underlying reasoning for by causing problems to his fellow Greeks, especially the Milesians, he reminded them of his presence and perhaps in time they would consider him an asset to their cause. No doubt the Ionians knew of his presence but reconciliation did not occur.

Meanwhile, the Persian commanders decided to combine all their forces for a major assault on Miletus instead of tackling a number of cities simultaneously. The strategy was surely that with the loss of Miletus, regarded as the leading city of the rebellion, they would rapidly bring about a termination of the hostilities everywhere. A fleet was gathered probably somewhere northwest of Cyprus along the coast the Pamphylia and brought together contributions from the cities of Phoenicia such as Tyre and Sidon, the Cypriot cities, by now re-conquered by the Persians, Cilicians and Egyptians (Herodt. 6.6). The Ionians must have been aware for some time that the Persian war machine would eventually be galvanized into action on a scale that they could not match, yet they were not prepared to come to any terms that would result in peace in the region. It is quite probable that the leading figures in this revolt, perhaps not necessarily friends of either Aristagoras or Histiaeus but who had benefited from the rebellion, knew that they had everything to lose and nothing to gain by making peace.[63] The cities that were still free from Persian control – Clazomenae was now in enemy hands – met at Panionium on the peninsula of Mount Mycale across the Bay of Latmos from Miletus and close to Priene.[64] They knew that on land they were no match for a Persian army that may well have numbered fifty thousand or so in total. The strength of the Ionians, especially the islanders but also Miletus, with its long history of overseas trade, was in their naval arm. The meeting at Panionium broke up with the decision not to try a relief of Miletus by land but rather risk a major sea engagement in the belief that a victory over a Persian fleet would ensure that the city could be maintained by supplies brought in by ship and that in time the Persian attackers would run short of supplies themselves and be forced to withdraw. Herodotus says none of this but it seems to be the most likely thrust of any argument put forward by the leaders of the Greeks on this occasion. Invading forces unless they had a rapid victory and overran a besieged city were often forced to retreat from a lack of supplies or if they were badly affected by the sorts of diseases that were integral to any large scale encampment of military forces without sanitation. The strategy made the best of a difficult situation but was one which could not possibly produce anything other than a pause in the Persian attempts to reincorporate Ionia. The Greeks were therefore playing for time so what can they have considered possible longer-term advantages? The first and most obvious would have been to use a victory at sea to obtain more lenient terms from Darius who did not have the reputation as a vengeful ruler. It is perhaps less likely that secondly they considered trying to win over new allies. The closest neighbours in Caria and on Cyprus had been lost to them, while the cities around the Propontis and in the Troad were also now under Persian control. They may have sent delegates to mainland Greece, although such a mission is not recorded by Herodotus nor is it present in any other account such as Diodorus. If they did send envoys their pleas must evidently have fallen on disinterested ears and there seems to be no memory at all of discussions about aiding the Ionians at this time. It is just possible, however, that some message was delivered and discussed at Athens in 495. The rejection of any aid to the Milesians after a heated public discussion may well account for the explosion of grief which is reported at the production of Phrynichus' play about the destruction of Miletus later in the decade (Herodt. 6.21). The heated response of the audience may in part have its origin in a guilty conscience for not sending aid when it was needed.[65]

While the Persians mustered their land forces, which may indeed have already advanced on and invested Miletus since this was now the summer of 494 BC, the Ionians began to gather their fleet.[66] The Persians would usually have advanced west from Sardis and not further afield, but the rest of Asia Minor needed to be secured first. Thus the war in Caria seems to have been concluded only in the previous winter months and the Hecatomnid ruler of Mylasa, Pixodarus, was able to extract favourable terms from the Persians to make peace.[67] It is also quite clear that the Persian campaigning in Caria, which earlier on had brought support from Miletus and other Ionian cities, must have lasted nearly as long a time as the entire Ionian Revolt. This view seems plausible since the events in Caria that conclude Herodotus' narrative in Book 5 (5.121) must be temporally closer to the sea battle at Lade and the Persian assault on Miletus which brought an end to all but mopping up operations than to the attack on Sardis. It is quite likely that the Carians, including leaders such as Pixodarus, like their neighbours in Ionia, retreated into their various strongholds, each of which then withstood a siege by the Persians and witnessed heavy fighting at all stages.[68] The fleet of the Persians, as was usually the case for campaigns they conducted at the western edge of the empire, had to sail long distances from their main harbours in Egypt and the Levant. There may have been opposition from the Rhodians at Lindos but this does not appear to have caused much delay in the Persian arrival.[69] On the other hand, while no great distances were involved for the few remaining free Greek cities the rendezvous for their combined forces was the Island of Lade at the mouth of the Gulf of Latmos, and within sight of the walls of Miletus.[70] The Ionians who were still free from Persian control were joined by a contingent from Lesbos, who Herodotus describes as ethnic Aeolians (Herodt. 6.8). The Greek fleet and its various assigned divisions are recounted by Herodotus in much the same as he does for all the major battles in his history. For the sea battle at Lade Hecataeus was probably his source. Herodotus relates that the Milesians was given the eastern end of the line or the left wing that was closest to the shore, and that they provided eighty warships. Next to these were their neighbours Priene and Myus with a total between them of fifteen triremes.[71] In addition, the citizens of Teos north of Ephesus sent seventeen vessels and next to them were the Chians with one hundred warships. Erythrae, still evidently free, and Phocaea, had sent eight and three ships respectively.[72] Next to the Phocaeans were the men of Lesbos with seventy ships and finally on the right or western wing were the Samians with another sixty triremes. The total for the combined Greek fleet was three hundred and fifty-three warships.[73]

The total number of warships in the Greek fleet may sound impressive, and it is claimed that the Persian generals were surprised at this number, but it was probably still heavily outnumbered by the opposition. Herodotus (6.9) gives a figure of six hundred for the Persian fleet, a figure that has been challenged, but it is not likely to be far from correct since Darius would surely not have countenanced any further weakness in his military forces after a war that had dragged into its sixth year.[74] On the other hand the Milesians evidently had found eighty warships when they apparently had no ships to contribute for Aristagoras' campaign against Naxos less than a decade earlier.[75] Had new ships been built in the interim and more importantly would these have been of the new design and size that have become known to us as the trireme? If these new warships were the larger and far more formidable triremes this fact would have been of grave concern to the Persian commanders. Both fleets no doubt were a mixture of larger and smaller vessels hence the seemingly high totals. At this stage in the history of the Aegean, war fleets were not yet of the homogenous nature they became during the course of the fifth century BC. The confidence of the Greeks suggests that they had at least a fair number of the newer warship types. On the other hand is Herodotus' evidence about the Cypriot vessels in the Persian fleet to be taken seriously? In the rebellion on Cyprus the rebels there appeared to be lacking a substantial naval arm, which was why they had summoned the aid of the Ionians. The answer to both questions is simple enough: that ships could easily be constructed if the raw materials were available and that warships could be readied for active duty within a season. It is also plain that in the Greek fleet many of the crews were unfamiliar with the work that would be necessary to have even a chance of victory.

Dionysius of Phocaea may have been in command of just three warships, but he claimed to have the knowledge of the sorts of tactical movements needed to obtain a victory over a numerically superior opposition. He persuaded the assembled crews and their commanders of the value of employing synchronized manoeuvres across the entire line of attack. Naval battles down to this time if they took place on the water at all – ships rarely ventured far from the shore and fighting between fleets often took place on beaches – would have involved fairly simple grappling equipment and then joining the fight between infantry carried for this purpose across two or more stationary vessels. However, Dionysius seems to have been a proponent of the *diekplous* or the breaking of the opponent's line and obtaining the advantage by attacking the broadside of the enemy's ships. Quite how this was accomplished is never stated and it clearly did not occur at Lade.[76] The *diekplous* is plainly a less refined version of the *periplous* or more general encircling movement attempted by the wings of opposing fleets that came to be drawn up like an army on land.[77] The *periplous* became a fundamental battle strategy in ancient sea warfare from the fifth century. This manoeuvre like the *diekplous* depended on whether or not the warships had rams or beaks attached to their prows. The triremes certainly possessed this armament, but it was probably also present on the smaller galleys. If a warship was rowed by its oarsmen into an enemy this beak could cause sufficient damage either to disable or even sink the opponent. But there was as much danger for the offensive movement as for the defence since acute precision was needed to avoid severe damage and disaster to one's own ship. Later on when an encircling movement was accomplished the vulnerable broadside of the opposing galleys became easy prey to the beaks of the attackers, who at the same time disabled many of the oars and oarsmen on one side of the rammed vessel.

It seems on the whole unlikely that senior figures in either fleet were unfamiliar with such tactics even if they were not used to employing them battle. Dionysius might have learned these tactics from the Carthaginians operating in the western Mediterranean, with whom the Phocaeans clashed, but the Carthaginians also maintained close links with the cities in Phoenicia and their ships must have been familiar sights in most ports across the region. Yet Herodotus asserts, perhaps to add colour to his narrative, that the Greeks were unaccustomed to even acting together. Considering the Ionians' recent success in Cyprus this again strikes the reader as a little contrived unless the historian was aiming to illustrate the rawness of the crews in their new vessels. According to Herodotus, it soon became apparent that the crews were also unhappy about the extent of the training Dionysius demanded, especially insisting that the ships remained anchored at sea for battle readiness instead of being drawn up on a beach overnight and for much of the day. The crews rapidly grew weary of his orders and after just seven days of intensive training they all but mutinied, went ashore, made encampments and ignored further demands to be ready in the event of a Persian attack.[78]

The Persian fleet had arrived near Miletus, perhaps further along the coast to the south where there are suitable places for beaching ships. They knew that the Greeks had assembled but the Persian commanders were under orders to defer battle for the time being. It transpires that Artaphernes, perhaps wanting to avoid another costly engagement, summoned for meetings the former rulers of the Ionian cities who were in his entourage. He suggested to these ex-tyrants that they should try to persuade their former citizens to desert the Ionian cause and individually come to terms with the Persians. Messages were to be carried to their cities inviting collaboration with the Persians which, if rejected, also came with the stark warning that their cities faced imminent destruction, their families reduced to slavery and certain death for all the men. There was certainly no attempt to entice these cities back into the fold and, moreover, since the messengers were sent out in secret each community thought it was the sole target and so dismissed the intrigue out of hand. However, as a result of the lack of discipline by their fellow Ionians and their contempt for Dionysius' advice the Samians wavered in their loyalty to the common cause.[79] Aeaces, a son of the former Samian tyrant Syloson, promised leniency for the city, and respect for the temples and homes if the Samians deserted to the Persians.[80] The Samian generals were not at all confident that they could now defeat their enemy and considered it very likely that even if they did so they would soon be faced with another force just as strong or even more formidable. But instead of announcing their disquiet and intention to withdraw, they remained quiet, which suggests that in fact there was no general agreement about their future action. And so when the Persian fleet moved at last into action and the Ionians set out from Lade to meet them the Samians took up their allocated position in the line. Unluckily for the Ionians, as soon the ships began to engage the Samians, as arranged, withdrew from the line and turned for home. In fact, Samos lies at the end of the peninsula on which Mount Mycale is situated and is within sight of Lade. It was not far to sail. There had clearly been some major disagreement among the Samians for, of their sixty ships eleven remained in the line and, says Herodotus, disregarded the orders of their commanders. The loss of forty-nine warships might just have been carried by the others in the fleet, but the crews of the seventy ships from Lesbos, seeing the desertion of the Samians, followed suit with the result that the entire western or right wing of the fleet, nearly a third of the fleet, was entirely lost. Herodotus also states that the other Ionian ships also fled at this point, but that would surely leave at least the Milesians, who had no choice but to stay and fight, the Chians, whom he singles out for particular praise, and the eleven Samian and the Phocaean ships.[81] This still represents nearly two hundred warships and the fight that developed proved to be a long and bitter one.

Herodotus highlighted the earlier lack of discipline among the Ionian crews and that this was a major factor in causing the desertion of the Samians. It is very strange therefore that he ascribes to the remaining warships precisely the tactics that had been promoted by and practised under the tutelage of Dionysius. It is possible that the historian had knowledge of two sources for the battle at Lade, one more negative than the other and this would account for the obviously inconsistent coverage that has come down to us.[82] He says without any comment that although the Chians in the centre had become isolated and that they suffered the worst casualties, they also behaved in an exemplary fashion, they attacked the Persian line, broke through on numerous occasions and captured many enemy ships. Yet at the same time the opposing fleets must also have engaged in grappling their opposite numbers with fighting across adjacent decks. Herodotus' description of the Chian contingent gives a clue to the use of this tactic, which was presumably commonly employed in sea battles of this time. He says that each Chian warship included forty heavily armed infantrymen (Herodt. 6.15). During the course of the fifth century it became normal practice to include thirty *epibates* or marines on each trireme along with one hundred and seventy of so oarsmen, the pilot and the trierarch, but it was possible to crowd more fighting men into each ship as Thucydides indicates in his description of the battle between the Athenians and Syracusans in the Great Harbour of Syracuse in 413 (Thuc. 7.60).[83] Still, forty hoplites for each of the one hundred Chian vessels would suggest a complement of four thousand heavy infantry standing above or among the rowers. It also suggests that the ships involved in the battle could not have been the smaller pentekonters or biremes because they would not have been able to carry such numbers and make effective use of them, which must mean that they were using the new trireme construction. This would also indicate that the Chian force alone, rowers and infantry, consisted of over twenty thousand men, which was no mean contribution to any fleet in this period of Greek history.[84] The battle seems to have carried on for much of the day. Finally, those Milesians who survived, at some point, must have retreated to their own harbour, Dionysius and his three Phocaean ships after capturing three enemy vessels retreated but not to their city, which they knew would soon be in enemy hands but to a life of piracy first in the Levant and then from a base in Sicily.[85]

Some of the Chian ships were able to extricate themselves from the fighting, probably only at sunset, and sailed for their homes, but many of their ships are described as being 'disabled', which probably means that they had lost many of their oars or indeed rowers, and since they could not outrun their pursuers, they made for the beaches at Mount Mycale and abandoned their vessels. Herodotus recounts (Herodt. 6.16) that these Chians intended making for home overland, which would have taken them through the friendly territory of Ephesus, Colophon, Lebedos, Teos and finally Erythrae where they would have found a means of crossing over to Chios. However, the Chians moving quite rapidly probably arrived in the territory of the Ephesians well after dark, probably within hours of the battle ending. The Ephesian women were celebrating the feast of the Thesmophoria, usually celebrated around harvest time, almost certainly outside the city walls at a shrine of Demeter, the goddess of fertility. Herodotus clearly relates the Ephesian version of events since it is claimed that the arrival of unidentified newcomers at night caused great alarm and that since these were considered to be marauding robbers the citizens of the city rushed out to intercept them. The surviving Chians were all massacred at the hands of fellow Greeks before the error was discovered. The citizens of Ephesus were apologetic but claimed that they had heard nothing of the defeat of their fellow Ionians near Lade. Yet from Ephesus to Miletus or Priene was not such a great distance, as noted above. A major battle, and one pivotal to the future course of the revolt and in which not many fewer than a hundred thousand men were engaged including some of its closest neighbours and allies the result of which did not reach the Ephesians by that same evening does stretch the boundaries of credulity a little and points to a later invention to protect any criticism against their honour. Indeed the episode as Herodotus retells it may well disguise the reality of the situation: that the Ephesians were well aware of the results of the battle and had either already deserted to the Persians or decided to ingratiate themselves with the winners by finishing off some of their fellow Ionians and so provide evidence for where their future allegiance lay.

The rebellion was all but over and the Ionians if they were not actively seeking some accommodation with the Persians were now fighting for the survival of their cities and no longer for their independence. Miletus was probably already under siege and with the Greek failure at Lade its fate was sealed. It seems to have withstood an assault for some weeks, which is perhaps surprising since Miletus does not occupy a strong natural position lying as it does on the flood plain of the Meander's estuary, while any chance of supplies or aid would have been prevented by the Persian blockade. The end was inevitable once the Persians brought down a section of the circuit wall and the city was subsequently sacked (Herodt. 6.18). One section of the city alongside the harbour may have been so ruined, perhaps the sector that saw the most severe fighting, that it was never rebuilt and the city's orientation was altered in later developments of the urban area.[86] Herodotus also notes that the sack of Miletus occurred six years after Aristagoras began his rebellion, either late in the autumn or early in the winter of 494, and that a substantial part of the population was forcibly relocated to Susa, and the city left deserted (Herodt. 6.22).[87] A word of caution also needs to be voiced about this reported destruction because Diodorus (10.25.4) appears to place Hecataeus in or near Miletus at the end of the revolt or soon after the Persians captured the city. It is interesting to note that this outspoken opponent of Aristagoras should have survived for so long and remained in his own city. The episode in which Hecataeus is described as an envoy to Artaphernes has been dismissed as a construct but it is actually not out of place in the circumstances. While the city was under siege or when it had been taken representations could easily have been made to the satrap about its future. The fact that Miletus did not suffer permanently in this affair suggests that its 'destruction' has been somewhat embellished in Herodotus' account and that in fact for the city and its citizens, although they may have endured considerable disruption, there may well not have been the catastrophe that is usually transmitted in the tradition and in modern accounts.

More shocking for the Greek world as a whole was the fate of the temple and precinct of Apollo at Didyma. This was completely destroyed in revenge for the Greek desecration of the temples at Sardis six years before.

> The Persians learned to burn down temples from the Greeks, giving like for like the same violence to those who had first committed the wrong. (Diod. 10.25.1)

All the treasures stored in the temple were taken away as plunder. Meanwhile, the Branchidae, an extended family or clan, who had nominal control over this Milesian site, and who provided the hereditary temple priests, if they survived, and Herodotus is silent on this issue, were relocated elsewhere in the Persian Empire.[88]

In this tense and volatile situation following the Ionian defeat at Lade Histiaeus reappeared at Chios with his fleet of borrowed or captured ships. The numbers of ships at his disposal must have grown a great deal since he was very quickly able to take control of the chaotic situation on Chios. Herodotus places the death of Aristagoras sometime before the arrival back in Asia Minor of Histiaeus and so this central figure of the revolt was no longer a player in the events. Moreover, Histiaeus was notably not considered welcome when the Ionians went to the defence of Miletus. He remained at the Bosphorus, although it might have been a wiser move to bring him into the Greek camp prior to the hostilities such was his intimate knowledge of the Persian command. After Lade Histiaeus' supremacy on Chios was brief, although he established a foothold at a place named Polichne and then took the city of Chios itself since, following their losses in the war, its defenders had been seriously depleted in strength (Herodt. 6.27). After he had installed himself as ruler of Chios, Histiaeus immediately led a force of Ionians and Aeolians against the island of Thasos (Herodt. 6.28), probably mostly supporters from Lesbos. Still this is a strange move and is perhaps not historical for it makes no strategic sense at all when Chios was already under threat from the Persians. It is possible that Histiaeus hoped to divert attention away from Ionia to the northern Aegean, although it seems a strategy not likely to have enticed the Persian commanders from their primary task of recapturing the entire seaboard of the western Aegean.[89] And so when a Persian force was reported to have left Miletus heading north Histiaeus gave up this venture and returned not to Chios but to Lesbos. Histiaeus may have found that Chios had already been occupied by the Persian fleet, and badly in need of supplies he crossed to Atarneus to plunder the harvest there and along the coast of Mysia as far south as the estuary of the Caicus River.[90] He was caught at a place named Malene by a Persian force commanded by Harpagus and although his forces were heavily outnumbered, they put up a determined resistance but were scattered when Persian cavalry detachments were deployed. After the rout Histiaeus was captured and taken as a prisoner to Sardis. Artaphernes and Harpagus knew that they should send Histiaeus to Darius but at the same time they were well aware that the king held the Milesian in high regard and was likely to forgive his recent activities. If indeed that did happen their lives would immediately be in danger if Histiaeus regained the confidence of the king. Therefore they decided on his execution and his head was sent to Susa (Herodt. 6.30). Darius was angry with his satrap and general and gave orders that the head be buried with all the honours due to a man who had been a close adviser and friend of the king.[91]

In the spring of the following year the re-conquest of the remaining rebels took place (Herodt. 6.31). Chios, Lesbos and Tenedos fell without much opposition and on each of these islands a massive displacement of the populations took place, more so than on the mainland according to Herodotus.[92] When the Persians occupied an island they appeared to have used their soldiers almost like beaters in a hunt rounding up or netting refugees as they formed up in a line and systematically walked across the open country. Some criticism of this supposed method has been voiced since the mountainous islands are deemed unsuitable for such a procedure but in all likelihood this pursuit and capture of people was confined to the lower-lying areas near the towns. Herodotus does dwell on the issue by stating that netting these runaways was less effective on the mainland and this is surely because there was simply more land in which they might disappear. While Herodotus sometimes indulges in tall tales in other places his descriptions should be taken very seriously indeed. Which Ionian cities were retaken at this time is not stated and there were probably not that many who remained defiant in the face of the formidable Persian forces now deployed throughout the region. Those with a view to survival will have reached a settlement and it was those leaders perhaps who had the most to lose who held out for a short while longer. Lade was the supreme dramatic event of this stage of the war and all events afterwards pose something of an anti-climax. The Ionian cities and others in Asia Minor all survived and thrived after the re-conquest. Therefore, Herodotus' tale of young men and women being dragged off into captivity in Persia is largely an embellishment to the account but was appropriate for its context of oriental despotism reasserting its control over the Greeks. Still it is clear that the Persians were not content to confine their activities to the Asia side of the Hellespont but used their fleet to plunder and destroy settlements on the western Hellespont and Propontis. Herodotus specifically mentions attacks on the Chersonese, Perinthus, Chalcedon, and Byzantium, and that many of the inhabitants of these cities fled before the arrival of the Persian fleet. He also describes how at Cardia the Athenian Miltiades who becomes a central character in the subsequent war and hero of the victory at Marathon and who then still ruled in this part of Thrace fled to Attica.[93] This was the same Miltiades who had nearly twenty years before advocated the destruction of the Persian bridge over the Danube and for making a bid for Ionian freedom. Histiaeus on that occasion had argued against the proposal and it was his advice that had prevailed. Herodotus does not explain how Miltiades was able to remain as ruler of the Chersonese if his anti-Persian sentiment was apparently so open; the whole episode looks as if it was invented to prove Miltiades' credentials, and that of his family, for Athenian leadership against the Persian attacks of both Darius and Xerxes. Miltiades had obviously been cooperating with the Ionians and other rebels for him to be in fear of his life after Lade. So when he heard that the Persian fleet had taken Tenedos (Herodt. 6.41) he left Cardia with his family and as much of his fortune as could be transported in five ships.[94]

Artaphernes was keen to restore peace in Asia Minor and also to regain the trust of Darius after his complicity in the murder of Histiaeus. Long-term retribution against the Ionians and other Greeks in the region was not to be a feature of future policy, and Herodotus notes that no further aggressive acts occurred against the Greeks in 493. Indeed, to Artaphernes is credited some attempt to alleviate the financial burden on the communities of western Asia Minor. The annual tribute was to be levied according to the size of each community's country or *chorē*, and this measure remained in force until after Xerxes' defeat in 478 when many of the cities in the region then broke free of Persian rule and switched their allegiance to Athens and the new League of Delos. Artaphernes also introduced a system of arbitration for the peaceful settlement of disputes between the cities, probably throughout western Asia Minor, although Herodotus seems to think it applicable only to Ionia (Herodt. 6.42). Such a measure draws the observation from Herodotus that the Greeks habitually raided and plundered each other's territory and that peaceful co-existence had to be imposed from above. The statement has drawn little modern interest but does deserve some attention. It appears to be some form of window-dressing of the restoration of peace from a Persian view seeing that the relationship between the Hellenized communities of the region had been characterized more by cooperation than division during this lengthy war.[95] No details emerge about this judicial process but there was peace in the region for the next fifteen years.

The fragment of Diodorus' history (10.25.4) regarding Hecataeus' interview with Artaphernes at the end of the siege of Miletus preserves still another tradition. Hecataeus is supposed to have asked Artaphernes for the reasons why he placed little trust in the Ionian Greeks and received the reply that the satrap feared that they would retain grudges against the Persians for any injuries they had brought upon themselves. Hecataeus is said to have responded with the advice that if severity breeds resentment then kindness would produce contentment and loyalty. Hecataeus' advice, which highlights extremes of behaviour and therefore probably represents a topical element in philosophical discourse, has necessarily been dismissed as a deliberate construct in Diodorus' account, although simultaneously the same historian is also accused of lacking the ability to create such hypothetical situations. Of course, Diodorus may have simply copied this scene from one of his sources such as Ephorus or Timaeus, the latter certainly possessed the talent for recreation and invention of interaction between famous individuals. Moreover, a close inspection of Herodotus' narrative reveals Hecataeus being portrayed in much the same role as he is given by Diodorus and so the idea that he might just have advised a course of reconciliation to Artaphernes should not be ruled out of hand. Indeed, given the role that Hecataeus had played in Miletus as an opponent and critic of Aristagoras his advice may well have been taken seriously by the satrap keen to be seen as bringing peace to the region.

And so we return to the whole question of why the Milesians and Aristagoras and Histiaeus especially did not take more notice of the oracles when the oracle to the Argives must have become common knowledge and when Didyma was situated so close. The key may lie in Herodotus' choice of the word *hubris* in his description of the Persian treatment of the shrine at Didyma, which was a response to the equal 'pride' or 'violent action' of the Greeks at Sardis. The Ionians, Aristagoras in particular, were too consumed with *hubris* either to have bothered to have consulted Apollo or chose to misinterpret or ignore the warnings of future failure. The destruction of Miletus had been foretold by an oracle from Delphi some years before when the Argives had considered sending aid to the Ionians, perhaps at the request of Aristagoras (Herodt. 6.19). If the outcome of the war had indeed been foretold by Didyma there might have been an attempt to suppress such a negative message or the advice was not sought since only a positive response would have suited the leaders of the undertaking. In conclusion, some points that are ignored in accounts of this war should be noted here. It should also strike a note that Histiaeus was not allowed to return to Ionia until five years after the rebellion had begun, which may point to a number of issues. He had pleaded to be allowed to act as peacemaker yet the Persian war machine was gradually winning the struggle in all quarters. His presence was therefore unnecessary unless Darius was concerned about the financial costs – yet his kingdom was undoubtedly one of the wealthiest in human history – but also about material losses in regions of his rule, which were important to maintaining that financial security. And so is it possible to assess just how influential was Histiaeus in promoting rebellion? The answer is that he was almost certainly far less than is made out in Herodotus' account. Why the historian decided to give such prominence to Histiaeus is unknown but personal factors may have intruded since Herodotus used Hecataeus' account and may have found a negative view which he incorporated without, as elsewhere, too much criticism. Finally why were the Persians so long in regaining control of the situation and their satrapies from the Taurus Mountains to the Hellespont? Darius may have had good reason to suspect that other regions of his rule might rise in revolt if the instability in the west continued for much longer, but the strength and commitment of the Greeks may have come as a surprise. In the end the Persians needed to have a pacified Caria before they attempted to reunite Ionia with their empire in order to avoid a possible recurrence of the revolt that would have cut their supply lines and communications with Susa as had occurred earlier in 499/8 BC.

Chronology

522/1	Darius became Persian king.
514/2	Darius in Asia Minor, campaigned in Thrace and Danube region.
505/4	Naxian exiles in Miletus.
503/2	Persian expedition against Naxos.
502/1 (or 499)	'Message' of Histiaeus to Aristagoras.
500/499	Aristagoras fermented the revolt in Ionia and sought allies in Greece.
499 (summer)	Persian attack on Miletus.
	Eretrians played a major role in an Ionian victory off the coast of Pamphylia.
	Athenians and Eretrians participated in the sack of Sardis.
	Defeat of Greeks near Ephesus; Athenians returned home from Miletus.
499 (summer)	Revolt spread to Cyprus and Caria.
	Victory of Ionian fleet over the Phoenicians but defeated and death of Onesilas at Salamis.
499/8	Soli besieged for five months by Persians. Its capture marked the end of the rebellion in Cyprus.
496/5	Recapture of Cyme and Clazomenae by Artaphernes and Otanes.
	Aristagoras left Miletus for Thrace where he was killed.
	Histiaeus returned to Sardis and then Ionia.
495	Persians gather an army and fleet against Miletus.
	Peace restored in Caria.
494 (summer)	Battle of Lade.
494 (winter)	Miletus captured and sacked (Herodt. 6.30).
493 (spring)	Chios, Lesbos and Tenedos retaken by the Persians.
493 (spring)	Ionian cities sacked and burned.
493/2	Miltiades fled to Athens following vigorous Persian intervention in Thrace and the establishment of a satrapy on the European side of the Hellespont.
	Darius made Mardonius satrap of Hellespontine Phrygia and Thrace.
492	Phrynichus' tragedy *The Fall of Miletus*.
	Mardonius campaigned in Thrace.

Chapter Two

From Marathon to Thermopylae
Expurgating Persian War Myths (490–480 BC)

The report that Sardis had been captured and burned by the Athenians
and the Ionians was brought to Darius and that Aristagoras of Miletus had
instigated that joint action. It is said that when Darius heard of his affair
… he asked who the Athenians were. When he was he told he called for his
bow. He took it and loosed an arrow into the sky saying 'Gods grant that I
shall be allowed to punish the Athenians.' He then ordered one of his slaves
to repeat the following words three times every time he dined: 'Master, do
not forget the Athenians!'

(Herodt. 5.105)

T he story is amusing but fanciful, appealing to the audience perhaps
but not that convincing when searching for authenticity.[1] Darius had
campaigned in Thrace and further north, had in his court many of
Greek origin and was close to Hippias, the former tyrant of Athens who when
expelled in 510, had gone into exile at Sigeum on the Persian side of the
Hellespont. Darius needed no reminding about the Athenians and the fact
that he appointed Mardonius as the new satrap for Hellespontine Phrygia
and Thrace, with instructions to take the Persian presence into Greece
just months after the Ionian Revolt had been quelled plainly indicates that
a general subjugation of the Greek mainland including Athens had been
contemplated for a long time.[2] The battles at Marathon and Thermopylae,
ten years apart, but between the same foes, certainly remain the two most
easily recalled military engagements of ancient Greece, if not in all antiquity.
Yet there is much less modern attention on the battlefields themselves and the
historical contexts of each episode, which usually draw just a few sentences
in a general coverage of the wars between the Greeks and the Persians.
The campaigns that led to battles at Marathon in the summer of 490 and at
Thermopylae in early August 480 have become famous partly because the
expansion of Persian Empire in a westward direction was thwarted, although
its resources were much greater than those available to the Greek cities, and
partly because of the stature of the main source material, which again hinges

on Herodotus' *Histories*. Notwithstanding the fame of the work in question, its seemingly inchoate narrative regarding these battles, provided by history's first historian, poses numerous puzzles, which for any sense to prevail about them require some critical analysis. Although there is a decade between Marathon and Thermopylae the campaign that led to the latter began almost immediately after the Persian defeat in 490 and continued down through 487 when dealing with a revolt in Egypt took precedence (Herodt. 7.1).

Darius had every intention of enlarging his provinces on the European side of the Hellespont, but the defeat at Marathon, although no catastrophe, upset his plans and before he could regain the initiative in that quarter he died in 486. It was only in 485 after the Egyptian rebellion was quelled that an invasion of southern Greece again became a primary objective of the Persians and their new king Xerxes. He wanted to redress the failure of 490, which implicitly was an affront to the dignity of his kingdom and although he massacred the Greek defenders of Thermopylae this proved to be just another minor victory in an overall campaign that became a Persian debacle. Yet Marathon and Thermopylae far more than Salamis and Plataea dominate the popular imagination, and so the focus here will be to trace the two battlefields to place events at them in a realistic and historical context. The reason for concentrating on just two battles and not the entire war is firstly that geographically they are very close, secondly that both although land battles were heavily influenced by events on sea, and thirdly both involved one or both forces of small size. These were not the great displays of manpower and military might expected of the pitched battle.

Within months of peaceful conditions being restored along the coastal fringe of western Asia Minor, Darius ordered his new satrap Mardonius to continue the work begun by Megabazus and proceed to campaign further along the northern Aegean coast with a view to subduing the entire mainland of Greece (Herodt. 6.44).[3] Before Mardonius crossed the Hellespont he visited the cities of Ionia and Herodotus notes a most unexpected gesture on the part of this new satrap in that he installed democratic governments in the cities that had recently been reconquered. Tyranny of the kind previously favoured by the Persians in these parts was no longer to be permitted. Bearing in mind that this course of action is precisely what Hecataeus urged Artaphernes, the Lydian satrap, to do, according to Diodorus (10.25.4), it ought not to have come as such a surprise.[4] Furthermore, while Herodotus noted that some former leaders had been restored to their cities along the Hellespont he makes no mention of any in Ionia, which suggests that the Persians recognized that the imposition of governing through single rulers simply did not have popular support. Mardonius' decree was not entirely motivated from a desire to please the local populations, however, for he knew that in the campaign he planned to wage he would need financial and material support from these cities. Therefore to avoid further civil unrest it was of a little substance to him whether the people ruled themselves or were ruled by tyrants just as long as they were compliant to his wishes and needs. Herodotus presents it as an amazing event, but it was actually simply a matter of sensible politics and part of the planning of the logistics for a new venture in Europe.

In the early summer of 492 Mardonius moved quickly by transporting his army, which Herodotus states was impressive, from Abydos to Sestos, the narrowest point on the Hellespont. From there a Persian army marching overland had little hostility to be concerned about since Megabazus had already imposed Persian rule from the western shore of the Propontis to the Chersonese, and then in Thrace as far as the River Strymon. Therefore, it must have been clear to all that Mardonius' objective can only have been Greece and since the Macedonian king had already made a treaty with Darius the way through to Thessaly lay open. However, things did not go according to plan. At first there was a successful occupation of Thasos, which was taken without opposition, but then the fleet that had accompanied the army was caught in a gale off Mount Athos in the Chersonese. The northern or etesian winds of the summer months can be violent and were especially dangerous to ancient shipping. On this occasion Herodotus records that it was said that three hundred ships were sunk and as many as twenty thousand men from their crews were killed, some because they could not swim, others became the victims of shark attacks, and others were caught on the rocks (Herodt. 6.44).[5] The army too suddenly encountered a setback when the Thracian tribe the Brygi made a surprise assault by night. The Persians seem to have been taken completely unawares and Mardonius himself was injured. The general, however, refused to advance further until he had punished this tribe but the result seems to have been that the campaigning season drew to a close without any further positive results and Mardonius led his army back to the Hellespont. Herodotus states that Mardonius' army hardly behaved in a glorious fashion (Herodt. 6.45), although fault for the disaster to the fleet could hardly have been on account of incompetence of the commander. Later Herodotus (Herodt. 6.94) confirms that Darius had relieved Mardonius of the command against the Greeks.[6]

In the winter of the same year Darius ordered the citizens of Thasos to demolish the fortifications to their city and send their ships to Abdera (Herodt. 6.46). The Thasians had been besieged by Histiaeus some years before, but being a wealthy *polis* which, says Herodotus had an annual income from its Thracian gold mines of between two and three hundred talents a

year, the citizens had responded to external threats by expanding their navy
and strengthening their city's walls. In 492/1, however, they recognized the
futility of a war with the Persians who had occupied much of Thrace and all
neighbouring islands and so obeyed the commands of the dominant power
in the region. Darius also wanted to test sentiment in Greece not because
Mardonius had accomplished little of note in the previous year but to avoid
further losses to the Persian treasury. Darius is well remembered as being
a prudent ruler, and evidently decided to try diplomatic means to obtain
his goal, however at the same time, ever the realist, he gave orders for the
preparation of a further military campaign and demanded that the cities
of western Asia Minor have warships and transport vessels in readiness.[7]
Meanwhile, heralds were sent to the islands of the Aegean and to all the
cities on the Greek mainland demanding fire and water from each of these
communities as a sign of their submission. The island communities were
quick to comply since most if not all of them were within hours of Persian
held territory. One of the islands to offer submission to Darius was Aegina
(Herodt. 6.49) situated in the Bay of Salamis and within sight of Athens itself.
The Athenians appealed to Sparta to intervene in what they considered to be
a hostile action by the Aeginetans who were members of the Peloponnesian
League under the leadership of the Spartans.

The Spartan king, the same Cleomenes who had rejected the appeals of
Aristagoras of Miletus for military aid, arrived in Aegina soon after and took
hostages who were then despatched to Athens for safe keeping. This was to
ensure that the Aeginetans went no further in their attempts to curry favour
with Persia. The Persians would have had cause to regret not being in a
position to intervene in Aegina's internal affairs since that city had a strong
fleet and its harbour would have made a useful base in the event of a Darius
launching an attack on Attica and the Peloponnese. But the Spartans were
not the immediate target since they had not fought alongside the Ionians like
the Athenians and Eretrians, and so this opportunity to gain a foothold in
southern Greece was lost, irrevocably as it turned out. Evidently, an attack
against at least one ally of Sparta, however loosened the bond between the
Athenians and Spartans had become since the expulsion of Hippias in 510,
was also regarded as a threat to the Peloponnese. The Spartans recognized
that threat and acted at once. The citizens of Aegina may have considered the
Spartan king's action high-handed and may have begun planning a retaliation
but the hostage-taking had the required effect and nothing more is heard
about Aegina for the next five or six years. The Peloponnese and Attica seemed
united against any involvement with Persia, although elsewhere medizing as it
became known was common enough.[8]

In the meantime, in the early summer of 490 Darius ordered the rendezvous of a new army and fleet in Cilicia, near Tarsus. The land forces consisted of infantry and a large contingent of cavalry and the army was reviewed on the Plain of Aleia by the joint commanders Datis and Artaphernes, son of the Artaphernes who had been the previous satrap of Lydia.[9] The appointment of two or more generals to a command was plainly a common enough practice among the Persians and had been employed effectively in the war in Ionia, but in this instance was also probably a conscious decision in reaction to the recent failure of Mardonius who had been granted sole command in Thrace. From there the army sailed to Samos. Herodotus describes this force as a powerful one but just how large was it? A fleet consisting of six hundred triremes (Herodt. 6.95) would require 102,000 rowers, some of whom could have been utilized as light armed troops in the field, plus a further 18,000 heavy infantry, thirty carried by each warship. Still this total of 120,000 appears to be unrealistically high and problematic in logistical terms especially supplies. A fleet of this size would have required almost as many transport ships carrying food and fodder since local communities compelled to provide material aid would have simply buckled under the strain. A fleet of 1200 in 490 is not credible nor can the Ionians and the islanders of the Aegean had delivered sufficient supplies. Another reading of the text is therefore required. Herodotus must be using the name 'trireme' in a loose or careless fashion forgetting that whereas by his day, this was ubiquitous 'ship' employed for all purposes, that was not the case in the campaign to Marathon. In 490 the trireme was still a relatively novel construction and since the historian refers to transport ships for the horses ('horse–carrying ships') these were almost certainly not warships. A cavalry force of as little as one thousand would have required about forty triremes, and double that number of smaller vessels, especially if there was more than one horse for each trooper.[10] It means that of the six hundred in total, perhaps one hundred or more were smaller transport ships. Moreover, some of the warships were undoubtedly of the older bireme or pentekonter construction. Altogether a fleet comprising a mixture of shipping would reduce the total to perhaps 80,000 rowers, 10,000 infantry and 2000 cavalry. The force was certainly powerful but this was not intended for a full invasion of mainland Greece but as a punitive expedition against Athens and Eretria to cause havoc before a still more powerful force could be sent to enforce Persian rule over the broader region. Herodotus has perhaps inadvertently inflated the size and power of the Persian force, which can be corrected here but for his audience it would have sounded much more impressive than it actually was if they thought in terms of contemporary triremes.[11] The fleet probably called at Miletus before making the short crossing to Samos, but instead of heading north towards the Hellespont and the usual crossing points between the two continents sailed out in a south–westerly direction across the Icarian Sea.[12] Herodotus affirms that this route had been chosen since the Persians were still shaken by their severe losses around Mount Athos in the previous summer and had decided to avoid that route altogether. The transportation of an army, especially one with cavalry units across the open sea, even keeping close to the islands was yet another innovation by the Persian generals, and perhaps of Darius himself.

The 'Marathon Campaign' began almost as a carbon copy of the Naxos expedition, and indeed Naxos was one of the first objectives since the fleet sailed west from Samos. The Naxians will surely have been alerted to this imminent threat yet unlike their spirited defence against the Persian attack, led by Megabates and Aristagoras, they offered no defence at all. The size of this latest expedition may have been just too intimidating for the Naxians who apparently abandoned their city and fled into the hills. The Persians plundered and burned the city and the temples and continued on their way. The episode must have occurred over a matter of days and is given little coverage by Herodotus, although there is perhaps more here than the narrative yields to the reader. The Naxians had been confident of withstanding an attack a decade before but in 490 made no attempt to do so. This can be attributed to a number of reasons, that the attack came early in the summer before the harvest was gathered and when food supplies were at their lowest after the winter so that there were simply insufficient supplies to see out a blockade or that there had been a change in the political leadership at Naxos, which was less opposed to an entente with the Persians. Herodotus (6.49) claimed that all the islands had offered fire and water to Darius, so the attack may have been unexpected and unprovoked. Finally, the example of the fate of some of the Ionian cities was still fresh enough to make a defence the island seem a worthless proposition.

Datis also occupied the island of Delos, although the population fled before the Persians arrived. On account of the cult to Apollo and Artemis, which was also held in esteem by the Persians, the island was not plundered and its people were invited to return.[13] The Persian fleet then had a short distance to cover before they landed on the southernmost point of Euboea at Carystus. Datis had already enforced the submission of all the islands he had visited and collected troops and hostages from each. He now demanded from the citizens of Carystus that they also join the war against their neighbours but, even in the face of what must have appeared overwhelming odds, they refused. A siege commenced and the land around the city was devastated and the people of Carystus surrendered to the Persians and the city was spared destruction.[14] The Eretrians will have had some days' warning that they were about to be attacked but will surely have heard reports of the Persian expedition from well before the attack on Carystus. They sent messengers to Athens requesting aid and the Athenians responded immediately by sending a force of four thousand who, according to Herodotus, were from families that had been settled on lands belonging to Chalcis some years before.[15] Such a prompt and positive reaction was not copied by any similar action by the Eretrians who were divided in how they should meet the Persian threat. One group wanted to flee from the city and make for the safety of the surrounding hills – which they probably did – another group with their sights set on future personal gain was conspiring to turn the city over to the enemy without a fight. An Eretrian citizen named Aeschines was alerted to this treachery and he informed the Athenians who at once withdrew and crossed the straits to Oropus just in time to escape the disaster that followed.[16]

The Persian fleet made land at a number of beaches close to Eretria (Herodt. 5.100) and they prepared to make an assault on the city, which remained well defended since many of the citizens had chosen to remain but were not confident enough to offer battle outside their fortifications. The Persians appear to have attacked the city but there is no mention of any specialist siege equipment and it is likely that they concentrated on undermining a section of the circuit walls. The fight went on for six days with heavy casualties but with no obvious conclusion in sight until certain Eretrians who were pro–Persian opened a postern gate or successfully connived to leave a section of the walls unguarded. The Persians sent troops in and opposition seems to have completely collapsed as the sack of the city began. The traitors are named by Herodotus (Herodt. 5.101) as Euphorbus and Philagrus who were no doubt well rewarded, but may not have been allowed to remain in Eretria but rather resettled elsewhere. Xenophon in his *Anabasis* (8.7), written after 400 BC, which describes the events of a rebellion and its aftermath against the Persian king Artaxerxes II by his brother Cyrus in which the writer participated as a mercenary, mentions a meeting between himself and descendents of a certain Gongylus of Eretria. Gongylus had participated in the betrayal of Eretria in 490 for which he had been granted lands in Mysia. His widow who was named Hellas still lived in one of these possessions in the Caicus Valley, which later became the city of Pergamum.[17]

Eretria was neither a major settlement nor especially well defendable, although it possesses an impressive acropolis on a steep hill above its theatre. The population was probably hardly more than twenty thousand so its seizure by the Persians was predictable. Those who were caught were taken as prisoners to Asia Minor and resettled.[18] The temple of Athena Daphnephorus was burned and plundered by the attackers in revenge for the destruction of the burning of the temple at Sardis. Datis was certainly carrying out instructions but it might have been wiser to have been more generous in his treatment of the city. In fact, the severity of the punishment meted out to the Eretrians may, like that to the Milesians, have been exaggerated by the Greek writers of history. Like Miletus, Eretria quickly recovered, its citizens, many of whom must have fled to safe havens elsewhere on Euboea, returned and rebuilt their city, although the temple of Athena appears to have been a long time in restoration.[19] Just ten years later, in the allied Greek fleet that saved the mainland from Persian domination, the Eretrians provided the same number of warships as they had sent to aid the Ionians in 499. This is a clear indication of the dramatization of the episode in Herodotus and as it was received in the later literature.[20]

After a few days the Persians re-embarked their troops and sailed for Attica, but there was absolutely no chance of catching the Athenians unprepared since the events at Eretria will have been keenly observed from Oropus. The Persian fleet was probably shadowed by scouts as it made its way down from Eretria, past Rhamnous and into the Bay of Marathon, where an army of almost entirely Athenian citizens was encamped and waiting. The plain at Marathon stretches for at least five kilometres (2 miles) in length between two steeply sided headlands, especially that of the Mount Pentelicon range to the southern edge.[21] The depth of the plain is roughly two kilometres (2000 yards) from the hills that give access into central Attica from the sea. The landscape including the sea level has not altered much from the time of the battle. The tumulus in honour of the dead Athenians is as prominent today as it would have been in 490 (see plate) and will have be clearly visible to travellers passing by land or by ship. Obviously today the landscape has been altered by modern developments in housing and farming but the general nature of the battlefield remains the same. The land usage in 490 probably consisted of small subsistence farms with scattered bush and trees but which was easily level enough for the effective deployment of the cavalry that had been so carefully transported from Asia.

The forces assembled by the Athenians seem hardly to have made for a strong opposition or made a protracted campaign likely. An army of roughly ten thousand drawn from each of the tribes of Attica marched out from Athens to meet the attackers, which as a force is just two thousand more than the Naxians,[22] who had seen off the Persian attack just over a decade earlier, but who had recently surrendered without a fight. The enemy must certainly have had an overall numerical superiority especially in cavalry units, although that military arm constituted a problem in itself since the nature of the land in

Attica was mostly unsuitable for large cavalry deployment. The northern and western quarters of Attica and hence the route for any force whose objective is Athens itself is particularly hilly with narrow valleys and steep sides gorges. This means that the Persians were extremely limited in the places they could effectively operate out from. Marathon on the western coast of Attica and Phaleron just to the southwest of Athens had the available space for making the superiority of the cavalry count and had the space for beaching the fleet. Otherwise, the use of cavalry could easily become a handicap and a structural weakness for any attacking army. And this is clearly what actually happened. The Persians were guided to Marathon by Hippias who knew the area well and at least was able to give some specialist advice but he must also have had qualms about the ultimate success of the venture. If he did not voice this concern it may only have been to ensure that any negative remarks were not held against him later on. Hippias like the Persian commanders knew that unless they controlled the battlefield the enemy would start with a major advantage and quite simply they allowed the Greeks with a smaller force mostly of infantry to start hostilities from higher ground while their cavalry does not appear to have been fully disembarked or brought into action.

One can also easily discern the extent to which the Marathon campaign became as much myth as history when the tale of the courier Pheidippides is encountered in the narrative. The Athenians had received reinforcements from just one of their allies, namely Plataea on the southern edge of Boeotia, a small community that probably sent most of its available manpower. The Plataean contingent numbered approximately a thousand and was to be stationed on the left wing on the northern side of the plain. The Athenian generals were also counting on the support of Sparta. If the Spartans sent troops the other cities in the Peloponnese that looked to Sparta for leadership would follow. Herodotus states that before the Athenian army had fully mustered in the city and therefore perhaps as much as a week before the battle Pheidippides was ordered to run to Sparta and appeal for aid. Why the appeal was left until the last minute when the Athenians could have sent requests some time beforehand is not explained and exposes the extent of dramatic invention in the text. The distance between Athens and Sparta is approximately one hundred and fifty kilometres (100 miles).[23] Twice Herodotus says (Herodt. 6.107) that Pheidippides twice encountered the god Pan, either a personification of Dionysus or the god himself while on his way. The presence of Pan or Dionysus in this account is not a random event that was added for entertainment but was linked to the origin of the cult of this god at Athens and his cave on Mount Pentelicon, which rises to the southwest of the plain of Marathon. The runner is said to have met the god, a habitué of the mountainside, this time on Mount Parthenium just above the city of Tegea in the Peloponnese and on the frontier with Laconia. Pan addressed Pheidippides asking why he was not given honours in Athens when he had helped its people in the past and would again in the future. The Athenians did not forget this and when times were more favourable they built a temple dedicated to this deity beneath the Acropolis and from 490 held sacrifices and games in thanks for his intervention during this crisis. Again, myth has entered the account for Marathon when it is noticeably absent from the record of the Ionian War.

Pheidippides arrived in Sparta just twenty-four hours after he left Athens and in his appeal for Spartan aid he specifically noted that Eretria had just been destroyed. This pinpoints the episode to within a matter of days in the mid-summer of 490, and indeed Herodotus states (Herodt. 6.102) that the Persians remained on Euboea only for a few days. The Spartans are said to have been sympathetic but in accordance with their laws and because they were celebrating the festival of the Carneia celebrated between the seventh and fifteenth of the month Carneus (the Athenian month Metageitnion and roughly August) in honour of Apollo (Apollo Carneus), and since it was on the ninth day that Pheidippides addressed them they were unable to leave for another six days to join their allies. Pheidippides returned with a promise for future aid but nothing more. The runner's mission also exposes the absence of Athenian planning and the ad-hoc nature of their preparations. The institutions of the democracy, while only recently inaugurated in Athens, tended to preclude rapid decision-making. The planning of the defence of Athens could easily have been placed in motion some months before particularly since the Athenians had known for some years that Persian revenge would come. They also had Mardonius' campaigns of the previous year when contacts with trading partners in the Euxine had surely been affected. All in all, the myopic attitude of ancient communities to the outside world prevalent in antiquity is very plainly revealed here.

While the delay to their departure is attributed to a scrupulous observation of religious principles, there may have been suspicions that the reluctance on the part of the Spartans may also have been based on political grounds.[24] And so a delay was also imposed on the Athenians, although there was no consensus. This is again clear from Herodotus who gives a glimpse of infighting among the ten generals and perhaps the rather ambiguous or very cautious approach of the person in command, Callimachus the polemarch (Herodt. 6.109),[25] whose home town, Aphidnae, was just on the other side of the mountains from Marathon. Among the eleven was the same Miltiades who had fled from the Chersonese three years before and who had acquired the office of general on account of his exploits and family background.[26] Herodotus writes that Miltiades, supported by four generals – there was deadlock about the best action to take – was for an immediate engagement with the enemy. This made some sense since the Athenians already held the higher ground and the Persians had to disembark.

The Athenians and their allies are said to have already encamped among the hills to the south of the bay. The Persians having rounded the northern headland, Cape Cynosura, into the bay of Marathon beached their enormous fleet, approximately two kilometres away from their enemy who must have been in full view of the attackers. Herodotus' account is not coherent and some guesswork is needed to understand the events of the next few days. The Persians evidently disembarked and although the plain might have been suitable for employing cavalry units it would have taken a great deal of time to offload the horses and supplies and form them up into effective units. This will account for several days since not all the ships will have been able to beach at the same time and some complex schedule would have been enforced besides making an encampment for the troops and sending out foragers to meet all the needs of soldiers and animals alike.

The Athenians and their allies must have watched all these proceedings from their vantage point. The problem was one of waiting for the Spartans to arrive and thereby having battle-hardened troops among the front line. The Athenian citizen hoplites will have had very little recent experience of a battle, especially against a force that had obtained recent victories across the Aegean and on Euboea. Miltiades was the leading advocate, or so Herodotus claims, of an immediate engagement and this must be connected with not allowing the invaders to become comfortable in their new bridgehead. He persuaded Callimachus to vote against delaying any further and seems to have been concerned that some of the generals were secretly in contact with the Persians (Herodt. 6.109).[27] It made good sense to catch the Persians and their allies unsettled and unprepared but there was also the adoption of some interesting strategy, attributed by modern scholars to Miltiades but in fact probably one that was discussed at length by the commanders, that of weakening the centre while adding extra troops to both wings of the army. This would result in the centre being deliberately allowed to withdraw in the face of superior weight from their opponents but also allowed the right and left wings of the army to rout their opposition and then sweep round to attack the enemy's main concentration of troops from the rear.

This plan was put into effect in a most shattering manner and gave the battle of Marathon the fame it has enjoyed ever since. The Athenians occupied the centre while Callimachus as the senior commander occupied the right wing, which was closest to Mount Pentelicon, while the Plataeans were assigned the very end of the left wing, which was probably supplemented with some of the Athenians or possibly other allies.[28] These duly advanced down into the plain where no pronounced gradient is noticeable and once the level ground was reached the Greeks did not possess an advantage in terms of a slope down towards their opponents. Hence all speed was necessary. The Greek army numbering 11,000 opposed an opponent of about the same number, although the Persians probably had additional light armed skirmishers. It is evident that with these numbers they could not possibly have filled the entire plain as is often illustrated on maps in discussions about this engagement. A single horseman or heavily armoured infantryman might occupy as much as a metre each but neither side on this occasion stood in such a thin line. Each side will have formed up its troops in ranks that for infantry by the end of the century varied from eight to sixteen deep. On a plain that extends in length for some five kilometres the battle was confined to just the southern end near to where the tumulus in honour of the dead Athenians was erected. This is closer to the Pentelicon range of mountains where a tumulus to the dead Plataeans was also erected and which still stands near the site of the modern museum. It shows clearly enough that the battlefield was on the small rather than on the grand scale.[29] While a Persian encampment to the northern end of the bay where the hills behind offered protection Herodotus appears to describe the Greeks attacking ships that can only have been beached at the southern end of the bay, although once again a dramatic element may be present.[30]

At this point, it seems appropriate to voice some scepticism about the usual perception of the battle in that Marathon is represented as a great victory for the hoplite or heavily armoured infantry over the Persians whose force must have in some measure consisted of cavalry, or Herodotus would not have made the point about the horse transports. Descriptions of Marathon tend to dwell on the prowess or training of the hoplite but whether this was a vital factor at all is questionable. The terrain was ideal for cavalry being employed interspersed with light armed troops, which was indeed a feature of battles elsewhere in the Ancient World.[31] The Persian invasion force was clearly a mix of cavalry, heavy and light armed infantry, and such a combination would surely have been most successfully met by a similar composition in the Athenian led defence. Furthermore, the Persians had with them Greeks from Asia Minor and the islands and therefore the ethnic composition of the two sides would not have been that discrete. The landscape quite clearly indicates that the battle took place on more or less a level space and this may well indicate, although Herodotus makes no mention of this, that the Athenians made use of cavalry among their ranks as well. To counteract any superiority their enemy possessed the

Athenians could naturally draw on their own cavalry especially since they were well informed about the nature of the invaders long before they arrived from not only reports from Eretria and Oropus but also observation of the Persian fleet from Rhamnous.[32] Finally, some strength in cavalry also then makes the account of the Athenians moving rapidly back to Phaleron to intercept any Persian attempt at landing there afterwards more understandable. This would have been more easily accomplished by cavalry units than by exhausted hoplites.

The battle according to Herodotus was hotly contested, although it is likely that a later and more heroic interpretation that became the tradition crept into the account of what was probably a short and sharp encounter. The Greek attack caught the Persians and their allies on the back foot, which is surprising if the latter had superiority in cavalry but comprehensible if they were evenly matched with similar troops moving rapidly towards them from the southwest.[33] A late afternoon assault by the Greeks, as Munro suggests,[34] would have placed the sun in the eyes of the enemy. Yet if they moved out of the Vrana Valley in the direction of the beach, a distance of not less than eight stadia states Herodotus (6.112) or roughly one thousand six hundred metres (a little under one mile) would such a long approach have caught the Persians in disarray? The Persians would have been caught unprepared only if they had not secured a bridgehead, although that seems improbable. If that were the case then Herodotus' account of the Athenians waiting at Marathon becomes meaningless since a sudden attack would imply that the Athenians met up with their allies closer to Athens, marched down the Vrana Valley and went immediately into battle. The Persians would have had too short a time to fully organize their forces and were particularly badly beaten on their right and left wings by the unexpected superior numbers sent against them by the Athenians. In such a situation neither army could have formed up in much of a fashion if the Greeks were charging across the plain while their opponents hastily drew up their lines. This is not what Herodotus recounts since he is categorical about the components in each line, which suggests the usual drawing up of army formations prior to engagement. It is true that Herodotus claims (6.112) that the Greeks possessed no cavalry or archers but since this is contained in a section that is mostly devoted to material that is of dubious historicity it can probably be dismissed.[35] Munro suggested that the Greeks advanced at a rush to avoid Persian archers but that tactic would only be effective if there had been none in position and this supposed charge in full armour was for nearly a mile.[36] As regards the Athenian centre, right and left wings, Van Wees is rightly sceptical about the tactics ever working, as they are described by the Herodotus, simply because in the confusion of battle to have the two wings acting in perfect unison is at best implausible.[37]

Once the Athenian wings had supposedly turned their opposites to flight but had not pursued them and instead turned together to attack the Persian centre from the rear the rout in which the enemy casualties are given precisely as six thousand four hundred began.[38] The fugitives were pursued to the beach and attempts were made to capture or destroy the enemy ships. It was during the fighting around the ships that Callimachus and two of the other generals, Stesilaus and Cynegirus, were killed.[39] If this is an accurate account by Herodotus why, if there had been a really serious rout with a substantial number of the enemy dead, were the Persians able to disengage with very little trouble? It is more likely therefore that the Persians put up a stiffer resistance on the field and at their ships, most of which they launched successfully from the beach. The senior Athenian commanders were killed in fierce fighting, which was certainly not against terrified fugitives who had thrown away their weapons.[40] The loss of Persian ships was minimal, seven out of six hundred, and even if the fatalities given appear to be high in fact the Greeks probably inflicted more casualties on non-combatants and unarmed camp followers among the Persians trying to evacuate the beach than military personnel. This would naturally enough have not been remembered by any of the participants or entered the later historical accounts. Whereas large numbers of casualties were to be expected whenever a rout took place in the later stages of a battle, unlike in modern conflicts camp followers intermingled with the troops during the fighting in the hope of finding good plunder. It is these who are more likely to have been killed.[41] The fact that the cavalry was clearly not much affected by the defeat has led some to believe that the Persians were about to sail and were in the process of loading their horses on to the waiting transports. This is an equally odd interpretation of the events since it presupposes such a lengthy delay between the beaching of the invasion force and the battle that the Persians rather than risk a battle on prepared ground were instead prepared to venture into less well chartered territory, even if they had Hippias with them who obviously knew Attica well enough. If the cavalry escaped largely unscathed then it must mean that the Athenians did not, in fact, manage to cause much damage to this section of the army.

To sum up, it seems probable that the Athenian attack was staged in the late afternoon brought on possibly by seeing the Persians about to sail off.[42] The Athenian command may have assumed that the Persians either intended to return to Euboea or sailing on to Athens. If the first, the intention must have been to at least gain some credit before their enemy departed, if the second, then to disrupt any further invasion of southern Attica. Thus the Greeks erupted out of the Vrana Valley mostly in two columns of a rapidly moving combination of cavalry, heavy and light armed infantry. This meant that the

Persians did not have the time to draw up their entire force especially since the cavalry may well have been already on the transports. They then paid the penalty for not taking the offensive when they could have marched south into Central Attica before the Athenians arrived or decided against forcing an assault on higher ground where the Athenians are said to have camped if they were there already waiting for the allies to arrive.

With very little certain detail to go on it is possible to suggest that, contrary to Herodotus' statement (6.102), that the Persians remained in Eretria for only a few days, and that this period extended over some weeks. The Persians could have believed that the Athenians like the Eretrians would place their trust in their city's fortifications rather than risk a battle. The fact that both sides made for Marathon shows that the Athenians had been forewarned of the Persian arrival and that it was one of two places that could accommodate the invader's fleet and cavalry. Similarly, the Persians would probably have also been happier with an early battle before the Spartans arrived and had purposely landed during this Laconian festival because they had been informed about its significance by Hippias. Assuming that the Athenians were already encamped on Mount Pentelicon when the Persians beached at Marathon and refused to do battle they effectively debarred the Persians from attempting a march inland and once that route was denied then Datis and Artaphernes had to make for the alternative, which was the bay at Phaleron. Before they could make for southern Attica the Athenians had a successful engagement behind them, which may not have weakened the Persians by much but a defeated side was psychologically less willing to risk a second battle so soon after the last. A retreat would have seemed sensible in order to plan a more comprehensive second assault, perhaps the following spring.

The Athenian victory at Marathon was therefore no seminal point in the history of ancient warfare, but it provided and excellent opportunity for propaganda, as the subsequent offering to Apollo at Delphi and which was proclaimed on an inscription erected at the Treasury of the Athenians, just below the temple (see plate).[43] The *tropaion* or trophy consisted of armour taken from the Persian dead and was arranged on a triangular ledge on the lower side of the treasury building. The shape of this pediment probably intended to resemble the prow of one of the captured enemy ships, albeit that there were very few of those. Moreover, the victory became in later times attributed to the heavy infantry, although the evidence, such as it is, hardly supports that contention. And so the historical tradition clearly shows that this version became canonical but quite contrary to what was, in reality, just a moderate success and merely a setback for the enemy. The tumulus erected to the dead Athenian soldiers also provided another propaganda coup for the

Greeks who admitted to just one hundred and ninety-two killed. Although Herodotus gives no figure for the Plataean dead these were also honoured in a similar fashion at the entrance to the valley of the Vrana River.[44] However, it is likely that many other Greeks combatants died but were not honoured in the same way as those who possessed an elite status. The difference between the two casualty lists is probably far less than is presented by Herodotus.

The prominence in the deliberations before the battle given to Miltiades and the heroism attributed to the polemarch Callimachus (Herodt. 6.108; cf. Pausanias, 1.15.1) stems from the fame of one of the three frescoes in the *Stoa Poikile* ('The Painted Colonnade') in the Athenian agora which was commissioned by Cimon, the son of Miltiades, whose wife was also of the same family as Pericles.[45] Although he died in disgrace soon after the battle, his relationship with Cimon and Pericles, the most prominent Athenians in the generation following the defeat of Xerxes, goes far to explain the fact that his fame endured.[46] But Callimachus was also honoured with a *stele*, or dedicatory inscription, on the Acropolis, which suggests that for contemporaries of the victory he was regarded as a more significant figure than Miltiades, and that this memorial was in part erected to counter any alternative version put about by the latter.[47] Herodotus has little to say about the two thousand Spartans who were sent out to help the Athenians after the end of their festival. Although they hurried to take part in the defence of Attica and reached Marathon just three days after leaving their home, they were still too late (Herodt. 6.120), but they nonetheless wished to view the scene of the hostilities.[48] After they had viewed the dead and complimented the Athenians on their victory they returned to the Peloponnese. There is no mention about the identity of the commander of this force and whether or not it was one of the kings as would have been the standard practice. Indeed, there is also no clarification about whether this number represents the Spartiates alone, which if it did would mean that a substantial army had taken the field or whether this was the total number in this force. Also left unclear is whether or not Sparta had summoned its allies in the Peloponnese to provide troops to join this expedition.[49]

Having made the point that cavalry were an important element in the Persian force Herodotus then makes no mention of their use by either side at Marathon. Yet there is a source that does highlight the importance of the cavalry (*hippeis*) in Athenian society and since that evidence is a commemoration of the Persian wars, especially Marathon, then it must surely indicate that the Athenian army had a strong element of mounted troops in its army. This would go some way to explain why the Persians were so at pains to transport their cavalry such a long distance from Cilicia. They had been warned what to expect from the Athenian exiles such as Hippias. Thus while the Athenian force is usually considered to have consisted of hoplite heavy infantry there is no mention of hoplites on the frieze of the Parthenon on the Acropolis that commemorates the victories over the Persians.[50]

Besides Herodotus' account there is little of substance about Marathon in later accounts. Diodorus covered this event in Book 10 of his history but a single fragment (10.27.1–3) remains in which an incident is related to be placed just prior to the start of the battle where Datis sent heralds with a message to the Athenians demanding their surrender.[51] In this message he claimed that all Athenians were descendants of Medus, king of Media, just as he was and that he had come to reclaim his ancestor's land from which he had been expelled. Miltiades, speaking on behalf of the Athenians generals, rejected Datis' claim to Attica and stated that, in fact, the Medes ought to swear allegiance to Athens. Once rebuffed Datis prepared for battle. The episode is probably an invention but it does add certain points of interest, not least the prominence again given to Miltiades in the affair and reflects probably his dominating place in Diodorus' overall coverage of this battle, which he obtained from Ephorus and not from Herodotus who does not retell this tale. The preparation for battle suggests that Ephorus or perhaps Diodorus did not believe the Athenians had taken their enemy unawares and that some time did elapse between the arrival of the Persians at Marathon and their departure to Phaleron.

Pausanias, writing still later, adds a further element to the mythical aspects surrounding this battle when he describes the Sanctuary (*temenos*) of Nemesis at Rhamnous and a costly error of Datis. He says that the deity was depicted on a block of Parian marble that the Persians brought with them to inscribe their victory over the Athenians and is therefore another instance of *hubris* (pride) meeting *nemesis* (downfall), which is so evident throughout Herodotus' text. The origin of the marble block is interesting since Paros was occupied by the Persians after they had subjugated Naxos and Delos. Herodotus merely says that after they left Naxos the Persians took the remaining islands on their way to Euboea, but next after Delos is Paros. Yet if this block already contained the image of Nemesis then it may well have been pillaged from Rhamnous, which is not recorded, but would show that the Persians were active around the Bay of Marathon for some time. The authenticity of the statement is much less certain since Datis had taken particular care not to offend Apollo at Delos so why succumb to sacrilege elsewhere? Yet, with Hippias in his entourage Datis would have listened to any advice and a shrine to Nemesis almost visible from where the Persians were proposing to land would surely have made any show of arrogance in the vicinity, an act to avoid at all costs. The tale given by

Pausanias is probably an invention designed to appeal to the Roman tourist of such cult sites in the second century AD rather than a reflection of Datis' character. Meanwhile, Herodotus who had a predilection for such drama would have found it irresistible for inclusion in his narrative had he known it.[52]

Datis immediately sailed for Athens hoping to find the city undefended but probably took several days to sail around Cape Sounion.[53] Plutarch (*Arist.* 5.4) adds some interesting evidence about the Persian intention and of the date and timing of the battle. In his life of Aristides who was one of the generals at Marathon he states that when the Athenians saw the Persians setting their ships towards the south and clearly about to aim for Athens itself, the tribe commanded by his subject was left to patrol the battlefield to prevent looters and to bury the dead. This in itself was normal practice but he also claims that the Persians were obliged to head south because of the prevailing wind, which must have been blowing from the north. The etesian winds blow mid–May to mid–September and could make sailing very difficult, even impossible, in the Aegean hence the Persian command may have had no choice in their destination. Moreover, the winds are at their most severe in the afternoon and tend to die away overnight picking up again in mid–morning. Strong gales are more likely in the middle of the summer than towards autumn, which again places the battle in August rather than in September, but also in the afternoon. Datis arrived at Phaleron early in the morning perhaps and stayed only a short time in order to beat the afternoon winds, which would have hindered his easterly course towards Asia.

In 490 the broad crescent of Phaleron Bay, to the southwest of the city, was the main beaching place for vessels either bringing merchandise to Athens or of Athenian ships and even its war fleet. In 493/2 the archon Themistocles had supported a measure to relocate much of the city's commercial activities to the Piraeus, which offered more secure harbour facilities and which could be fortified and protected in time of attack. This was mainly in response to the raiding of the coast of Attica by their neighbours the Aeginetans but since Aegina had recently been pacified at roughly the same time the work of the Piraeus was unfinished. However, the Athenians' war fleet, by then at least forty triremes, had probably been moved to the new harbour especially when the Persians were reported to be moving down the coast from Marathon.[54] For the Persians Phaleron would have been the obvious point for disembarking mounted and infantry troops. From there it was a short distance to the city's fortifications which, without the army sent to Marathon, would have been inadequately defended and unable to withstand an assault. The walls of Athens were no doubt reasonably secure but it is worth remembering that in

490 they did not consist of the elaborate defensive circuit, which was to be completed only fifty years later by Pericles. Furthermore, any sympathizer of the Pisistratids or the Persians would have been ready to open a gate as had occurred at Eretria and may well have been planned in advance with Hippias and Datis. Indeed, the drawing away of the Athenian army to Marathon has an element of planning about it even if the Persians suffered a defeat. This was clearly not a disaster and perhaps been factored in as a tactical reverse to win the ultimate prize. It was Hippias who advised the plain of Marathon as the best suitable place for collecting the invaders' forces before these advanced towards Athens from the northwest. Herodotus (6.115) was also aware of some reports that gained some credibility then or later that the family of Cleisthenes and Pericles possibly favoured a Persian occupation of the city and which understandably as an admirer of the latter he dismissed out of hand. The Alcmaeonids, descended from tyrants and probably not averse to desiring outright power themselves, may have been pro–Persian while at the same time hardly sympathetic towards their great rivals Hippias and Miltiades. For a generation, Pericles was a quasi-tyrant and his rule was benign with all the acceptable trappings of senior statesmanship than of an absolute ruler. Invective about his family's activities during past events such as Marathon still became an inevitable accompaniment to the possession of power and influence from those who envied Pericles' position or who wished to emulate him. Still, in 490 there were surely others in Athens who might have been or could have been persuaded to betray the city by a promise of wealth or power. This is indeed hinted at by Herodotus through the words he gives to Miltiades when speaking to Callimachus when urging him to attack the Persians.[55] In ancient sieges at a time when siege machinery was either not transported with an army or was not available the easiest way to capture a town or city was by bribing a resident to allow the enemy entry. There are numerous examples of such conclusions to siege events, the capture of Athens might also have been accomplished in this fashion.

Herodotus (6.116) states that the Athenians reached Phaleron and made their camp at Cynosarges near the precinct of a temple dedicated to Heracles before the Persian fleet rounded Cape Sounion.[56] The Persians seeing the Greeks in possession of the beach chose not to attempt a landing, and perhaps rode the waves until such time that they were able to sail away. Where did they go? The first news of the Persians' whereabouts comes in Herodotus' account of another supernatural event, this time a vision or dream only when Datis had reached the island of Mykonos. Yet it is very unlikely that the Persians can have gone far from Phaleron before they would have been obliged to beach in order to rest the crews and attend to the horses. Carystus seems a likely harbour on their route to Ionia, which was not at too great a distance from Phaleron assuming that the coast of Attica was avoided altogether. However, depending on the time of day the Persians reached Phaleron then a halt in Attica perhaps near Sounion seems probable.[57] During the retreat from Phaleron when he was at Mykonos Datis is said to have had a dream, the details of which were never spoken of, but as a result of this he ordered a search of the ships in the fleet. As a result of this search an image of the god Apollo was discovered (Herodt. 6.118) on a Phoenician vessel and he heard that it had been stolen from Delos. Datis immediately set sail for the island where he returned the image to the Delians, who had taken up their former residence but he requested that they transport it to its original home, which was at Delium on the Greek mainland opposite Chalcis. The Delians failed to fulfil this request probably because they knew that Datis was in no position to enforce it and wanted the image for their own cult centre.[58]

There is a great deal of fabricated material in accounts of Marathon yet there is no mention of an oracle in connection with the battle. The Ionian War possesses neither oracles nor mythical material. It would seem therefore that there was a great deal of scientific evidence available for events in Asia Minor between 500 and 493, but much less secure information for Marathon.[59] This again contrasts a great deal with the account of the invasion of Greece by Xerxes where oracular material is highlighted as indeed is the physical presence of the Persians at Delphi. Immediately after the end of his coverage of the fight at Marathon Herodotus goes on to describe the last year of Miltiades' life in which he led an expedition against Paros, a campaign lavishly funded by the Athenians on the promise of great gains from the attack but which ultimately yielded very little. Miltiades' *hubris* or pride, which led to a loss of popularity, and death soon after from an infected wound was, however, foretold by the oracle to the Parians (Herodt. 6. 135) and gave them the resolve to resist any Athenian attack on their island. It is therefore unlikely to have been merely by chance that Herodotus chose instead to dwell on more supernatural elements that he regarded in some way as more relevant to Marathon than for either the preceding or the following wars.[60] Instead it is the presence of the gods themselves whose enmity is on occasion incurred or whose possible future anger must be avoided at all costs that is the more telling aspect. Thus the fear of and respect of deities is perhaps meant to reveal something about the beliefs of the time or the places which feature in the war. The god Pan puts in a physical appearance, Heracles and his cult centres are alluded to on more than one occasion, the goddess Nemesis was offended by the actions of Datis – according to Pausanias – who was concerned to ensure the goodwill of Apollo both at Delos and at Mykonos, while ghostly figures are also said to have joined the fight at Marathon. The battle of Marathon achieved mythic substance and the ingredients of myth filled up the gaps of an otherwise brief and unremarkable event.

The attempted submission of Aegina in the late 490s to the Persians ought not to have caused the surprise Herodotus claims since the Aeginetans had been hostile towards Athens over a long period of time. They were close neighbours and their commercial interests and ambitions clashed so the goodwill of Persia would have given Aegina the edge. The intervention of the Spartans denied the Persians a base on the island in 490 and while a section of the population in Aegina which would have wanted revenge on Athens for holding hostages from among its citizens, the Athenians wanted to ensure that the Aeginetans would not be a source of trouble and possible enemy in the future. Intervention in the affairs of Aegina occurred in the middle years of the next decade and the defeat of Aegina came as a result of the Athenians investing in a much larger war fleet than they had possessed up to that time in order to strike at least a parity with their neighbour. In about 487 Themistocles persuaded the people to vote to build an extra one hundred triremes to be funded from the silver bullion produced from mines in Laurion near to Cape Sounion in which rich deposits had recently been discovered.

Naval matters must also have been prominent in the thoughts of Darius following his latest failure to move the Persian frontiers westward. It was quite clear that the failure of Mardonius' campaign in 492 was not the result of the fighting with the Brygi but had everything to do with the loss of ships at Mount Athos. This point is emphasized in Herodotus' account, although he does not explain that it impacted negatively on supplying a large army when the movement was meant to be rapid and even when there were allied states along the route. Climatic conditions also draw no comment from ancient writers yet one poor summer, or worse a series of cold summers, resulting in a failure in the harvests and hence the depletion in local supplies placed heavy or impossible burdens on communities who had to supply armies on the move. A lack of locally produced supplies placed a heavier reliance on an accompanying fleet and when that was severely damaged it put paid to Mardonius' plans, and explains Darius' decision to launch a seaborne expedition instead in 490. After Marathon, Darius is said to have planned (Herodt. 7.1) a new expedition against the Greeks, which would have involved a far greater army and fleet. Xerxes' decision to make use of Darius' plans meant also that the logistics had to be solved before he actually took command of his army and fleet. This, of course, meant that newly levied forces had to be moved from Asia to Europe and, while this could have been accomplished by ferrying men, animals and materials and many camp followers across in transport ships as Mardonius had done, the ambitious Xerxes chose another spectacular and ultimately memorable way. He ordered the bridging of the Hellespont. It is often forgotten that, in fact, he was not the first to bridge the waters between Asia and Europe since Darius had ordered this to be done at the Bosphorus thirty years before in his campaign against the Scythians. On that occasion the architect or engineer had been a Greek from Samos named Mandrocles (Herodt. 4.87).[61] The first bridge at the northern end of the channel joining the Aegean to the Euxine was in effect an elongated pontoon construction probably of pentekonters or biremes lashed together with some sort of covering to allow the crossing of men and animals. The Bosphorus is a relatively narrow channel, and is today bridged at Istanbul, and probably in extent not that much larger than Darius' bridging of the lower Danube later in the same campaign.[62] Herodotus gives the impression that Xerxes, clearly wished not only to emulate but also to surpass Darius by instructing engineers to erect two bridges over the Hellespont (the Sea of Helle), which opens into Aegean (The Chief Sea or Archipelago).

For Herodotus the immensity of the project, which matched or was made to match the ego of the king, was, even so, successfully accomplished only at the second attempt. He says that the Hellespont was spanned by two bridges of almost fantastic design, and modern scholarship is divided between those rather sceptical of the historicity of this episode and those who see elements of historical fact admittedly mixed with the historian's desire to denigrate the character of the Persian king.[63] The scepticism arises from the scale of construction in an age when such technical knowledge did not exist. Large buildings could be raised on land using stone with little or no use of concrete, bridges over streams and rivers could be accomplished but the Hellespont or the modern Dardanelles is a rather different proposition. The depth of the channel and the strong current plus the length of the construction all combine to make the venture extremely hazardous with a good chance of failure. Of course, seventy-five years later in September 413 BC the Syracusans threw up a barricade of ships across the entrance to their Great Harbour in just three days, according to Diodorus (13.14.2).[64] These ships were almost certainly aging triremes, numbering about forty and linked bow to stern by chains and planks of wood and the entire cordon was garrisoned with troops. In contrast to the Hellespont, the main harbour at Syracuse has quite a gentle swell with little obvious current and in the event of a storm the ships could easily be disengaged and moored in safety in the smaller harbour to the north of Ortygia. This does not seem to have been necessary during the fairly short period that the boom was in place and which effectively prevented the escape of the Athenian besiegers. The entrance to the harbour at Syracuse is approximately fifteen hundred metres (just short of a mile), and forty triremes each a little less than forty metres or roughly forty yards in length uses up that space in a single boom ($40 \times 40 = 1600$ metres). The Hellespont between Abydos and Sestos at the point stipulated by Herodotus (Herodt. 7.36) was roughly seven stadia across (1400 metres, about three quarters of a mile) and he states categorically that the bridges were brought from the Asia side of the channel to a headland between Sestos and Madytus (Herodt. 7.33–34). Herodotus (Herodt. 7.36) is also firm in claiming that the more northerly of the two bridges required three hundred and sixty vessels of both pentekonter and trireme design, while the southern bridge required three hundred and fourteen ships. Unlike the fortified boom that the Syracusans built across their harbour mouth this Persian bridge cannot have had the ships linked bow to stern on account of the strong current running into the Aegean, which means that the ships must have been joined by their beams facing the Bosphorus. Triremes had a beam of five metres and pentekonters a metre less, so the northernmost bridge if using all three hundred and sixty triremes measures 1800 metres (roughly the same in yards), the southern bridge with three hundred and fourteen pentekonters 1256 metres. This means that Herodotus' figures are either incorrect or that a bridging point a little to the north of Abydos must be sought. This is also difficult since good stretches of beaches were also needed on both sides and where these exist, the current is markedly less but the distances at 3.87 and 3.39 kilometres for the two bridges would require more than double the number of vessels specified. In the end Herodotus' position probably comes fairly close to the actual bridging point but neither the specific situation nor the number of ships employed in the construction can have been accurate.[65]

The number of ships claimed for the bridges is remarkable since the figure must be double that stated by Herodotus since the first attempt to bridge the Hellespont failed. This is assuming that a large number of the original six hundred or so ships were destroyed in a violent storm and that even if some were salvaged for the second attempt then the total number of ships must exceed one thousand. Where did Xerxes' engineers lay their hands on so many warships? According to Herodotus (6.8–9) there were about six hundred Persian warships and three hundred and fifty-three warships manned by the Ionian Greeks and their allies in the battle of Lade in 494. A number of these vessels would have been destroyed in the fighting but the majority would have remained operational. Xerxes had access to massive resources but he does not appear to have ordered the building of new ships as the foundation for the bridges, whereas he certainly ordered cables to be manufactured to join the vessels together.[66] Therefore the ships were already in service or in harbour and must have been requisitioned from the cities in the region. Ships in any age have a limited working life but with limited technology the use of wooden vessels was fairly brief. A trireme probably served as a warship for no more than ten years, perhaps less, and after that as a transport for men or horses. Triremes or pentekonters would probably not have been re-employed as merchant ships because of the lack of space in the hold and the need for so many rowers. Twenty years' use would have been followed by decay on a beach or reuse as firewood. But decayed ships would have been useless for the bridging project since they would be unstable in the water – especially in the strong current of the Hellespont – and highly susceptible to damage in adverse conditions. The engineers appointed by Xerxes for the second attempt, perhaps Ionian Greeks,[67] at the bridging point must have sought out ships in good condition and either of relatively recent construction but not much more than ten years old. In 481 BC this points to warships from the 490s and a little later. Many of the warships used at Lade were no longer available since Mardonius lost at least three hundred at Mount Athos in 492. Any that survived had probably been retired from service. The Persian fleet that went to Marathon came back virtually unscathed and consisted of at least six hundred warships. Warships built after Mardonius' Thracian campaign and any built on the orders of Darius in the months following the defeat at Marathon were therefore the building blocks of the bridging project and not much older. Xerxes will also have ordered new warships to be built for his campaigns in Egypt from 487 and still more once he had decided on the new invasion of the Greek mainland. This all points to almost frenetic activity in the regions closest to the future theatre of war, but also indicates that there were financial benefits from funding a new war and the investment this brought from the centre of the empire. The communities in Asia Minor especially benefited from Xerxes' territorial ambitions. These same communities in the 490s had suffered from the lengthy war with Persia but would now have seen a full and rapid recovery in their wealth.[68] It is hardly surprising that among Xerxes' war fleet that accompanied him to Greece between a quarter and a third came from Greek-speaking cities.

Still, it is extraordinary that Xerxes was able to dispose of about a thousand warships of trireme or pentekonter design that were deemed too old or ruinous, but were still usable for bridging the Hellespont. Besides these he also had in service another twelve hundred warships, mostly triremes of recent construction for his fleet.[69] The disparity in the size between the two ship types indicates that if there were two bridges then the triremes placed beam to beam comprised one, the pentekonters beam to beam the other. The difference in height and width using the two types would have resulted in an unusable structure. The trireme with its five-metre beam was at least nine metres in height to take account of its three tiers of rowers, while the pentekonter was a much smaller vessel with a single line of rowers not that much shorter at twenty-eight to thirty three metres, with a beam of four metres, but its height was not much more than three metres. A bridge consisting of a haphazard combination of both types seems quite impossible. It has been argued that the Hellespont, which today has a depth in places of up to one hundred metres, was in antiquity about one and half metres lower at the Abydos to Sestos crossing. Yet it is also clear that the sea has retreated quite dramatically further south in the Troad; at Troy the citadel once at the beach is now five kilometres inland. If the channel further north had a lower level in antiquity then the crossing distance would also have been somewhat less than the seven stadia ascribed to it by Herodotus.

It is possibly fairest to conclude that as far as the bridging of the Hellespont is concerned that, although there are clearly invented elements in Herodotus' account, the assertion that the channel was crossed by Xerxes seems irrefutable simply because it is stated so firmly. Still, it may well be that there may have been just one rather than two pontoon bridges available to Xerxes and his army for crossing the channel in the late spring of 480, and that the crossing was a combined operation using bridge and ferries.[70] This seems plausible if only because of the waste of resources that building two bridges would have consumed. Thus one should not forget that quite explicit in Herodotus' account is the glorification of Xerxes' ambitions employed by the historian to elevate his subject's pride so that the victory by the Greeks can be equally enhanced. Finally, Herodotus states (Herodt. 9.114) that when the Greek fleet arrived in the Hellespont in the summer of 479, by then victorious over the Persians whom they had fought and defeated on the beaches around Mount Mycale just across the Latmian Gulf from Miletus, 'they found the bridges broken up', but provides no further details.[71]

Regarding Xerxes' war fleet, Barker, for example, believes that Herodotus' figure of one thousand two hundred and seven triremes (Herodt. 7.89) included those six hundred and seventy-four that had been used in the construction process of the bridge, hence leaving approximately another six hundred to accompany the invading army.[72] However, as Wallinga has shown this will not do, and the six hundred ascribed to the Persian fleet in 481/0 is drawn from a comparison with the fleet of Darius in his Scythian expedition and the Persian fleet at Lade, but it is clear that Xerxes' fleet was very much larger and meant to be greater than any employed in this region before. And indeed Herodotus is at pains almost to describe how Darius ordered the building of not just warships but also of other vessels (Herodt. 7.1) when he began to make plans for another attack on the Greeks in the aftermath of Marathon. Herodotus' numbers are extraordinarily precise and he must have drawn these from an earlier source, perhaps one of the early Ionian writers of history who may have remembered details and recorded them. Xerxes' fleet suffered considerable losses en route to Attica, especially at Artemisium (see below). Even if some of these were exaggerated by Herodotus to glorify the achievements of the Greeks there were still over six hundred ships in the Persian fleet at Salamis. Hence the starting total was not far from the figure given by the historian.

The total numbers in Xerxes' army have also been the subject of apparently endless debate and while clearly there is again much elaboration in Herodotus' narrative, the lowest possible totals for his army and navy make extremely impressive reading and as reports and rumours emerged about the numbers to the Greeks highly intimidating.[73] The crews of even a thousand triremes add up to about two hundred thousand men and these were mostly rowers not expecting to be involved in land battles. This figure would not be much less if there a sizeable number of the smaller pentekonters in the fleet. The fleet moving in tandem with the army west from the Hellespont also had to beach at the end of every day's progress for the ships' hulls to dry off and for the crews to eat and rest.[74] And this number does not take into account the huge number of civilian craft that would have accompanied the army in the hope of economic gain along the way. Merchant shipping may have relied more on sail than rowers but the crew of another thousand vessels may well have added another one hundred thousand to the sea borne element alone. The army was clearly a large one and Herodotus gives a breakdown, taken presumably from a source that either remembered this occasion or drawn from knowledge of the various regions that came under Persian rule. The list of the various contingents may appear impressive (Herodt. 7.61–81) but simply illustrates the wide variety of armed troops that were available and could be levied by a Persian king. It says nothing about their military capability. Herodotus surely provides the list for the amazement of an audience who would not have seen such a sight, but he was also consciously emulating Homer's catalogue in the *Iliad* of the participants in the protagonists of the Trojan War.[75] Homer's Trojan War was the portrayal of the supreme conflict, Herodotus' war between the Greeks and the Persian Empire was meant to equal or even to surpass that ancient myth with one of his own time and perhaps crafting. The Persian army is therefore given a fabulous total number but it is worth remembering that at the final land battle at Plataea in the summer of 479 the invaders must have at least have equalled the Greek armed forces, which are said to have numbered one hundred thousand. The crossing of the Hellespont in the late spring of 480 and the end of the next summer casualties and the division of the army after Salamis between Xerxes and Mardonius must surely indicate armed forces somewhere in the region of two hundred thousand. Mardonius was left with the task of securing Greece by Xerxes so required sufficiently large numbers to overcome any opposition while the king could not be seen to return without a suitable bodyguard. Put the land forces total with the total from the fleet and merchant shipping and the number approaches half a million, not to mention camp followers, slaves and servants, plus all the pack animals and wagons and one can easily see why the total might be inflated further since such a force would blot out the landscape and appear almost like a swarm of locusts.

Because of the difficulties Mardonius had encountered in 492 and perhaps as a solution to the problem of sailing with Mount Athos first directly ahead and then to the right with strong tailwinds the decision was taken to bypass the peninsula altogether (Herodt. 7.24). The plan was to excavate a canal across the isthmus leading from the city of Acanthus to the peninsula on which Mount Athos is the dominating natural feature. As with his detailed description of the bridging of the Hellespont Herodotus is particularly precise about this as can be gauged from his narrative (Herodt. 7.22–24):

> The Persians Bubares, the son of Megabazus, and Artachaees, the son of Artaeus, supervised the construction.[76] For Athos is a great and famous mountain and comes down to the sea and is inhabited. At its furthest limit on the side of the mainland the mountain is a peninsula ('chersonese') and the isthmus at this point is twelve stadia.

The Persian engineers chose what may already have been an existing causeway and since the distance is less than two and half kilometres (about a mile and a half) and land mostly level, the construction ought not to have been that formidable. Yet Herodotus states (Herodt. 7.22) that work on the canal began three years before Xerxes' army crossed the Hellespont. There was no shortage in the numbers of men available and many of these were drawn from the armed forces and transported to Athos by ship. The local communities were also obliged to provide labourers. Gangs of workers seem to have been collected along ethnic lines since the Phoenicians are said to have shown particular skill in the segment of the canal assigned to them. Finally, at the entrances to the canal breakwaters were built to prevent silting from the prevailing sea currents (Herodt. 7.37). Remains of the canal have been excavated but whether it was much more than the existing causeway with some water flowing through parts of it is questionable. Furthermore, the number of ships that passed this way when Xerxes had seen the canal is likely to have been a fraction of the ships in the fleet. Most captains would have taken the risk of sailing around the headland in mid-summer when the chance of gales was not as great as later in the year.[77] It was, however, another instance of the overweening pride of the oriental despot, as Herodotus claims that the building of a canal was quite unnecessary (Herodt. 7.24) because ships could be easily dragged across the isthmus. Still, in the narrative it adds to the drama leading to the ultimate Persian failure and the humbling of Xerxes. The evidence suggests that the canal remained in use for a very short time, mainly because there was no city nearby to maintain the facility. It is surprising perhaps that the Athenians never showed the slightest interest in the canal when they were major importers of grain from the Euxine and when the shipping route from there to Attica was a very busy and lucrative one. This too possibly points to an unfinished or temporary project rather than one that was intended to last or that could easily have been utilized later.

The question of supply dumps in the campaign to Thermopylae is a very important issue and has seldom if at all been addressed by modern scholars.[78] Herodotus places great emphasis on the incredible size of the Persian armament, both on land and on the sea; and, while some element of exaggeration is obvious in order to enhance the later victory of the Greeks, it is clear that the Persians came in force. But the campaign required intricate planning, which evidently took four years before the king even set foot in Europe and preceded the crossing of the Hellespont. Herodotus notes the placement of supplies along the march probably collected at the end of the summer in 481 since much of the material stored was perishable grain for making bread. Other supplies such as meat and fodder for the horses and other pack animals could be requisitioned from local towns and cities. Merchants accompanying the column sold all kinds of goods, and bought others, chiefly slaves. This enormous body of troops and camp followers is in modern parlance easily comparable to a moving hypermarket/superstore on foot! Xerxes was advised that there must be the placement of supplies along any route that initially lay through the Persian satrapy of Thrace and from there, via Macedonia whose king had made a treaty with the Persians, into Thessaly. The use of supply dumps seems an innovation, although Darius may have employed such measures on his march to the Danube in 513/12. Its use may be related to the fact that there were few wealthy cities along the route of advance through southern Thrace and the western border of Macedonia. Xerxes' army and fleet marched or sailed from Cilicia, some of the ships or land forces from very much further afield, but there is no mention of the same exercise elsewhere because the route possessed sufficiently wealthy communities for requisition or market places.[79] Herodotus names five places where supplies were brought by ship from Asia: Leuce Acte, Tyrodiza, described as 'of the Perinthians', Doriscus, Eion at the mouth of the River Strymon, and in Macedonia. Leuce Acte is said to have been chosen as the base for most of the equipment, raw materials or foodstuffs, which were transported by ship mostly from Asia Minor (Herodt. 7.25).[80] Strabo in his geographical survey of the region lists the places along the western shore of the Hellespont from its southern entrance, and Leuce Acte is given as the fifth town after Aegospotami, which is two hundred and eighty stadia north of Sestos. The first and most important supply dump was therefore perhaps no more than four hundred stadia (80.8 kilometres, roughly 50 miles) distance from the Persian bridging point of the channel. If the intention had been to situate the supply depots along the route intended for the invasion force then Tyrodiza seems out of the way since Perinthus was situated towards the centre of the Propontis and lies six hundred and thirty stadia (127 kilometres or roughly seventy-five miles) from Byzantium and about twelve hundred stadia (250 kilometres or a little under 150 miles) from Eleus (Strabo, fr. 57). Ideally a supply depot should have been sited towards southern Thrace, but Herodotus' text suggests that Tyrodiza was a harbour of Perinthus.[81] Barker has made the attractive suggestion that Tyrodiza actually lay at the head of the Melian Gulf (Gulf of Saros) near or at the mouth of the Melas River.[82] There is no evidence to support this conjecture but it is attractive in terms of the logistical placement of Persian supplies; and Xerxes' army had to cross the Melas before moving into southern Thrace. Incidentally, Herodotus says (Herodt. 7.58) that the Melas River, like the Scamander River in the Troad (Herodt. 7.43), ran dry on account of the number of Persian troops and animals who camped there, which shows that it was one of the main halting points in this early part of the expedition. This point would also make tactical sense since it lies further along the direct route from Leuce Acte. No major urban centres are attested in this area, although Strabo (7.7.6) states that Greeks had settled there. Perinthus was a colony of Samos and therefore the Samians may also have been active at the Melas River. After the Gulf of Melas the next supply base is said to have been at Doriscus on the Hebrus River. Doriscus was clearly an ideal site since the beach and the surrounding country were flat (Herodt. 7.59). The fleet could be hauled ashore to dry off and there were sufficient land for an encampment of the entire army. That being the case, Herodotus claims that Xerxes insisted on carrying out a tally of his forces (Herodt. 7.60; cf. 7.87), which is said to have been one million and seven hundred thousand infantry and eighty thousand cavalry not to mention mounted camels and teams of chariots.[83] The fleet consisted of three hundred warships from Phoenicia, two hundred from Egypt, one hundred and fifty from Cyprus, one hundred from Cilicia, thirty from the Pamphylians, fifty from Lycia, seventy from Caria, thirty from the Dorians living in Asia,[84] one hundred from the Ionian Greeks, seventeen from the islands, and sixty from the cities of Aeolia; the cities of the Hellespont provided another one hundred but the citizens of Abydos were instructed not to accompany the fleet but were to guard the bridge (Herodt. 7.89). Besides this total figure, Herodotus states that there were another three thousand smaller vessels and transports.[85] Diodorus (11.3.9 cf. Herodt. 7.184) claims that there were eighty hundred and fifty horse transports and about three thousand smaller vessels he names as triaconters or thirty-oared ships. Like Doriscus, Eion on the Strymon River, was in Persian hands and had been fortified by them since Darius had ordered Megabazus to occupy the region after the expedition against the Scythians (Herodt. 7.108).[86] After Eion, Xerxes spent some time at Acanthus before moving on towards Macedonia where he ordered his fleet to await his arrival at Therme (Herodt. 7.121).

Compared with the difficulties encountered by Mardonius in 492 Xerxes' advance across southern Thrace and into Macedonia went without any major mishaps. Still, between Acanthus and Therme, Herodotus notes (Herodt. 7.125–126) that lions attacked camels in the baggage train but not the usual pack animals. He is at a loss to explain their partiality but at the same time provides evidence for lions being common all the way between Abdera in southern Thrace to Acarnania in western Greece and almost to the northern shore of the Corinthian Gulf.[87] The supply depot in Macedonia, and there may have been more than one, is not attested but is likely to have been at the coast rather than inland. The ruler of Macedonia at this time was Alexander I who had a treaty of friendship with the Persians and so was expected to provide help to Xerxes whose route lay through his kingdom. If the Persians sent supplies here in advance it may indicate that Macedonia was unable to provide for the numbers that were anticipated to gather there before moving south into Thessaly. Moreover, at this time the Macedonians had limited access to the sea since the best harbours in the region at Pydna and Methone were independent states.[88] The fact that Xerxes was able to encamp his entire force at Therme (Herodt. 7.127) shows plainly enough that the final supply depot, although not initially specified, must have been at or near Therme.[89] And the Persian forces occupied the coast from Therme all the way to the Haliacmon River, which marked the southern boundary of Macedonia at this time. The distance from Therme to the Haliacmon River was about fifty kilometres (30 miles) and must have been filled with the various camps of the contingents in the army and the ships of all sorts drying off in the summer heat.[90] The Persians evidently remained in Macedonia for a number of days if not weeks (Herodt. 7.131) for during this stay Xerxes went on ahead of his forces to explore the various possible routes by which he might enter Central Greece through the mountains, which mostly barred his way. Mount Olympus divides Macedonia from Thessaly and only one or two passable routes linked the two regions. The most feasible of these was the road, also the most obvious, which hugged the coast and ran between Mount Olympus and Mount Ossa – the gorge at Tempe – and seemed the logical course since the army and fleet needed to move in tandem. But there was another route about which Xerxes had been informed, which lay to the west of Olympus. Xerxes therefore sailed south to the mouth of the Pineus River to view his options. He was very surprised at the size of the river and when informed by local guides that all the rivers of Thessaly joined the Pineus before it entered the sea wondered if the river's course might be diverted by some artificial means. When the king was told that Thessaly was surrounded on all sides by high mountains and that this was the sole possible exit a river might make to the sea he is said to have declared that by just damming the river at its gorge through the mountains before it reached the coastal plain the whole of Thessaly could easily be swamped. And Xerxes observed that the Thessalians had been clever to offer themselves as his allies and subjects knowing that their land was vulnerable to conquest such were his resources.[91] The king's curiosity was satisfied but not his plans for it must have been clear that another bridge or number of bridges would be needed at the mouth of the Pineas and that such construction would delay the invasion further. Apparently no longer interested in the coastal road into Thessaly Xerxes returned to Therme and gave orders that the inland route south was to be taken by his forces. This also meant that army and fleet would be separated for a number of days. Herodotus adds the rather odd information (Herodt. 7.131) that the forests, presumably to the west of Therme, were cut down by one third of Xerxes' soldiers in preparation for their advance. It is far more likely that local timber was consumed in huge amounts by the fires needed in the various camps and for repairs to the ships. It is possible, although hardly credible, that wood might be carried for fording streams and rivers when the mountains through which they were about to depart were also forested unless Herodotus means that the forests were so dense that a road had to be cut through them. While the forest clearance was taking place heralds who had been despatched by Xerxes to the Greek communities further south demanding fire and water, the traditional signs of surrender, returned from their assignments, not all by any means successful (Herodt. 7.132). Still, among the Greeks to offer formal allegiance to the Persians were those who lived in Thessaly, Locri, Magnesia,

Thebes and most of the cities of Boeotia, and Perrhaebia (through which the Persians were about to march on their way into Thessaly).[92]

Herodotus' account at this point appears to have been derived from more than a single source since having stated that the Thessalians submitted to Xerxes while the king was at Therme. Later in the narrative (7.173) as something of an apology Herodotus also claims that the Thessalians only deserted to the Persians when no alternative remained to them. This appears as if his source wished to exonerate Thessalian activities, although in the narrative it is explicitly stated that these Greeks served Xerxes well in the subsequent war.[93] The Thessalians had earlier summoned help from the other Greek communities intent on fighting the Persians, and the response had been a combined force of Athenians and Spartans numbering about ten thousand hoplites. This force went by sea along the cost to Halus in Achaea Phthiotis and then crossed inland into Thessaly. Themistocles was in command of the Athenian troops, a Spartan named at Euaenetus of the Peloponnesian forces, and they took up a defensive position at the gorge at Tempe. The route through the gorge was narrow and overhung with high cliffs and even without opposition would have held up the Persian advance, although at that stage Xerxes had yet to cross the Hellespont. But the Greeks are said to have remained at Tempe only for a short time and retreated after they were advised by the Macedonian king Alexander that they would be vulnerable to an attack from the rear by another route from Macedonia and ran the risk of being caught on two fronts by the invaders. The Greek force marched south again and returned to their ships and the safety of Attica and the Peloponnese. What is not clear is just how long this force remained in Thessaly and must have withdrawn before Xerxes went to reconnoitre a way south for his army. Xerxes went in a Sidonian trireme, which Herodotus states was the ship and crew the king favoured (Herodt. 7.128). He was accompanied by a sizeable force, although probably not his entire fleet as Herodotus claims, and sailed to the mouth of the Pineus near Tempe. The date of Xerxes' visit here is probably late June some weeks after the Greeks had departed and following the submission of the Thessalians. Xerxes does not appear to have remained at the Pineus for any length of time and returned to Therme before directing his army by the inland route into Thessaly. The Greeks may have missed an opportunity of intercepting the Persian king. But why would the Greeks have withdrawn in May when Xerxes had yet to march through Thrace unless Herodotus' chronology is suspect and the defenders actually remained at Tempe until the Persians arrived at Therme?[94] In May there was no need for a rapid withdrawal before the Persians were actually close at hand, unless it became known to Themistocles and his fellow commanders that the Thessalians were about to medize. There are missing details in Herodotus' account and the chronology may require some alteration to make the Greek retreat and Thessalian desertion of the defence of Greece more causally related.[95]

Herodotus states that it took a full month for the completion of the crossing into Europe and then another three months before the Persian took Athens.[96] The distance from the Hellespont to Athens is, however, just eight hundred and fifty kilometres (about 530 miles). This means that with the frequent halts for the pack animals to recover and for the various reviews of the land and sea forces an average daily march of a maximum of perhaps fifteen kilometres (10 miles) is indicated and probably less on most days. The slow rate of the advance had much to do with the size of the forces involved and the number of camp followers, but Xerxes seems to have also wanted to display his power to these new subjects who, says Herodotus (Herodt. 7.44–45) suffered greatly from the financial burden placed on them for entertaining the king and his immense entourage. The importance of the fleet in supplying the land forces cannot be underestimated and was probably high on the agenda of the deliberations among the Athenians and the Pelponnesian Greeks about what was the effective means of disrupting Xerxes' advance to such extent that he would have to withdraw from his objective. Inflicting damage to the Persian warships and merchant shipping therefore became a priority and the place best to achieve that result was thought to be Artemisium at the northern end of Eubeoa. The combined fleet of the Hellenic League was sent north to intercept the Persians moving south along the coast. The command was given to the Spartan Eurybiades but Themistocles may be identified as the main architect of the strategy.[97] To delay the Persian land forces long enough to cause maximum disruption to the accompanying fleet, another army was sent under the command of Leonidas, one of the Spartan kings to hold the pass at Thermopylae on the mainland opposite Artemisium (see map).

Herodotus gives precise figures for the pass (7.175–177) and had plainly visited the site, although he does not claim to have been there. He states the road that ran through Thermopylae in Trachis was just 16 metres (50 feet) wide. It was a coastal road rather than a gorge as at Tempe with high cliffs on the left looking north and the sea to the right. In some place both north and south of Thermopylae the way was even narrower and barely sufficient for a single wagon to pass safely.[98] This seemed an ideal spot to make a defence where superior numbers would count for less, and it was only when the Greeks arrived there that they discovered a major Achilles' heel in their strategy, which was a mountain track that would be used by the enemy to attack defenders along the road from the rear. This revelation seems remarkable and hardly credible if the southern Greeks were joined by citizens from nearby communities as Herodotus states. His figures for the Greek force are also specific: the 'official' total was three hundred Spartiate hoplites (the full Spartan citizens),[99] five hundred from Tegea, five hundred from Mantinea, one hundred and twenty from Arcadian Orchomenus, one thousand from the other communities of Arcadia, four hundred from Corinth, Phlius contributed two hundred, Mycenae eighty. These three thousand two hundred from the Peloponnesian League were accompanied by four hundred Thebans and seven hundred citizens of Thespiae and at Thermopylae were joined by one thousand Locrians, a thousand Melians, and roughly a thousand Phocians. The overall number of hoplites was seven thousand two hundred but there would also have been almost the same number of light armed troops not to mention the non-combatants and camp followers.[100] There is no mention of any contribution of troops from Athens or Plataea.[101]

Later Herodotus (7. 215) gives some of the history of the use of this 'secret path' in former times by the Melians and Thessalians. This track was hardly a best kept secret! It also illustrates that this was a known weakness in any attempt to hold Thermopylae or that the southern Greeks were really extremely careless in their strategic planning. Themistocles who is usually credited with being the architect of Xerxes' downfall and a tactician of genius was surely aware of such an alternative route, which Herodotus reveals to have been quite a straightforward route to tackle, beginning in the valley of the River Aesopus (7.215–218). Therefore, it can probably be assumed at the root of the description of what was ultimately a glorious failure for the defenders are some negative impressions about Themistocles and praise instead for Spartan courage on land. The Phocian contingent offered to guard the track, but Leonidas must have known from the time he arrived at Thermopylae that at best his role would be of a brief delaying nature. There cannot have been any thought at all of a victory on land against the Persian forces at this stage, although Herodotus suggests that the choice of Thermopylae had much to do with limiting the use of enemy cavalry (7.177) and that some use could be made of an existing but dilapidated defensive wall that the Phocians had erected many years before in anticipation of an invasion by the Thessalians (7.176).

The Greeks had probably been present at Thermopylae for some days and although this force consisted of some well-trained hoplites in terms of numbers – perhaps ten thousand in all – they posed no real threat to the Persians who ought to have been able to sweep them aside. Xerxes clearly recognized the problem of forcing a way through the defenders on the coastal road and waited four days (Herodt. 7.210) for the Greeks to retreat in safety. On the fifth day by which time he was exasperated he ordered an attack with Median and Cissian troops but when these had suffered severe losses they were replaced by the king's own Persian guard known as 'The Immortals'. These too were equally unsuccessful against the Greek forces. On the next day, events repeated themselves and the Persians were repulsed with heavy losses. It was at this point that a certain inhabitant of Trachis named Ephialtes came to the Persian camp in the hope of a reward for telling of the existence of a track through the mountains that would allow the Persians to outflank the Greeks. Xerxes was delighted and sent off a column of troops after nightfall. At daybreak the Persians had arrived at the spot where the Phocians were on guard. These were quickly scattered – a half-hearted defence seems implicit in the text – and these hurriedly brought the news that the Persians would shortly be attacking from the southern end of the pass. The Spartan king instructed most of the Greeks to leave because, says Herodotus (7.220), most were unenthusiastic about facing certain death, although he also notes that some claimed that many of the Greeks simply left in a panic. Neither claim is truly appropriate since Leonidas would have been able to command his Peloponnesian allies to remain if he had wanted them to do so while it was Boeotian troops that actually stayed.[102] It is therefore more likely that he dismissed his allies in order that they would be not be lost to the general cause while the Spartan force was to delay the enemy as long it could. This of course can hardly have been for more than a few hours especially since the Spartans are said to have abandoned the defensive walls in preference to a more open position. The day would have ended long after the Greek defeat. Twenty thousand Persians are said to have been killed. Most of the Thebans surrendered and were branded as slaves. The entire Spartan force of one thousand and the seven hundred hoplites from Thespiae were killed.[103]

The fleet of the recently founded 'Hellenic League' had been sent to Artemisium, the place of the Artemision or the *temenos* of Artemis, on the north coast of Euboea, which allowed close contact with the land forces at Thermopylae. But here the sea also became a narrow channel (Herodt. 7.176), which would reduce the effectiveness of Persian numerical superiority. There were two hundred and seventy-one warships (Herodt. 8.2) with one hundred and twenty-seven triremes from Athens, and so the Greeks were heavily outnumbered.[104] The choice of taking up a defensive position at this passage towards the more sheltered inner channel – the Euripus – between Euboea and the mainland is not remarkable, but it must certainly have resonated with an audience familiar with the geography that both land and sea forces took advantage of the landscape or here seascape to attempt to overcome the Persian threat. And if the Greeks could inflict some injury to their opponents' fleet it immediately deprived Xerxes of command of the sea and made supplying his army more susceptible to disruption. Hence the Greeks would impose their own will where up to that point the initiative had lain with the Persians. In 490 before Marathon, on account of their victory at Lade three years before, the Persians controlled the sea lanes, but the vigour of especially the Athenians seems to have inspired a confidence to defeat this enemy navy. Perhaps they were spurred on by the fact that they had emerged the victors from the encounter at Marathon, although to what extent this apparent bravado is historically accurate and not written with the benefit of hindsight is difficult to judge. Herodotus possibly indicates that the Greeks were in fact far less enthusiastic about giving battle at sea than later became the tradition for when the fleet's commanders heard of the approach of some Persian warships they immediately withdrew to Chalcis (7.183). Ten Persian triremes had been sent on in advance of the main body from Therme to reconnoitre and approached the island of Sciathos where there was a flotilla of three Greek ships. The latter turned tail but two were captured with their crews while the third beached at the mouth of the Pineus and the crew escaped overland into Thessaly.[105]

From the Haliacmon River to Thermopylae the distance is roughly two hundred and seventy kilometres (about 170 miles) and it would have taken Xerxes' army nearly three weeks to advance to a point where they came into contact with the defenders at Thermopylae. The army is reported to have departed eleven days earlier than the fleet (Herodt. 7.179), which seems like an accurate report. But Xerxes' strategy had already begun to unravel because of a change in the weather. The fleet encountered no problems sailing south along the coast from the Thermaic Gulf and arrived between the town of Casthanea and Cape Sepias on the coast of Magnesia (Herodt. 7.183). There the earliest arrivals beached but the size of the fleet meant that there was no space and the majority of ships were forced to anchor offshore in eight lines (7.188). It should be assumed that the warships had precedence and were the quickest vessels in the fleet and so were brought ashore while the transports and the other ships lay at anchor. On the very next morning Herodotus claims (7.188) a storm blew up from the east known as a 'Hellespontine Gale', and those ships closest to the beach were brought ashore but those forced to ride out the high winds suffered many losses.[106] Herodotus (7.190–191; cf. Diod. 11.12.3) claims four hundred triremes were reported as lost while large numbers of merchant vessels remained unaccounted for.[107] The figure cannot be an accurate one and, as later in his narrative, is an attempt to reduce the Persian fleet to roughly six hundred warships at the start of the battle at Salamis.[108] While a violent summer storm could wreak havoc with ancient shipping, mariners of the time would not have been taken entirely by surprise and so some exaggeration in the total losses may be expected from Herodotus especially since it does not appear to have been a cause of concern to the Persian command. The gale relented on the fourth day by which time Xerxes had issued instructions to take the war to the Greek fleet. Having observed the withdrawal of the Greeks south to Chalcis, two hundred Persian triremes were despatched to cover the southern end of the Euripus Channel perhaps aiming for Carystus or Eretria. The main body moved to Aphetae (Herodt. 7.193; Diod. 11.12.3) and arrived there two days after the Persian land forces had departed. Herodotus states categorically that the Persians arrived there early in the afternoon and that on the next evening the Greek force stationed at Artemisium went on the attack using a circle formation with their bows outwards. With this tactic, which prevented them from being rammed, they captured thirty Persian ships but how was this accomplished? The Greek ships were not in a position to grapple the enemy but they might have dashed out of the defensive circle and rammed amidships any encircling Persian vessel that came too close. However, these enemy warships were more likely to have been disabled or sunk rather than have been captured. That same night there was another violent storm that brought ashore the debris from the recent battle with the Greeks and seems to have unnerved the Persians at Cape Sepias. The following day the Persian fleet put to sea again and confronted the Greek fleet now reinforced from Chalcis but again when the sides broke contact it was the invaders whose losses are said (Herodt. 8.16) to have been severe but no figure is given except for the warships sunk by the previous evening's storm as they made their way along on the Aegean coast of Euboea. On this second occasion the Greeks, although in a stronger position than in the first encounter, were still obliged to retreat to the safety of Salamis since reports arrived telling of the catastrophe at Thermopylae (Herodt. 8.21). Still, it is stormy weather as much as fighting that is noticeably the constant theme in the account of the battle of Artemisium, and which accounted for more casualties than the fighting itself. Herodotus ominously reports (8.14; cf. Diod. 11.13.1) that it was as if the deities, offended by Xerxes' pride perhaps, were determined to reduce the numbers of the enemy fleet so that the Greeks would in future be more evenly matched.

Any detailed recollection of the encounter or rather series of encounters at Artemisium was quickly lost. Indeed as soon as the Greeks scored their great victories at Salamis, Plataea and Mount Mycale, all thoughts about the indecisive affair off the northern coast of Euboea ceased. Thermopylae remained as an example of heroism in the face of adversity and overwhelming odds, but the Greek inability to hold the Persian advance on sea before Attica could easily be suppressed. The defeat at Thermopylae happened when the

Greek and Persians fleets were still engaged on what was probably a second day of fighting. They were warned by messengers of the defeat on land and that Xerxes was already advancing south. Tactics dependent on synchronized action between two forces were always a problem in antiquity and success could hardly be guaranteed, especially when one was on land the other on the seas. The battle at sea needed to be won so that Xerxes would think twice about venturing further into Greece, and this did not happen. Xerxes may have faced problems on land and on sea but he had accomplished his objective of penetrating the obstacles to an invasion of Attica and the Peloponnese. Still, a brief but curious interlude full of the supernatural intruded before the Persians occupied Athens their ultimate goal.

After forcing his way through Thermopylae Xerxes' army marched south through Boeotia causing immense damage and devastation. While on the march the king's attention was drawn to the fact that he was very close to Delphi, a place whose contents, says Herodotus (8.35), Xerxes was more familiar than he was with the contents of own treasury. Of particular interest to him were the treasures dedicated to Apollo by Croesus, former king of Lydia, whose kingdom had been conquered by the Persian king Cyrus in 545 BC. He ordered a force to attack and sack Delphi and to return to him with its treasures.[109] There was perhaps another reason for the attack since Xerxes hardly needed the wealth of Delphi but he knew that recent oracular messages delivered especially to the Athenians urged the defence of Greece and promised victory against the Persians. The oracle regarding the defence of Athens by the employment of a wooden wall (Herodt. 7.141), which Themistocles had presented as a case for investing in the construction of a hundred new triremes as late as 483, would by then have been known well enough in Susa. The sack of Delphi and destruction of the temple of Apollo might have seemed an appropriate action to take after the victory at Thermopylae.

The Delphians were well aware of their danger and sought oracular advice of whether to hide the temple treasures or take them elsewhere for safe keeping only to be told that Apollo would look after his own possessions (Herodt. 8.36). The citizens of Delphi nevertheless were not convinced that the god would also look after them as well and so families were evacuated across the Gulf of Corinth to Achaea or into the mountains around Parnassus and Amphissa. As the Persian troops approached Delphi from the northwest, still the main route inland from Orchomenus, defence of the *temenos* lay in the hands of Apollo's priest and just sixty volunteers. As the Persian troops reached the shrine of Athena Pronaia the priest noticed that at the temple of Apollo arms that were dedicated to the god were lying before his shrine.

At the same moment it was claimed that loud thunder was heard and great boulders fell from the cliffs high above the Spring of Castalia crashed down and killing many of the attackers. Besides this two phantom giants were said to have emerged to fight with the Delphians who had taken advantage of this intervention by the god and scattered the invaders who fled. Later reports also spoke about two gigantic warriors – supposedly local heroes from ancient times – who also joined in the rout killing many of the Persian troops. If the attack took place at all, and there is considerable doubt about this since the political sentiment of many of the members of the Amphictionic council, which oversaw the management of the Delphic Games, second in importance only to those held at Olympia, had already joined the Persian cause, then a fortuitous earthquake, common enough in these parts, would have been a sure sign of the god's displeasure.[110] Historical the episode is not but here once again the narrative has that unlikely mix of fact and unreality that pervades Herodotus' account of the campaigns to Marathon and Thermopylae.[111]

The fame of Thermopylae unquestionably matches that of Marathon, and rather in the same way that the latter's renown is constantly reinforced by the running of the 'marathon race' every four years at the modern Olympic Games, the former has remained in the public imagination through continued cinematic interpretations. The development of an elaborate modern myth takes its starting point from the epitaph to the dead Spartans for whom this was held up as the apex of not exactly famous victory but glorious defeat.[112] Herodotus, of course, records the inscription and had almost certainly visited the scene of the fight and observed the memorial (Herodt. 7.228):

Oh stranger on the road announce to the Lacedaemonians that obeying their words we lie dead here.
Once here four thousand from the Peloponnese fought against three hundred times ten thousand.

The result of the engagement between the Greeks and the Persians at Thermopylae clearly provided another opportunity for propaganda and an entry into the historical tradition. But was it really like it was recorded by Herodotus and to what extent have modern versions altered the ancient accounts?

For such an apparently great victory Herodotus' coverage of Marathon is remarkably brief (Herodt. 6.112–115) and is barely any longer than his account of the sack of Sardis at the start of the Ionian War (Herodt. 5.100–102). This brevity probably indicates that the writer was not in a position to retrieve any more than the barest outline of a military engagement, and that his own sources, whether oral or written, were almost completely deficient and that much of what he was obliged to provide his audience with therefore a gloss to cover this shortfall. And what Herodotus relates has long been recognized as both inaccurate and incompatible with any scientific study of the episode. He may wished to have bypassed any detailed account but could hardly ignore Marathon entirely; however, he was in possession of much more material for Xerxes' invasion and that was where his main focus rests in the later parts of his history. The date of the battle of Marathon (mid–August 490[113]) plainly illustrates the slow progress of the Persians and indicates that this was no lightning strike. The Persians must have left Samos only in May or June and did not arrive on Euboea until early August and so six to eight weeks were spent subjecting the Cyclades to their rule and ensuring a stable line of communications with Asia Minor. The planning up to departure had been meticulous and Datis and Artaphernes can hardly be criticized for poor management of the expedition up to their beaching at Marathon. However, the organization of the troops and especially of the cavalry detachments is open to censure for once landed there seems to have been insufficient attention to the possibility of a hard fight. It should also be remembered that the heavy emphasis on cavalry use indicates not a whim of Darius but that he had discussed the expedition with Hippias long before it set out or before the first preparations were ordered. This gives an insight into this ruler's habit of consultation and being prepared to accept advice from specialists who knew the region and the inhabitants. The Persians might be forgiven for being over-confident following the ease with which the expedition had gone thus far, but they must surely have realized, especially with the presence of Hippias as adviser, that the encounter here would be much more fiercely contested. It was either this lax discipline or perhaps a decision to go forward to Athens itself without a fight at Marathon that proved the expedition's undoing. The Persians may simply have decided that with the hiatus in the hostilities and the chance that the Athenians would not engage that they faced a better chance of outright victory by sailing without a further delay to Phaleron. This decision allowed them to be caught without their cavalry in a position for best utilization. The Persians clearly had well trained infantry and these were almost certainly outnumbered by their opponents, yet they did initially well in repulsing and turning the admittedly weakened Greek centre before falling into the trap designed by the Athenian commanders. Finally, the tenacity of the defence of Attica must have surprised the Persians after the ease with which they had taken the islands and especially much of Euboea. Hippias may well have given over an optimistic assessment of the reception the invaders would have received.

For the campaign to Thermopylae it is again the question of supplying an invading army and insuring an easy progress which dominates the narrative in Herodotus and later sources. Admittedly there is a great deal of fanciful and entertaining material about the *hubris* of Xerxes or the participation of the deity in saving his temple at Delphi or the role of oracles in foretelling defeat for Persian and triumph for Athens. As with the campaign to Marathon, the text has an almost eclectic mix of fact, pseudo-fact, and fiction, but remain the ingredients of a highly successful narrative composition. Its survival intact attested to that success! The defence of Thermopylae, for it was that rather than a battlefield in the true sense, seeing that two opposing armies were not on this occasion drawn up in the classical manner of infantry or cavalry drawn up as a centre and wings, and the tactic of encirclement being attempted by either side. The importance of holding Thermopylae is plain because the main north south route into Attica, Boeotia and the Peloponnese lay through this narrow one sided gorge. The road ran beside the sea to the left as one approached from the north with high overhanging cliffs on the right. There are others routes into Central and Southern Greece, for example via Amphissa to the north of Mount Parnassus but for an army of the size that accompanied Xerxes that was almost impassable so the Persians were forced to go by Thermopylae. And so the interface between sea and land in these campaigns continued as the protagonists regrouped after Thermopylae and Artemisium and events inexorably moved on to Salamis, Plataea and Mycale; but that is another story. And indeed the stage was set for the final showdown but the form those encounters took and the logistical problems that were overcome in undertaking such ambitious adventures were solved in the Persian expedition to Marathon and along the road Xerxes took to Thermopylae. But perhaps most important again in both Marathon and Thermopylae has been overcoming the problems of logistics for an army on the move, the placement of the battlefield in its geographical context and the affect the weather can have on the outcome of any military campaign.

Chronology

493/2	Mardonius satrap of Hellespontine Phrygia and Thrace.
492 (summer)	Mardonius in Thrace where his fleet was destroyed by gales trying to round Mount Athos in the Chalcidice.
491	Datis and Artaphernes appointed to joint command of an expedition to Greece.
490 July	Persians attacked and captured Carystos and Eretria on Euboea.
August	Persian forces landed at Marathon and were defeated.
August	Persians failed to land at Phaleron.
September	Persians returned to Asia Minor.
487/84	Rebellion in Egypt against Persian rule.
486	Death of Darius. Accession of Xerxes.
483	Start of construction of a canal across the isthmus to Mount Athos.
481	Xerxes ordered the 'double bridging' of the Hellespont.
480 May	Xerxes crossed the Hellespont.
May	Themistocles at Tempe.
June	Persian army and fleet in Thrace and Macedonia.
July	Persian victory at Thermopylae, sea battle at Artemisium. Persians attacked Delphi.
September	Persians defeated at Salamis.

Chapter Three

Caesar's Campaigns to Ilerda in 49 BC

... validissimas Pompei copias, quae sub tribus legatis M. Petreio et L. Afranio et M. Varrone in Hispania erant, invasit, professus ante inter suos, ire se ad exercitum sine duce et inde reversurum ad ducem sine exercitu. Et quamquam obsidione Massiliae, quae sibi in itinere portas clauserat, summaque frumentariae rei penuria retardante brevi tamen omnia subegit.

... (Caesar) attacked the most powerful forces of Pompey, which were in Spain under the command of the three legates M. Petreius, L. Afranius and M. Varro, and he said to his friends beforehand that he was going to fight an army without a leader and from there would return to fight a general without an army. And although he was delayed by the siege of Massilia, which had closed its gates against him while he was on the march, and by an extreme lack of supplies in a short time nonetheless he was successful against all his enemies.

(Suetonius, *Julius Caesar*, 34.2)

The focus of this chapter is the campaigning undertaken by Caesar following his successful occupation of Rome and Italy in the first half of 49. This field of battle is situated in modern day Catalonia, which in the Roman empire of the first century BC was in the province of *Hispania Citerior*, the main city of which was (Tarraco) Tarragona. The battlefield to be retraced was outside the town of Ilerda, modern Lerida (Catalan Lleida), about one hundred kilometres (60 miles) inland from the coast in the foothills of the Pyrenees mountain range and on the route to one of the passes that linked this northern part of the Iberian Peninsula with the Roman province of *Gallia Narbonensis*.

Caesar intended to neutralize or annihilate all opposition to his rule in the western sector of the Roman Empire in order that he could not be attacked from especially Spain where his principal rival Pompey had legions commanded by legates loyal to him when the war was continued in the East. The campaign itself was fairly brief lasting just about six months with Caesar gaining an outright victory in all quarters of the conflict but has evoked little interest in comparison to the more famous military episodes that led to the battle of Pharsalus in the following year. Nonetheless, the conflict in southern Gaul and northern Spain is of considerable interest for again, as previously in this volume, it is the magnitude of the logistical problems and how these were overcome that show them to have been instrumental in securing Caesar's primacy in Rome. Of particular significance is the speed with which Caesar acted and how all aspects of military capability were galvanized into making this such an overwhelming victory for its architect. The main source for this conflict is not only primary, in the most precise definition of the term, in that it is contemporary but also it is a personal account in that the protagonist has provided a narrative that he wrote himself – Caesar's own *de bello civile* (*BC*) Books 1–2. Primary source evidence that is also autobiographical poses its own unique problem for the historian since it is likely to possess bias to a greater or lesser extent and so it inevitably has to be dealt with care and on occasion some scepticism. The secondary ancient literary evidence for this campaign, which involved the siege of Massilia and the event leading up to the battle of Ilerda, is also problematic since where it exists at all it consists of an adaptation of Caesar's own account.

The military campaign that culminated in Caesar's victory occupies a substantial part of the *de bello civile*, a detailed description of the civil war that he initiated on 7 January of that year.[1] It provides by far the most detailed evidence for an episode in Caesar's career, which hardly features in other ancient accounts and which also receives cursory modern treatment. The reason for the indifference or lack of interest about this campaign is that it interrupts the more significant war between Caesar and Pompey, which ended in the battle of Pharsalus in the early summer of 48. Caesar's autobiographical account breaks off in the autumn of 48 during his time at Alexandria; he never returned to his memoir and the work remained unfinished. The campaign clearly warranted Caesar's personal intervention and leadership in the field, firstly because of the calibre of the opposition commanders and secondly because of the need to safeguard his rear before he could undertake further operations against Pompey who had taken control of Greece and, on paper, had a superior number of land and sea forces at his disposal.

Caesar's account begins at *BC* 1.34 and ends quite abruptly at *BC* 2.22, or roughly a third of the entire manuscript of this composition, dealing with the war between himself and Pompey. Besides Caesar's own version of the events we possess very little. There is a brief mention in the biographies written by Suetonius (*Iulius*, 34.2) and Plutarch (*Caes.* 36) one hundred and fifty years after the event. Appian has an equally brief coverage, *Bella Civilia* (2.42–43) in his otherwise extensive history of Rome's internal conflicts. The account by Cassius Dio in Book 41 of his history is equally brief and dated one hundred years later again. There is therefore a heavy reliance on evidence that is necessarily partial since it was written by one of the participants in this war, although it has to be said that it was recorded when the outcome was far from certain. Nonetheless, memoirs of any sort regardless of the stature of the writer must be handled with care since human nature alone will compel a presentation of events in the most positive light when these reflect on the author. It becomes a particular problem when there is no corrective account to act as a balance. There must have been other accounts, notably by Livy and Gaius Asinius Pollio, neither of which have survived but which were written when this civil war was still within recent memory. Both also wrote when Caesar's heir, Augustus, had become sole ruler of the Roman empire therefore criticism of Caesar would probably not have been tolerated, however well connected the writer. The estimation of Caesar as a literary giant also reduced the possibility of a negative account while opponents of the dictator did not survive to advance their side's view of the campaign. Yet it is interesting how admiration for Caesar has tended to colour judgement of his actions in the twentieth century comments such as the 'narrative may be regarded as in the main trustworthy, though it is evidently intended by Caesar to justify his political action in the eyes of his countrymen, and sometimes he appears to misstate the political situation or understate a military reverse'.[2]

The enemy commanders were not negligible lightweights or novices and were well known to Caesar: L. Afranius, a former consul and long-time supporter of Pompey, M. Petreius a former praetor responsible in 62 for suppressing the rebellion of Catiline at the battle of Pistoia in Etruria, and M. Terentius Varro.[3] Afranius was the proconsul of Near Spain (*Citerior*) where the gubernatorial seat was at Tarraco. Although he seems to have abandoned that city in preference for Ilerda, Petreius seems to have been Varro's senior legate perhaps with a nominally separate command of Lusitania (mainly the southwest of the Iberian Peninsula). Varro governed Far Spain (*Hispania Ulterior*) with his provincial administration based at Corduba.[4] Between them they had eight legions plus a large number of native levies from a region that had a long warlike tradition and a large population to draw from. A legion at full strength is difficult to gauge at this time but was probably between three and four thousand heavy infantry in each unit, hence an overall total in excess of twenty thousand Roman citizen troops and perhaps another one to two thousand cavalry. The legates of Pompey could easily count on at least as many local troops, which indicates that Caesar faced a formidable opposition force amounting to roughly fifty thousand.[5] Afranius, Varro and Petreius met to discuss how they should proceed against Caesar and it was decided to follow the legal restraints placed on Roman governors in that they might defend their commands but not exceed them without senatorial or popular approval. Thus they decided to defend Iberia and not to be seen to vacate their positions or behave in a belligerent fashion and that Caesar should be viewed as the aggressor. It is interesting that Caesar omits all mention that he was in breach of the law, but he might have argued that the senate that he summoned on his arrival in Rome in January (March) 49 had sanctioned his move against the proconsuls of Iberia.[6] However, Caesar hardly faced a totally amenable gathering of fellow senators in Rome, which evidently came as a surprise. About two thirds of the senate membership had departed with Pompey and Caesar ought to have cause to expect those who remained to be either allies or supporters or, at worst, neutral or indifferent to either cause. He delivered a speech in which he justified his invasion of Italy and urged the senators present to join him in governing the state (*BC* 1.32) or if they felt unable to not to stand in his way. He quickly realized that there was a distinct lack of enthusiasm for his cause even from among those who had said they were sympathetic. And so when he argued that envoys should be sent to Pompey to negotiate a peace between them, various senators supported the proposal but not one offered to take part in such a legation, nor could be coerced, since Pompey had already stated that anyone who remained in Rome after his departure would be regarded as an enemy of the state and liable for immediate execution. Excuses for not participating were produced by individual senators and three days were consumed in fruitless discussions. Caesar clearly found this apparent absence of backbone frustrating and clearly believed that fear (*BC* 1.33) was the motivating factor in the senatorial response to his request. Furthermore, one of the tribunes, L. Caecilius Metellus, tried to veto the proposal entirely and proved to be an obdurate critic, and when he also attempted to foil Caesar's attempt to seize bullion from the state or public treasury (*aerarium*) in the Temple of Saturn (see plate) in the Forum he was arrested.[7] Caesar comments that 'having wasted some days in vain and in case he lost more time, having failed to achieved what he had urgently desired, he set out from the city and arrived in Far Gaul'.[8] The traditional view of Caesar as popular leader is clearly glossed in the later sources, while his own account betrays a certain peevish reaction to the cautious and vacillating approach of those senators who had chosen to remain in Rome. His constitutional and legal position in 49 was clearly highly irregular and any belief that he was particularly welcomed in the city may be dismissed. And the fact that he chose to leave Rome within a few days of his arrival illustrates his frustration and unease at the lack of cooperation he found, but at the same time he extricated himself from the immediate problem and went to deal instead with a pressing military matter that might upset his overall plans for the future.

Pompey had been awarded the Iberian Peninsula, or that part which had been conquered by the Romans up to that time, as his provincial command. This arrangement came as a result of the agreement between him, Caesar and M. Licinius Crassus at Luca in 55.[9] As a further concession Pompey had also been allowed to govern the two provinces in this region *in absentia* through his own nominees who acted as proconsular legates. Hence the position of Afranius and Varro and perhaps also Petreius, although sanctioned by popular vote was itself somewhat irregular. Still taken together they represented a formidable opposition, but they seem to have made the grave error of underestimating both the rate of Caesar's advance south and also the number of troops he had under his command. It was decided that Afranius and Petreius should mass their five legions and allied troops at Ilerda, while Varro with his three legions would remain in reserve in the south either at Carthago Nova (Cartagena) or Corduba. This was at some considerable distance from the theatre of war and much too far for him to be summoned very rapidly even if these troops were in fact ready to march at short notice.

Among the senators who remained in Rome note should be made of some senior figures such as L. Calpurnius Piso Caesoninus, consul in 58 and Caesar's father-in-law; one of the consuls of 56 L. Marcius Philippus who was married to Caesar's niece Atia;[10] and Ser. Sulpicius Rufus, consul in 51 and an acknowledged legal expert. The blame for the start of the hostilities is usually placed on a small number of enemies of Caesar who forced the passage of the *Senatus Consultum Ultimum* and, it is usually claimed, coerced Pompey into acting against his better judgment while at the same time intimidating a majority of the senate who would have preferred a compromise between these two leading figures. Yet few major or influential figures remained in January 49 and those who chose to remain were rather half-hearted in their support.[11] On the other hand, those most vociferous in their condemnation of Caesar such as Marcus Cato, Marcus Favonius, Q. Caecilius Metellus Pius Scipio (cos. 52), L. Cornelius Lentulus Crus (cos. 49) were either with Pompey or had been assigned various commands.[12]

The choice of Ilerda as the main line of defence is surprising to say the least. Our main and sole detailed source Caesar states that his opponents chose to defend this town because it was in a strategic situation (*BC* 1.38: '*propter ipsius loci opportunitatem*'). But was this really the case? The geography of northern Iberia comprises a high plateau that rises out of the coastal plain and which in turn lead north to the foothills of the Pyrenees and then the mountain range itself. The main river of the region is the Segre (Sicoris), which drains southwest from the mountains in a shallow valley at Ilerda before it joins the Ebro. Today the town of Ilerda straddles the river, but in the first century BC it was confined to the hill on which the cathedral is situated and which is both the historical centre and the acropolis of the settlement. The town was linked to its southern hinterland by a bridge. The river in the sweltering summer months can run almost dry but violent storms, characteristic of the region, can cause flash flooding and the snow melt from the winter precipitation and the rain that falls more commonly on the mountains can cause the Segre to be in spate even when the land through which it flows is completely arid (see plate). Movement of armies across this mostly level landscape would have been reasonably straightforward, although the more obvious line of advance into the Iberian Peninsula from southern Gaul was along the coastal road, the Via Domitia, as it remains today.[13] The Via Domitia branched just before the mountains in Gaul; one route was along the coast today from Collioure through Port Vendres and Port Bou before rejoining the main arterial road just south of the Le Perthus Pass at what is now La Jonquera. The road then runs directly south to Girona, Barcelona (Barcine) and Tarragona (Tarraco). But it is quite clear that Caesar's commander Gaius Fabius did not advance along the Via Domitia, and was instead ordered to cross the Pyrenees further west near to where the modern town of Prades is situated and make directly for Ilerda.[14] Caesar's own testimony is quite precise but gives no reason for this move other than it was intended to engage the enemy as quickly as possible. Caesar had obviously learned of the whereabouts of Afranius and Petreius but chose not to isolate them from the coast nor occupy what appears to have been undefended settlements along the Via Domitia. The choice of Ilerda seems baffling and perhaps an indication that neither Afranius nor his fellow commanders were of quite the same brilliance as Caesar, or points to Ilerda being a key point in the defence of the entire Iberian Peninsula. Yet Ilerda was not situated on a major route from the north; it did, however, give relatively easy access to Celtiberia and beyond that to Lusitania. Caesar had campaigned extensively just north of the Pyrenees in Aquitania in recent years and may have established contacts with various Celtiberian groups during the 50s. Moreover a little more than a decade earlier Caesar had been proconsul in *Hispania Ulterior* and he most certainly had friends and clients in the south, in numerous places such as Carthago Nova, Hispalis and Gades, who would join his cause once freed from the supervision of Pompey's generals.[15]

Caesar's account of the various military engagements around Ilerda is highly detailed and much of what he writes about must have been witnessed at first hand. Since he provides information that he cannot possibly have observed himself, especially about the siege at Massilia (see further below) this must have come through eyewitness accounts probably from the reports delivered to him by his subordinate commanders. Caesar sent Gaius Fabius, his senior commander in the region and then stationed at Narbo (*BC* 1.37), on towards Iberia with instructions to seize the mountain passes (*BC* 1.37) by which he presumably meant those three on the eastern end of the Pyrenees. Fabius accomplished this task quickly and moved his three legions to within sight of Ilerda. The speed by which Fabius moved an army consisting of heavy infantry, cavalry and an accompanying baggage train together with camp followers across the mountainous terrain indicates a commander of some expertise, but also that the opposition was weak and unprepared. Caesar states that the troops of Afranius guarding the particular pass by which Fabius advanced were quickly scattered (*BC* 1.37) and from there he was obviously unhampered on his march south from above the modern town of Prades. Once he arrived to the north of Ilerda it is evident from Caesar's account that Fabius crossed the Segre River (Sicoris) and established a camp on the same bank as the town. It is also clear that Caesar rapidly ordered three further legions to join Fabius (*BC* 1.39) with auxiliary infantry and cavalry, mostly of Gallic origin.[16] The Caesarian army was therefore at least forty thousand in total and about equal in number to the forces at the disposal of Afranius and Petreius, and each army had at least as many camp followers. So many additional mouths to feed placed a grave strain on local supplies at an early time of the year when the local population would still have been living off the results of the previous year's harvest.[17] This anticipated shortage was clearly behind Fabius' next moves, as recorded by Caesar, in that he is described as working to undermine the loyalty of local communities and bringing them over towards Caesar's cause (*BC* 1.40). This statement is closely followed by the news that Fabius' troops were ordered to build two bridges over the Segre River primarily to ensure further supplies, which confirms the timing of the campaign to the late winter or early spring of 49. The bridges were four Roman miles apart to the north of the modern town and give a good indication of the foraging area envisaged by the Roman commander.[18] Their location and the Caesarian camp illustrates the terminus of Fabius' line of advance from the mountains. The troops of Afranius were engaged in exactly the same activity also across the river, which runs from northwest to southeast before its confluence with the Ebro River. They had the advantage of occupying the town and whatever supplies it already possessed but these would not have supported the troops for long. The close proximity of the opposing groups meant that hostilities were bound to break out between foraging parties. Surprisingly this did not happen because the weather intervened. Fabius had two full legions and the entire cavalry posted out across the river by the bridge closest to the town to protect those men who were collecting supplies. A sudden storm brought a flash flood, which broke down this bridge and stranded the two legions and the men foraging on the southern bank of the river, while the cavalry seem to have become separated from them still on the north bank. The infantry and foragers without cavalry to give them protective cover were immediately vulnerable to attack and when this new situation was reported to Afranius and Petreius they took immediate action.[19] They ordered out four legions and their entire cavalry across the bridge that joined the town and their camp to the southern bank. It is interesting that during a storm they seem to have had their troops in readiness for an attack and perhaps this had already been planned and the destruction of the bridge merely accelerated their decision to move. Munatius Plancus in command of Caesar's stranded legions and foragers was faced with a dangerous situation and immediately drew up his heavy infantry in the hollow square formation on higher ground to withstand any attacks, especially from hostile cavalry. Caesar does not elaborate on exactly where his troops were but this ground must have been further away from the river and within this defensive formation the foraging parties who were probably unarmed and their pack animals will have taken refuge. The enemy attacked strongly using both infantry and horsemen but after a short time two legionary standards were sighted by the opposing armies and which were two other of Fabius' legions that he had ordered to relieve Munatius Plancus by crossing by the bridge further upstream and which had clearly survived the storm. These then marched down the right bank of the River Segre and once sighted, Afranius' troops withdrew, and both sides returned to their respective camps. No details of casualties are given but it is likely that Afranius' troops were able to inflict injuries to Caesar's infantry and so made a tactical but confident retreat to their camp in Ilerda.

Caesar arrived just two days later (*BC* 1.40) probably directly from Arelate and Narbo, a distance of some five hundred and forty kilometres (275 miles).[20] With him was his personal bodyguard, an additional force of nine hundred cavalry. Once in the camp he immediately took control of the situation and the incredible force of his personality is at once apparent.[21] He ordered that the rebuilding of the shattered bridge across the river, which was in the process of being repaired, should be completed that same night. By the next morning he had decided to move his camp forward and to within sight of Ilerda and so invite Afranius out to battle. He left a guard at the original camp and advanced in three lines, which was a formation much favoured by Caesar since it deprived the enemy of a complete view of the forces at his disposal. It also allowed the use of the third or rear line for other duties, which is precisely what occurred. Caesar offered battle but Afranius, although he led his own troops out and positioned them on higher ground, did not initiate any hostilities. Caesar says only that Afranius was opposed to any fight but offers no reason for that decision. Why did Afranius not engage? Caesar is hardly specific but gives the impression that Afranius dithered and was reluctant to engage with his opponents. It may simply have been that Afranius offered the usual sacrifices and found that these were not favourable for battle.[22] Afranius had taken up a defensive position immediately outside his camp and seems to have chosen the sound course of waiting for Caesar to attack him. Since Afranius' legions were drawn up on higher ground and Caesar's troops were on the plain near the river the latter also recognized that he was vulnerable, but also wanted to keep up the pressure on Afranius by not withdrawing to the camp originally constructed by Fabius, So he immediately ordered his third line of troops to prepare a new camp some four hundred paces (400 metres or 1200 feet) from the lowest level of the hill where the opposition was drawn up. Since these could not easily be observed by their enemy and were protected by the first and second lines they were able to accomplish their objective without fear of a surprise attack. To ensure that there was no sign of what was intended or any unusual activity that might arouse suspicions, he also ordered that the usual wooden palisade on a rampart should not be constructed and that only a *fossa* or ditch be excavated beyond which the entire army might withdraw by that evening.[23] This ditch was surely meant to make an attack by cavalry less effective but that meant it needed to be about five metres (15 feet) in width, as Caesar states, and at least two metres (6 feet) deep. That such a task could have been completed in a matter of hours probably by three to four thousand or even more heavy infantry indicates not only efficiency and organization but also the personal control Caesar had over his troops. When Afranius withdrew into his camp Caesar was able to do remain close by, although his forces are said to have rested under arms, presumably because they had no defences other than the ditch.[24] On the next day (*BC* 1.42) Caesar began the fortifications of a new camp by ordering the construction of further ditches, which would ultimately surround the fortified area. He assigned one legion to each of the three sides of the camp yet to have a ditch and the other three legions were to guard their fellow soldiers from attack. Afranius now appears to have realized his own danger and instructed his own troops to obstruct this work but these do not seem to have made much effort over a sustained period before withdrawing again. By the next day Caesar considered that his new position was sufficiently strong enough to give orders for the camp of Fabius to be abandoned and that any troops or camp followers who remained there to be transferred.

Caesar says (*BC* 1.43) that the camp of Afranius and Petreius was on a hill (*collis*) and that a plain of some three hundred paces or metres (900 feet) separated it from the town. About half way across this flat area was a tumulus or mound, and Caesar decided that it would increase his chance of success if he could place a garrison on this mound. By doing so his opponents would be isolated from the town, its supplies, and the river crossing, which not only allowed necessities to be brought in but also contact with the coast. Caesar initially led out three of his legions and arranged them in battle order but in such a position that his intention was not immediately clear to his adversaries and he then ordered a picked force from one of the legions drawn up to charge for the mound.[25] When Afranius recognized this strategy and the predicament he would be faced with in the event that he lost his link to Ilerda and the river, he immediately ordered countermeasures. Afranius had drawn up at least a sizable section of his army outside his camp on the hill to be prepared for any engagement in response to Caesar's actions on the plain below. When it was duly noted that an attempt was being made to gain the mound Afranius ordered out a detachment – Caesar's account has 'cohorts' by which should be understood infantry – and these reached the tumulus first by a shorter route. This suggests that the hillock in question was closer to Afranius' camp and that his troops ran downhill to reach the spot earlier than Caesar's legionaries. These two groups engaged but since the Pompeians had the advantage of being on the more elevated ground they were able to throw back Caesar's soldiers and even though these were reinforced they were eventually driven back. The reason given by Caesar for this reverse was the enemy's tactics, which seem to have been copied from Iberian tribes, specifically the Lusitani (*BC* 1.44) which essentially consisted of skirmishing rather than fully engaging in a line. Rather than advancing to clash in a solid rank the soldiers grouped together at some distance from their opponents, here the top of the mound, and then individuals dashed out to fight either throwing their javelins, or in close combat and then retreating to join the main body of troops. This is said to have thrown Caesar's legionaries off balance since they had not come across this form of fighting, although there are clear references to similar strategies being employed by the German tribes commanded by Ariovistus in 58 BC (*BG* 1.52) and by the Britons led by Cassivellaunus in 54 (*BG* 5.16).[26] Yet Caesar states that he had personally to intervene with *Legio* IX (*BC* 1.45) who turned the situation around and pursued their enemy who retreated and regrouped outside the walls of the town. However, there was another twist to come since although Caesar was in command, his troops charged up towards Ilerda, on the adjacent hill and when they wanted to retreat found they were attacked by the Pompeians who could now hurl themselves downhill again. To compound Caesar's problem he could not draw up a full line for battle since the route taken by his troops – perhaps the main track into the town – seems to have had ravines of either side and he states that just three cohorts in length ('*tres instructae cohortes*') could be deployed in the available space and as a result of the narrow site no relief could be brought up on either wings. There seem to be two main options here from Caesar's rather obscure description. He meant either that the way up was a spur of land that had steep slopes to either side or that the way up was through a steep–sided ravine. Actually neither really appears to fit the geography of the town today since the centre is perched on a hill of no particular height but is prominent because of the flood plain around it (see plate). The text, as is often the case with geographical features in ancient historians, is a problem even when the writer was supposedly an eyewitness. The limitations of Latin as a language in this instance perhaps does not allow for a strictly accurate description, on the other hand the writer is possibly somewhat lax in his comments, which are more concerned about the valour of his troops than about the situation in which they found themselves. On balance it would appear as if Caesar intended his audience to visualize his men caught in a defile with the enemy dominating on three sides and above their enemy.

The final charge seems to have caused the Pompeian troops to withdraw into the town after a fight that had gone on for five hours probably more from sheer exhaustion than the 'terror' ascribed by Caesar (*BC* 1.46). Both sides claimed a victory, Caesar for pushing his enemy into Ilerda and coming off best in the fight around the town, and Afranius' troops for capturing the mound, which they now fortified and garrisoned. The Pompeians maintained their line from their camp to the town and the river, while Caesar had now camped further to the south and the bridges across the Segre built by Fabius were some way off and could be reached only by a rather circuitous route. Afranius had easier access to the land south of the Segre but Caesar won over the allegiance of native communities further to the west and southwest around the Cinga River and so still acquired supplies from this quarter. Then the weather played a part again with what Caesar describes as the worst storm experienced in those parts. This seems to have been especially severe over the mountains where it accelerated the spring snow melt, which added to the heavy rainfall causing swollen rivers and extensive flooding. The bridges constructed and repaired by Fabius were swept away but not the crossing at Ilerda. Both the Segre and Cinga became impassable because of the height of the flood waters and so Caesar's army became cut off from supplies. Yet the crossing point at Ilerda was clearly constructed of more durable material and survived this adverse weather, which meant that Afranius still had contact over the river and a means by which supplies could continue to arrive for his troops but that he also had already taken the precaution of filling all available warehouses and granaries. Caesar's rapid deployment without an eye on possible setbacks now placed him in a dangerous position. Supplies very soon began to be scarce and the grain was used up quickly, while the local communities appear to have had the foresight to move their livestock, which could also have been consumed, far from the vicinity.[27] The harvest was still months away and the inhabitants were still living off the stores they had collected from the previous autumn, a factor that compounded the problem of finding additional foodstuffs. Foragers sent out by Caesar therefore had to cover large distances to find any food and were therefore vulnerable to attack especially from the local tribesmen who were accustomed to the local flooding and were able to swim across the swollen rivers using either air-filled hides or stomachs from cattle or sheep. Quite why Caesar's allied troops or indeed any of those among his entire army were not acquainted with such elementary aids is not disclosed. More importantly, neither is any reason given for not attacking and trying to secure the bridge at Ilerda. It would obviously have been the focus of Afranius' defence and a major contributory factor to any victory over Caesar, but the latter seems to have decided against any assault in this sector and looked for other avenues, perhaps less costly in human terms, to alleviate his logistical problems. An assault on the bridge at Ilerda would have isolated Afranius from the south from which any aid might come and by which route lay the sole realistic avenue of retreat.

Caesar also states (*BC* 1.48) that supplies were being brought in from Italy and Gaul and that reinforcements had also been summoned (*BC* 1.51). Accompanying these were a large number of envoys and other civilians. Afranius was informed and he set out with a substantial force consisting of three legions and his cavalry to intercept this relief column crossing the bridge at Ilerda by night to avoid detection and from there went in a northerly direction towards the mountains.[28] The force approaching Ilerda appears to have been a mixture of allied troops that were mostly cavalry, some volunteers from various Gallic communities and a large number of camp followers with no single commander. This cavalry engaged with the horsemen sent out from Ilerda and put up such a good fight says Caesar that the rest of the column was able to take refuge in the hills before the main infantry led by Afranius could be deployed. Caesar gives a total casualty figure of rather more than two hundred, although he fails to make it clear to which of the forces this was to be attributed.[29] He was plainly preoccupied with the problem of finding a secure source of food and other supplies for his troops. Food had become particularly scarce and the demand for the limited amounts of grain available had caused an immense spike in prices from less than one denarius to the *modius* to fifty denarii (*BC* 1.52).[30] Such an escalation in price placed this basic foodstuff out of the reach of the ordinary legionary and while meat might be purchased instead there was also no steady supply of this commodity. After a number of days in which there was no change to the flood levels in the area and when attempts to repair the bridges north of Ilerda failed because of the height of the torrent and because any reconstruction work was hampered by enemy archers or javelin throwers, Caesar was inspired by a memory of his time in Britain to order the building of boats. These boats were lightweight since they had a basic body or skeleton of wood covered with a latticework of twigs, which then had an outer case of hide. These were transported after dark on wagons that had been coupled together (*BC* 1.54) twenty-two Roman miles (32.5 kilometres or 20.2 miles) across country to the river and were used to transport troops across who occupied a hill on the other bank. These boats may have been similar to those described today as coracles but they were clearly large vessels since they required a double wagon to carry them and they must have carried probably about twenty men in each. They were probably employed in much the same way as boats are today used in white-water rafting downstream from one bank to the other and not intended for reuse. Caesar obviously wanted to transport sufficient numbers across the river to establish a fort on the other bank. The number of such boats may have been fairly small perhaps twenty to thirty in number hence not at all like the individual coracles still used in parts of Wales. Such one-man coracles would have involved the construction of a large number and probably would have been totally inadequate for the flooded stream and likely to capsize and result in high casualties before the objective could be achieved.[31] But where did Caesar effect this crossing? Clearly not on the Segre near Ilerda or the bridges previously built by Fabius. Caesar is exact in his mention of the distance covered by the wagons and this surely in the opposite direction to Ilerda and hence down the valley of the Segre towards its confluence with the Cinga. Having established a base on the far bank, Caesar then states that he conveyed across or brought over a full legion into this new camp (*BC* 1.54). How was this done and where was the crossing point? Caesar gives the impression by using the verb '*traicio*' (to bring over) that he reused the boats that had recently been built, although that surely must have been impossible without skilled boatmen, and the boats were probably meant to last for just the single crossing. He also states that a new bridge was constructed at this place and so the level of the flood waters was actually diminishing, therefore some inaccuracy in the timeline is probably indicated for soon afterwards cavalry units were also conveyed across the river and this cannot have been other than by way of a bridge or a fordable point.[32] Once he had established a strong base on the other side of the river the supplies he was expecting could be retrieved, but these were not those expected from Italy and Gaul but from Iberian communities further west. A crossing point close to the Cinga River can reasonably be argued here since this stream joins the Segre about twenty-five miles south west of Ilerda, and five miles from where the Segre join the Ebro. Some degree of thought must have gone into the decision to ford the river at this point since it opened up a much larger area for foraging and for links with local allies. By sending substantial forces across the river Caesar was now able to disrupt the foraging of his opponents and harass their supply lines.[33]

This action, although a minor affair, appears to have had a profoundly negative effect on morale in Afranius' camp (*BC* 1.59) and probably was as much to do with the fact that Caesar had regained access to the south bank of the Segre. Caesar states that his enemy now wandered far less from their camp when searching for supplies, and indeed stopped foraging during the day and rather went out after darkness, which was a highly unusual practice. The balance seemed to be tipping very rapidly in Caesar's favour especially as several of the most important local communities, including Osca, Calagurris and Tarraco, all offered their support and allegiance (*BC* 1.60). This must have been a very worrying development for Afranius and Petreius especially since these towns would now send supplies to their enemy and from then on were no longer a source of aid to them. The loss of allegiance of Tarraco in particular must have come as a shock and a blow to their chances of success because it was at the coast and the main Iberian city in the north west of the peninsula.[34] Further local communities went over to Caesar who notes the change in fortunes of the two sides, and ordered that a ford be made across the Segre near Ilerda so that his cavalry did not have to cross the river by way of the bridge twenty-two Roman miles downstream. The river was made fordable by reducing its flow through the construction of several ditches dug along the bank, which drained away the water and proved a highly successful operation. Afranius and Petreius immediately took fright and considered a tactical withdrawal from Ilerda into Celtiberia where the support for Pompey remained strong and where they could still count on local supplies. With Caesar's evident strength in cavalry, which could patrol both banks of the river, they now had a serious problem in supplying their own army. A move towards the interior is perhaps surprising when the coast is less than one hundred kilometres distance (60 miles), downhill and quite a straightforward march. But with Tarraco now hostile there was no obvious urban centre to which to retreat north of the Ebro, while Terrentius Varro with three legions still held *Hispania Ulterior* and the major centres in the south, and this is clearly the direction they preferred. Afranius and Petreius clearly hoped to unite their troops with those of Varro and gain numerical superiority over Caesar and then aim to delay a major engagement until the winter or even the following spring (*BC* 1.61).

The route to the Ebro was downstream from Ilerda but this would also take them towards and past Caesar's camp near the Cinga River. Afranius gave instructions for transport ships to be gathered at Octogesa on the Ebro at some point after the Segre empties into this stream.[35] From there the army could be transported to the coast to a harbour such as Saguntum and from there unite with Varro's army in *Hispania Ulterior*. Octogesa was just thirty Roman miles (44 kilometres or 27.5 miles) downstream from Ilerda (*BC* 1.61), a march of no more than two days, but this would have to be accomplished in the face of stiff opposition from Caesar's forces. Caesar then gives some puzzling information:

> At this point in the river they (Afranius and Petreius) ordered a bridge to be made of ships lashed together and they brought over the Segre River two legions, and fortified a camp with a rampart twelve feet in height. (Caes. *BC* 1.61)

Caesar here and in the following section of the narrative has conflated material and refers back to events that appeared to have already been concluded. Thus he seems to mean that the Ebro was meant to be bridged, although this cannot be the case for this new crossing point must be over the Segre since Afranius' two legions crossed this river out of Ilerda.[36] These were to act as an advance guard and prepare a camp while at the same time the camp on the northern side of Ilerda was to be abandoned by the Pompeians. It had lost all significance in this campaign by now especially following the decision to retreat from Ilerda. Caesar apparently learned of this move by his opponents through scouts yet he had already stated that his cavalry had unhampered movement on the south bank of the Segre. Yet this was clearly not accurate since he then goes on to indicate that the construction of a ford across the river had not yet been completed, and that far from being an easy crossing the water levels were still high and dangerous. The cavalry crossed the river and heavy infantry followed but these waded through a shoulder-high torrent. The bridge over the Ebro seems to have been completed very quickly while the construction work on the northern bank of the Segre by Caesar's troops at last produced a decline in water levels (*BC* 1.62).

Afranius now ordered his army to move out from Ilerda with the objective of reaching the Ebro as quickly as possible. Two cohorts of allied troops were left as a garrison in Ilerda, which was hardly sufficient to withstand an assault by Caesar's full army but also provided a friendly base in the rear of Afranius' now moving column. The entire Pompeian army moved southwest along the southern bank of the Segre, the main Caesarian camp was situated on the north bank near Ilerda, but Caesar too had a camp on the south bank about twenty miles downstream. Caesar's only tactic at this point was to make selective attacks on the column and particularly the rear, which was always the most vulnerable spot in an army marching since it inevitably contained the slowest moving individuals including the wounded. Afranius had made an early start – the third watch – when Caesar's cavalry crossed the Segre and immediately began to slow the column's progress (*BC* 1.63). This had already occurred by dawn (*BC* 1.64; '*prima luce*') and could be observed from Caesar's camp outside Ilerda, and that already the rearguard was in danger of being isolated from the rest. To begin with the troops of Afranius counterattacked and the fight was evenly balanced. Caesar's troops angrily complained to their centurions and tribunes that the enemy was making an escape and the campaign was therefore being prolonged and they urged their officers to go to their commander and demand that he issue orders to cross the river. The river was still flowing swiftly and the feeling among the soldiers was not unanimous when it came to attempting to cross the torrent. Caesar therefore chose to allow the weaker men 'either in strength or enthusiasm' to remain in the camp and form part of garrison with one of the legions.[37] The remainder was ordered to cross the Segre between a cordon of pack horses, which was positioned to indicate the route and in the event of any soldier losing his foothold to act as a safety net. In this way, although a number of men did trip, none were lost in the river. With the army now on the south bank Caesar formed up in troops in the usual three lines for battle, and Caesar says (*BC* 1.64) they were so enthusiastic to engage the enemy that although they had marched from their camp and forded the still swollen river they caught up with the rear of Afranius' column before nightfall.[38]

Afranius was clearly surprised again by the rapid deployment of troops by Caesar and he and Petreius immediately drew up their main forces for battle (*BC* 1.65). Caesar took defensive action on what he describes as on the plain ('*in campis*'), which indicates that he was then on the wide low shelf of land that rises gradually from the south bank of the Segre (see plate 4), today covered with olive trees and fields of maize, but then easily able to accommodate armies of thirty thousand or more to draw up their battle lines. However, the end of the day arrived and although Caesar's troops were still eager to engage he ordered that the army encamp for the night. Afranius did the same, and Caesar states that they were disappointed that they had made so little progress because just five miles away their proposed route took them through a series of passes between steep-sided hills. This terrain would make them safe from cavalry attack and by leaving guards in these passes would allow them time to reach Octogesa and the ships to transport them to the mouth of the Ebro. Therefore in the middle of the night the Pompeian troops attempted to depart and hence steal some extra distance on their pursuers (*BC* 1.66).[39] Foragers from Caesar's camp brought this news to him and when the usual signals were given for calling the troops to arms his opponents decided to remain in their camp. Their lack of superiority in cavalry support meant that without daylight they were even more vulnerable when attempting to march as a column even if the distance to be covered was not great. When daylight came both sides sent out scouts to reconnoitre the route ahead. Petreius accompanied his men; L. Decidius Saxa was sent out by Caesar. It was clear at once how the landscape could be the dominant contributory factor to a disaster for one army and a victory for the other. The Pompeian army would have to cover the five miles to the hills as quickly as they could whereas the troops of Caesar had to slow the opposing column in order to overtake their enemy and occupy the hills before them.

Afranius and Petreius debated the problem with their commanders and although some proposed a second attempt to break away from Caesar by night others argued that the dangers were too great, that they were unlikely to avoid detection and their vulnerability to Caesar's cavalry was accentuated during a march in darkness. Instead it was decided (*BC* 1.67) to vacate their current camp on the following morning and advance fighting off any attacks on their flanks and rear and while casualties were to be expected the goal was not far and the army as a whole should come through safely.[40] Caesar's army made a surprising move out at dawn apparently breaking off contact with their enemy and in the process of a retreat. Caesar had also gone out to look over the geography of the area and concluded that it would be difficult to inflict a severe enough blow on Afranius' column to disable it and so it would make better sense to make for the hills and try to reach this strategic position first. The Pompeian troops were misled into thinking that they were witnessing a withdrawal and therefore an easy march to Octogesa, but they then saw the column of Caesar's army begin to wheel right and move at some speed as their baggage train had been left behind. At once the strategy sank in, unless Afranius ordered an immediate advance his army would be outflanked by Caesar who might then place his own troops between them and the safety of the hills. Caesar's vanguard was already bypassing Afranius' camp where

7. View from Miletus looking north across the Gulf of Latmos.

8. View from Priene south across the Latmian Gulf, now silted up.

5. Theatre at Miletus from the harbour, now silted up.

6. View from the theatre at Miletus towards Lade (top right).

3. The River Meander below Miletus (centre distance).

4. View of the acropolis at Miletus from the Meander River.

1. Halicarnassus (modern Bodrum) birthplace of Herodotus.

2. The Temple of Apollo at Didyma.

9. Acropolis of Sardis from the Temple of Artemis outside the city walls.

10. The fortifications at Eretria.

11. View of southern
Euboea from Rhamnous.

12. View of the plain of
Marathon from Rhamnous.

13. The tumulus at
Marathon in honour of
the 192 Athenian dead.

14. The plain of Marathon today.

15. Plataea with Mount Parnassus in the background.

16. Thermoplyae and the Gulf of Lamia today.

17. General view of Delphi with the valley of the Pleistos River in the background.

18. The Temple of Apollo at Delphi.

19. Fissures in the rocks above the stadium at Delphi.

20. Shrine of Athena Pronaia ('Athena before the sanctuary [of Apollo]').

21. Crossing from Oropus to Eretria.

22. View north along the Gulf of Leon from above Collioure.

23. Pyrenees from Agèle sur Mer (Caesar's route to Ilerda).

24. The River Segre (Sicoris) at Ilerda (Lleida) in spate (June 2013).

25. River crossing on the Segre submerged (June 2013). Caesar's camp lay in this vicinity on the north bank of the river.

26. The acropolis at Ilerda (Lleida) from the hills beyond the south bank of the Segre (Caesar *BC* 1.65).

27. Dry farming land on the south bank of the Segre (June 2013).

28. Tarraco (Cathedral of Tarragona).

29. The aqueduct at Tarraco (Tarragona).

30. The coast of *Hispania Citerior* (modern Catalonia).

31. The landscape of the Po Valley.

32. The roads on dykes with drainage ditches between them near Brixellum in the Po Valley.

33. Snow on the Apennines (November 2013).

34. The Apennine passes were blocked with snow, November AD 69.

35. View of the Clivus Capitolinus, from the Forum with Temple of Saturn, left.

36. The Gemonian Steps (two views).

37. The Roman Forum with the Via Sacra in the foreground.

a hurried call to arms had been issued and the Pompeian army started out leaving behind a 'few cohorts' (*BC* 1.69) as a garrison.

Speed was now of the essence and a race for the hills began in earnest. Caesar was evidently further south away from the Segre and was forced to go across land where there were no roads. Afranius' column was, however, hindered by Caesar's cavalry, which was out in force, and his troops also appear to have abandoned their baggage in the hope that the less they carried they quicker they could move but they also realized that if they gained the hills first the cohorts left behind would be lost to Caesar, and so a victory would come with a heavy price (*BC* 1.70). Caesar, nonetheless, won this race and after he crossed the first ridge of hills found himself on level ground again on which to draw up his army in readiness for battle. Afranius could see the enemy ahead and was receiving reports of casualties because of the attacks to his rearguard. His column halted and occupied a hill while he sent on another four cohorts of light armed auxiliary troops to take another higher hill, which he believed would give his troops another route into the Ebro valley and ultimately Octogesa. Unluckily for the Pompeians they were easily spotted in this move by Caesar's cavalry, which attacked and annihilated the cohorts before they were able to establish a presence on the objective (*BC* 1.70).

Caesar recognized that victory was within his grasp. His troops, especially his officers, were keen to engage with their opponents who had just suffered a demoralizing blow to their chances of escape. Caesar sensed that the failure of his enemy to send out aid to their own troops when attacked by his cavalry showed that they were already in a negative frame of mind. Now they also gathered on the hill clustered without much organization around their legionary insignia and intent on defending themselves against the relentless cavalry assaults rather than launching any sort of attack themselves. Moreover, Afranius had no access to water, which Caesar (*BC* 1.72) thought must mean that a conclusion to the campaign lay in sight, and without further loss to human lives.[41] His troops were not at all pleased when they were denied the opportunity of taking the fight further but obeyed when ordered to withdraw from the attack. Caesar deployed his troops some way off, which allowed Afranius to withdraw into the camp he had vacated that morning. But Afranius and Petreius were now surrounded and there was no way for them to move to the Ebro valley and Octogesa unless they were prepared to fight all the way since not only was their inferiority in cavalry a serious deficiency but Caesar also placed guards on all the routes to the south ('*ad Hiberum intercluso itinere*').

On the next morning, Afranius held another council of his commanders who were naturally despondent about their failure to reach the Ebro. Two options remained, either a retreat to Ilerda, which was still held by their troops, or a march to the coast at Tarraco. While they were discussing the possibilities, neither held much prospect of victory over Caesar and in fact it must have occurred to any present that all they were doing now was delaying defeat or surrender. The current encampment was extended to the river bank to ensure water supplies and deter attacks by Caesar's cavalry. Afranius and Petreius went out to supervise these defensive measures, a grave error on their part since in their absence fraternization began to occur between the two opposing armies. The Pompeian troops are given credit by Caesar for thanking his troops for their kindness the previous day in allowing them to regain their camp. The fact that Caesar's legionaries were actually much more bellicose than their commander is glossed without comment. Still it is evident that, as in the case of all civil wars among the protagonists were many friends, neighbours and acquaintances. These were armies that shared a common language, culture and heritage. The soldiers obeyed their commanders up to a reasonable point and that point seems to have been reached when Afranius could find no clear route to safety through the hills to Octogesa. The troops of Caesar were quickly won over to the pleas for clemency from the Pompeian troops they met and some of these men even went to their general to grant a freedom of passage for Afranius and Petreius in the event that they surrender to him. In fact, the degree of civility that suddenly infused both camps seemed likely to lead to a speedy conclusion to the campaign. Rank and file soldiers intermingled in both camps, and centurions, tribunes and local Iberian chiefs all paid calls on Caesar. The young son of Afranius who was with his father's staff interceded on behalf of his parent through P. Sulpicius Rufus, one of Caesar's legates. Caesar was only too happy to be seen to be conciliatory and generous. The senior Afranius heard of this fraternizing between the two camps and so hurried back to his own but is said to have been resigned to surrendering his command to Caesar.[42] However, Petreius was evidently made of sterner stuff or less concerned about his own future for when he returned to the camp he immediately armed his bodyguard and some other soldiers, mainly from among the Iberian allies, states Caesar (*BC* 1.75), and went around driving off the soldiers of his enemy Caesar and killing those whom he found inside the fortifications. Caesar claims that some of his men: 'grouped themselves together and frightened by the sudden dangerous turn of events wrapped their left hands in their cloaks to act as shields to defend themselves, drew their swords' and kept the hostile troops at bay long enough to make their way to their own camp and the support of the guards who were posted there (*BC* 1.75).[43] Petreius afterwards approached the officers and men demanding that they renew their allegiance with Pompey.[44] He started with

Afranius. Both he and Petreius owed a great deal to Pompey, and the senior commander, perhaps from sheer embarrassment, complied.[45] The other senior officers also followed suit and then the entire army century by century (*BC* 1.76) and orders were given that any soldiers of Caesar discovered to be still in the camp should be brought forward and executed immediately, but most had been hidden by friends and were helped to safety after night fell. The harsh and implacable attitude of Petreius, but also the ease with which he was able to enforce his will, showed that the time had not yet arrived for a surrender by the Pompeian army since no opposition appears to have been voiced to his actions at this stage.

On the other hand, any stray soldiers from the Pompeian side found in Caesar's camp were to be returned unharmed although it is said (*BC* 1.77) that some ('*nonnulli*') of the centurions and military tribunes preferred to remain and abandoned their previous allegiance for which they were rewarded by being retained in the same ranks as they had held before they deserted. Afranius' situation was by now bleak indeed for while his troops still had access to water from the Segre River, other supplies were running low. His heavy infantry had been ordered to carry enough grain for the march to Octogesa when they quit Ilerda and some of this remained, but the allied troops had little food and as a result many went over to Caesar's cause each day.[46] Afranius therefore decided that a retreat to Ilerda must be accomplished quickly for he still possessed a strongly fortified camp there and the supplies that had been left behind. This may well have been the most sensible plan available to Caesar's opponents but a retreat for any reason was bound to be accompanied with low morale especially since this further withdrawal simply exposed further weaknesses in the Pompeian army. Even so the commanders seemed to believe that regaining the ground to Ilerda would deny Caesar an easy victory and could open up a way to the coast via Tarraco. The rank and file were probably less enthusiastic and perhaps rather more resigned to what must have appeared almost certain victory for Caesar. Still, the camp they had occupied for just three or four days was also abandoned and the army moved slowly northwest followed closely by Caesar's powerful cavalry. As usual it was the rearguard that bore the brunt of the attacks. Caesar describes in some detail (*BC* 1.79) the tactics his cavalry and light armed troops employed and how these were countered by his opponents. The Pompeian commanders had light armed troops covering the most exposed section of the marching column but this was not quick to move.[47] Where the column advanced uphill those in front could offer help to those behind by shooting off missiles against those attacking from a lower level, but once the same troops moved downhill those in the rear became extremely vulnerable since those ahead could not now provide assistance against an enemy now above them. The solution it seems was to halt at the summit of any hill, launch a fierce charge against the attackers and then bolt downhill as quickly as possible before Caesar's cavalry had regrouped to make the next assault. Once on lower ground the column had to halt before tackling the next hill. This tactic may have been a sound one but no momentum or rhythm was being maintained and the psychological impact must have worn out the troops who clearly had no really effective way of dispersing the attackers. Furthermore, Caesar claims that what cavalry Afranius and his commanders possessed refused to play a full role in covering this retreat since these troops had lost all confidence against the greater numbers of their enemy who had recently defeated them. These apparently sheltered inside the column like noncombatants or civilians leading their mounts. This lack of loyalty exhibited by these men who whether Roman citizens or drawn from allied states were usually drawn from the political and social elite can hardly have impressed the common soldiers and must have contributed to the feeling of despondency among the army.

Caesar states (*BC* 1.80) that Afranius' advance was slow and hardly more than four Roman miles or six kilometres (3.5 miles) had been covered before a halt was ordered and a high hill was occupied for what the pursuing cavalry believed was to be a camp for the night.[48] This stop occurred even before midday when Afranius' troops began to excavate a ditch between themselves and Caesar, but they did not unload their baggage from the pack animals. Caesar's army also halted and started the usual preparations for an encampment by pitching tents and sending out the cavalry to forage for supplies. At this point, at the sixth hour (*BC* 1.80) or early in the afternoon, unexpectedly the Pompeian troops surged down from their hill and began their march again. This general movement by a whole army could not go unnoticed but Caesar carefully allowed his own men to rest before setting off in pursuit. It is also noticeable that, although he does not say so, Caesar evidently believed that the end of the campaign was now in sight for he ordered that baggage and supplies be left behind under guard (*BC* 1.80). The cavalry and any foragers were recalled and as the daylight began to fail the former once more took up their relentless attack on the Pompeian rearguard where the fighting was the fiercest and where several officers including centurions were killed. More serious for Afranius was that Caesar's column had caught up with his rearguard.

The Pompeian army halted at dusk and was so pressed in that they made camp some distance from accessible water, yet they were surely marching up the Segre valley. It may well be that they had been forced by their attackers to move inland some miles to the south of the river, a move that in itself must have been debilitating and demoralizing. Caesar ordered that his troops rest under arms and that no full camp be constructed so that he could continue to harass the enemy should Afranius try to move out under cover of darkness. The Pompeians realized that their position was untenable and seem to have tried to move their camp in piecemeal fashion, probably trying to find a source of water (*BC* 1.81), but as they extended their fortifications and defensive lines they actually found themselves further from supplies than before. Still these moves continued overnight and throughout the following day. On the second night Afranius ordered the entire army to remain inside its encampment and no water was provided. The weather, which earlier in the campaign had been instrumental in affecting events by excessive rainfall, now failed to produce any at all or none that is recorded. The following morning the whole army except for a garrison for the camp marched to the river where water supplies were collected but no attempt was made to forage for food for either the pack animals or the horses. The Pompeians were left alone by Caesar who hoped that deprivation would bring about a surrender rather than having to fight a battle. To accelerate the worsening plight of his enemy Caesar ordered that a circumvallation of Afranius' camp be started and maintained a sufficiently strong guard to dissuade any form of retaliation. Inside the Pompeian camp all the pack animals were killed, since there was no food and in the event of a break out all personal baggage was to be left behind.

These events apparently took place over two days, and by the third day Caesar's objective of encircling Afranius' camp with a rampart was nearly finished. The Pompeian response could have been predicted easily enough for they had two options: either to remain boxed inside their camp and face the prospect of being reduced to starvation and surrender or they could fight. Afranius chose the second option and towards late afternoon on the third day he led out his legions. In order that he could not be seen to be avoiding a confrontation with his enemy in the eyes of his own troops Caesar also drew up his army for battle and left off the siege works. However, he was still not inclined he says (*BC* 1.82) to order an engagement since he did not wish to be responsible for casualties and was particularly concerned about the lie of the land and the proximity between the two forces. The two armies were drawn up in front of their respective camps, which were not more than two Roman miles apart (*BC* 1.82: '*non ... amplius pedum milibus duobus ab castris castra distabant*').[49] Each of the armies possessed three lines of infantry, which filled much of this area leaving less than seven hundred paces between the opposing front ranks. Afranius' five legions were drawn up in a double line with auxiliary troops forming a third line in reserve. Caesar's first line consisted of four cohorts from each of his five legions (one legion had remained in the camp at

Ilerda), and behind these three cohorts from each legion, and in the third row again three cohorts from each of the five legions. Light armed troops described as *sagittarii* and *funditores* – bowmen and slingers – were placed '*media acie*', which could mean in the centre of the front line but probably means that they stood just beyond the first line of heavy infantry into which they could retreat when the main army engaged. Caesar's cavalry occupied both the left and right wings. There is no mention of cavalry in the line drawn up by Afranius, although they had been in evidence earlier in the campaign. Their mounts may have already perished from lack of fodder and this lack placed the Pompeians at a grave disadvantage. It is of interest to note at this point that the three ranks of each side had a depth of about 650 Roman paces, while the length of Caesar's line, because he is more specific about his own placement, can be estimated as follows: a cohort of about 200 men, hence 800 men from each legion, and a total of five legions would indicate 4000 legionaries each occupying about metre each, and with gaps between each cohort, 10 metres or so, to allow ease of movement in and out by auxiliary troops, would suggest a front line of approximately 4200 metres, a little more than four kilometres (roughly 13,000 feet and about two and half miles). The space between the two armies meant that there was no room for manoeuvre. Each commander will have known that in such circumstances a bloody hand–to–hand combat was in store for their troops, although Caesar points out that the defeated side had no distance to flee to gain the safety of the camp. Still the armies stood ready for battle until dusk when they both returned to their camps. On the following morning Caesar's troops again began work on completing the siege works against the enemy, while Afranius tried one further attempt to break out from this stranglehold. He ordered some of his forces – Caesar does not stipulate numbers or whether these were legionaries or auxiliary troops – to try to ford the Segre. This must mean that the Pompeian camp was probably within sight of the river. Caesar responded quickly by sending some of his cavalry across the river and ordered light armed troops to guard the banks of the river a regular intervals. Afranius clearly gave up the attempt very quickly.

There was now no way of escape for the Pompeian army hemmed in all sides, and so messages were taken to Caesar asking for the opportunity to discuss terms.[50] Afranius initially asked for a private interview but this was denied. The two armies were drawn up probably not under arms and the two commanders met openly. Afranius was granted the delivery of a brief statement (*BC* 1.84) in which he excused his actions, which he stressed had been based on his sense of duty and loyalty to Pompey, and that his troops had also carried out obligations to the best of their ability but that there was now no alternative to surrender. Caesar's response (*BC* 1.85) was considerably more elaborate in an address where he exonerated the actions of Afranius and his army, but also used the moment to advertise his desire to avoid excessive cost of life and therefore he displayed a compassion for fellow human beings.[51] His conditions for peace were simple enough: the Pompeian army was to be disbanded since, Caesar claims, the seven legions assigned to Pompey's Iberian command had originally been levied in the mid-50s with the intention of being a force to be used against him and not for any benefit of the region.[52] If this demand was met then the troops in Afranius' army would be allowed to depart as free men.

This proved to be a hugely popular gesture and welcomed enthusiastically by soldiers fully expecting some form of retributive penalty. The fact that this declaration was made in front of the armies made it impossible for commanders such as Petreius who might just have considered fighting to the bitter end from preventing it being ratified. The soldiers of the defeated army wanted immediate discharge from further service and made their opinions very clear by shouts and a show of hands (*BC* 1.86). Those who had homes in either of the provinces in Iberia were to be allowed to go at once. While those who were presumably from Italy were to be cashiered when they arrived at the Varus River.[53] Their safety was to be guaranteed and soldiers would not be under any obligation to swear an oath of allegiance to Caesar. Moreover, food was to be provided for the march to the coast, while the cost of any personal belongings that had been lost – and which had been verified as such – during the recent events was to be met by Caesar. Caesar also relates (*BC* 1.87) that the defeated legions were also at loggerheads with their former commanders, Afranius and Petreius, who were unable or unwilling to pay them disputed allowances ('*stipendium*') and that they took their cases to him for arbitration and that the matter was solved to the satisfaction of all. Apparently over 30 per cent of the Pompeian army disbanded at Ilerda within two days of the final confrontation. The remaining troops were escorted to the Varus River by a guard under the command of Q. Fufius Calenus, and once they reached the coast they too were discharged and probably went by ship to Italy.

Iberia was yet to be completely subdued by Caesar because one of the proconsuls, M. Terentius Varro, still remained at large with three legions in *Hispania Ulterior* (*BC* 2.17). He was less committed in his political inclinations towards Pompey and had long been a friend of Caesar.[54] Still, he fell in with his obligations to Pompey and fulfilled any expectations there may have been of him. Varro's legions were levied from among the Roman communities in his province, probably mostly from Carthago Nova and Italica (Santiponce) and their surrounding districts. Besides this heavy infantry corps he also raised thirty cohorts of allied troops, probably a mix of cavalry and light armed skirmishers. Supplies of especially grain were collected, some of which was despatched to Massilia, the rest to Afranius at Ilerda. He also instructed the citizens of Gades (modern Cadiz) to begin the construction of ten warships, and others to be built at Hispalis (*BC* 2.18).[55] Gades was suitably rewarded for this task by being assigned the income from the Gaditane temple of Hercules, but at the same time was obliged to carry the financial burden of a garrison consisting of six cohorts under the command of C. Gallonius.[56] Caesar also accuses Varro of indulging in scurrilous defamation because he stated in public that Pompey's enemy was losing the campaign against Afranius and that these enemy troops were deserting their general in large numbers. This tactic was designed to extort financial and material aid from the local communities. Thus Caesar states that Varro was able to raise eighteen million sesterces and twenty thousand pounds of silver bullion together with one hundred and twenty thousand modii of grain (*BC* 2.18). Any community that was regarded by Varro as potentially an ally of Caesar's was immediately forced to accept a garrison and individuals suspected of favouring his cause were arrested and their property confiscated. The entire province of *Hispania Ulterior* was obliged to swear an oath to Pompey, although this appears to have been quite ineffective for when the events at Ilerda became common knowledge Varro was forced to consider making a withdrawal to Gades. By doing this he hoped that he could hold the city for Pompey and that Caesar would in due course be obliged to leave Iberia for Rome. Caesar writes that there were compelling reasons for returning to Italy but that he considered pacification of the peninsula and victory over Varro more important. He believed that if he returned to Rome without completing his objective his enemies might regroup and pose future problems, hence only a complete victory in Iberia was to be contemplated.

Caesar ordered one of his legates, Q. Cassius, to lead two legions into *Hispania Ulterior*, whereas he set out with a guard of six hundred cavalry to Corduba (*BC* 2.19) where he had instructed the leading citizens of this city and all the other communities of the province to meet him.[57] Corduba immediately closed its gates to Varro and posted sentries in case he should try a surprise assault on the city. The Cordubans also appear to have won over to Caesar's cause two cohorts of regular infantry from one of Varro's legions, which happened to be or near the city. Nearby Carmona, described as '*longe firmissima totius provinciae civitas Hispania Ulterior*' or 'by far the most powerful state of the whole province', also switched its allegiance from Pompey to Caesar.[58] Varro was understandably alarmed by this turn of events and decided to make for Gades without delay, but was hardly on the march when messengers arrived informing him that this city too had deserted the Pompeian cause. The citizens of Gades had, in fact, conspired with some of the officers of the garrison to rise against and expel Gallonius who had been allowed to leave unmolested and was probably by then sailing along the coast towards Massilia. When this latest reverse became known one of the legions under Varro's command mutinied in sight of the proconsul and marched out of his camp and into Hispalis where they were enthusiastically received by its citizens who allowed them the use of the public forum and porticoes (*BC* 2.20).[59] Varro, by now very alarmed at his own deteriorating position, then made a snap decision to aim instead for Italica with his one loyal legion, perhaps as few as three thousand men, but no sooner had he got under way than news reached him that this town too had closed its gates and switched its allegiance.[60] Varro immediately sent word to Caesar offering to surrender the remnants of his army. In return Caesar sent Sextus Julius Caesar one of his legates to take command of Varro's legion and perhaps also the other unit that was camped out in Hispalis.[61] Varro made his way to Corduba where he met with Caesar and presented all financial accounts of the province and precise information on the whereabouts of grain warehouses and the location of warships. Caesar next summoned a meeting of the delegates from the communities of the province where he personally thanked the Roman communities, the Iberian states and especially the citizens of Gades for their prompt action is asserting their preference for his cause by closing their gates or expelling Pompeian troops. In return he stated that any financial commitment that had been demanded of them by Varro was to be overlooked and any contributions forced from them returned at once. Any citizen of any town in the province who had suffered confiscation of property for his political leanings was to have this returned. Individuals and communities were also given other rewards and generally a feeling of wellbeing was promoted which, claims Caesar, had been lacking for some time. Caesar spent just two days in Corduba and then went to Gades where the expropriated treasury from the temple of Hercules was restored to its shrine. Q. Cassius was appointed the proconsul of *Hispania Ulterior* and Caesar then proceeded within a few days to Tarraco by sea. With him went the warships that had been ordered by Varro and which would now serve a useful purpose elsewhere. At Tarraco he was met, understandably enough, by delegates from all the communities from the province of *Hispania Citerior*, most of whom had deserted the Pompeian cause before the surrender of Afranius. As at Corduba Caesar rewarded individuals and certain states that had been conspicuous in their loyalty to him (*BC* 2.21). He then made his way overland along the Via Domitia to Narbo and then onto Massilia. His intention now was to deal conclusively with the pressing problem of this city, which by then had withstood a siege for probably more than two months.

When Caesar had first arrived in Arelate on his way to Ilerda he apparently summoned the fifteen leading citizens of Massilia to meet with him and these had originally hoped to avoid becoming embroiled in the conflict between Caesar and Pompey by explaining their longstanding ties of friendship with both parties. In this way these envoys hoped that an impartial stance would be respected by both Caesar and Pompey, although it was by far the greater benefit to the former if the Massiliotes remained neutral. While discussions were taking place, however, a coup took place inside Massilia for a group of citizens more strongly in favour of Pompey decided to invite L. Domitius Ahenobarbus to take command of the city against Caesar (*BC* 1.34–35).[62] Caesar seems to have been aware that Domitius was on his way to Massilia from Italy losing no time in continuing his feud against a man whom he clearly loathed. Yet not long before Caesar had allowed Domitius to leave Corfinium, where the latter had been in charge of the garrison. But this act of clemency had evidently been construed as a sign of weakness rather than an attempt to reduce tensions between the two. Domitius felt no gratitude for Caesar's act of generosity but seems instead to have wanted to settle old scores. His attitude is easily exposed in Caesar's account, although there is always the chance that the writer has enhanced the hostility felt towards him in order to denigrate the character of his opponent. Domitius went to the extent of seizing seven merchant ships in Italy – at Igilium and Cosanum – to transport him to Massilia with what appears to have been just a small number of friends and personal retainers.[63] A little beforehand probably in January 49 (November 50) some envoys from Massilia to Rome – Caesar describes them as young men from leading families – were sent back to Gaul by Pompey who was about to leave the city and who strongly urged them to remember his various kindnesses to them and not to change their allegiance to Caesar.[64] These reached Massilia before Caesar arrived in *Gallia Transalpina* and once there while the more senior delegates were meeting Caesar successfully persuaded their fellow citizens to close their gates.[65] As a result of this decision, the Massiliotes felt they needed the aid of the Albici, described as allies of ancient standing, who occupied some adjacent hills above the coastal plain. Their numbers cannot have been a considerable addition to a city that was the greatest power in the region, but they probably contributed as much in food supplies as in military capability.[66] At the same time, feverish preparations were underway to withstand the anticipated siege: supplies were transported in from outlying storehouses, weapons manufactured and walls and gates strengthened. Domitius arrived in the harbour at Massilia it seems while Caesar was still negotiating with the Massiliote envoys and given complete command of the city and the forthcoming siege. Domitius sent out the

Massiliote fleet (*BC* 1.36) with orders to round up every available merchant ship, any not seaworthy were to be repaired, and with all this shipping further supplies of every sort were brought inside. Caesar in retaliation led three legions to Massilia, had twelve warships constructed at Arelate and brought up siege towers and other siege engines.

Caesar then went to Ilerda and assigned command of the land forces in his absence to his legate C. Trebonius and the fleet to D. Iunius Brutus.[67] Domitius meanwhile encouraged the Massiliotes to invest time and effort in enlarging their fleet so that they might break the efforts of the besiegers by keeping control of the sea (*BC* 1.56). A number of decked warships, probably quadriremes, although Caesar is not specific, carried archers and a great number of the Albici, but again the writer does not explain their role.[68] Brutus was greatly outnumbered but he was an experienced naval commander and had stationed his fleet off one of the islands situated to the southwest of the entrance to Massilia's harbour (see map).[69] The troops Brutus had on board his warships are also credited with a great deal of experience and courage. Not only this but they had with them grappling irons, hooks and javelins with the aim of obtaining close combat in which they knew they were superior. Still, the Massiliotes were initially confident and sailed out of their harbour to give battle since their warships were fast in the water and they possessed skilled pilots (*BC* 1.58). Their aim was to avoid closing with the enemy and if possible ram the ships of their opponents and rely on their archers to maintain a safe distance and so always have an escape route available. Brutus' warships had crews that were less experienced and therefore for some time the fight was evenly balanced. The Albici and the 'pastores' of Domitius may have lacked finesse in their approach to fighting but made up for this in bravery and in the case of the latter in their hopes of being freed from servile status if they were on the winning side. Many of Brutus' vessels were also newly built and so lacked their opponents' speed in the water since the timber was still unseasoned. Moreover, the crews were unsure of the local currents and natural obstacles such as sandbanks, which might impinge on their ability to ensure a successful outcome to the engagement.[70] Still, the discipline of the Romans gradually wore down their enemy especially whenever there was a boarding, and Caesar boasts (*BC* 1.58) that his ships often took on two of the Massiliotes at the same time. In the end the Massiliote fleet was compelled to withdraw into its harbour with nine of their warships either sunk or captured and having sustained heavy casualties. Caesar who was then at Ilerda was informed of this victory (*BC* 1.59) and although it may not appear to have been a decisive affair it was probably enough to deny the open seas to the citizens of Massilia and a further indication of the mediocre generalship of Domitius.

At roughly the same time as their naval victory, the Roman forces outside Massilia began to seal the blockade of the city on the landward side (*BC* 2.1). Trebonius had the usual ditches and ramparts excavated in order to prevent any supplies reaching the city and any escape possible overland. He is also said to have brought up siege towers and 'vineae' or battering rams covered with a pitched roof made of wooden frameworks and covered with hides. The city possessed a strong and defensible position surrounded on three sides by the sea, the delta of the Rhone to the west its strongly fortified harbour to the east and even the side that faced onto the land was protected by a hilly terrain. In order to have a fully effective blockade therefore the Romans needed to employ a huge number of labourers, probably more than just the legionaries, and pack animals used to bring in timber and brushwood, which was used to reinforce the earth as it was built up. Caesar's text has an earthwork rising to eighty feet, which does not fit the description of an encircling rampart but rather a ramp aimed at a specific point in the defensive walls. Up this ramp battering rams and siege towers could be hauled to bring an assault on a sector of the walls or a gate believed to be vulnerable. The Massiliotes were ready to defend their walls and had certainly been viewing the construction in front of them for some weeks and which allowed them to be ready with an effective response. As the covered battering rams were brought up against the walls the Massiliotes launched from catapults missiles twelve feet (4 metres) long with both ends having spikes to penetrate the roofs of the battering rams, even those with four layers of wicker-work, and with such force that they could become embedded in the ground. To counteract this threat the battering rams were then provided with an extra thick roof of timbers a foot thick (*BC* 2.2). Provided with this more secure cover any undermining of the walls could be undertaken in relative safety. Caesar refers here to a *testudo*, meaning a portable covering similar to that which covered the battering rams but which allowed labourers to clear the land ahead in readiness for the latter to be brought forward, rather than an ad hoc covering to the body with raised shields against injury by air-borne missiles.[71] The *testudo* was roofed with timbers and all manner of material designed to prevent it being burned or split open by the defenders who threw flaming missiles, rocks or anything they could lay their hands to from the walls.[72] Besides this tenacious defence, frequent sorties took place, most often by the Albici who may have suffered high casualties but severely disrupted the Roman attempts to gain a foothold in the fortifications. As a result of all these difficulties progress was slow.[73]

Pompey had apparently sent a legate named Q. Nasidius from Dyrrachium in Epirus (App. *BC* 5.139) in command of a fleet of sixteen warships, which seems to have consisted mainly of triremes, to aid Domitius, although such limited reinforcements were hardly likely to make a fundamental difference to the situation.[74] Still, running the naval blockade of Brutus' fleet would be a boost to the defenders' confidence. This fleet managed to escape detection as it passed through the Straits of Messina and even made an attack on the harbour there. Nasidius also captured and towed away a ship he found beached in a dockyard, but lacked the manpower to attack the city itself, although many of its leading citizens apparently fled on his arrival. At Massilia news came by way of a small boat sent ahead that Nasidius was approaching and therefore it was decided to challenge Caesar's fleet for a second time. The Massiliotes had repaired several derelict ships to replace the nine warships they had recently lost at sea and added to their total by converting some fishing boats ('*piscatoriae*') to take archers and javelin throwers and even small catapults on a deck above the rowers. Caesar states that the whole of Massilia went out either to offer prayers at the temple shrines or to wish the fleet well knowing that their future depended on a successful engagement. Trebonius and his troops were also able to witness these communal prayers and sacrifices from their vantage point on the hills above the city.[75] The Massiliote fleet slipped out of the city avoiding Brutus and sailed to a fortress named as Tauroeis (today the town of Le Brusc a little to the west of Toulon) where they rendezvoused with Nasidius and where they carried out some tactical exercises in preparation for battle. They formed up with the Massiliotes on the right wing and Nasidius on the left wing, while Brutus who had followed in hot pursuit joined battle as soon as he arrived. Brutus was now in a much stronger position than he was before since he had augmented his fleet with six warships captured in the previous engagement (*BC* 2.5). At first the Massiliotes fought with some courage as did the Albici on board as light armed troops, although Caesar's text appears to consist largely here of general comments applicable to any naval engagement. The skill of the Massiliote pilots is duly noted and that the two sides were equal in their determination to succeed, although there was far less pressure on Brutus' crews than on their opponents who knew that failure would accelerate the end of the siege in the favour of their enemy. Brutus' warship became the target for two of Nasidius' triremes who seem to have been intent on ramming this vessel. But Brutus ordered a rapid movement forwards, which left the smaller triremes behind; they missed their prey and rammed each other.[76] As a result troops from Brutus' fleet were able to grapple aboard and sink both disabled enemy ships. This appears to have been the seminal point in the battle since the remaining crews of Nasidius' detachment seem to have lost heart and began to sail off in the direction of Iberia, although it is claimed that they were citizens of

Massilia (*BC* 2.7). Caesar also states that Nasidius' ships were useless ('*nullo usui*') but this probably means that they were smaller vessels than the larger warships possessed by Brutus and therefore mostly ineffective rather than that the crews were lacking any ability. They had after all sailed from Epirus. Without Nasidius' support the Massiliote defence quickly crumbled and they proceeded to have five warships destroyed, four captured by Brutus and one joined Nasidius in sailing away along the coast to Iberia after breaking off the fight.[77] Brutus' fleet did not go in pursuit possibly because his warships were slower than Nasidius triremes, but he was probably under orders to maintain his blockade while the enemy might be dealt with elsewhere.[78] The news was brought to Massilia where the people immediately went into mourning. Although the losses were not catastrophic, the attempt to break the blockade had failed and there now remained the prospect of fierce fighting.

Caesar's text (*BC* 2.8–12) now becomes rather puzzling for he gives an extremely detailed account of siege tower building without any attempt to contextualize this material; it could indeed be a description that fits a hundred sieges in antiquity. Caesar was not present and while he may have obtained some accounts from those who were there, this section looks more as if it was extracted from a manual on how to conduct siege assaults and the dangers that lurked in constructing towers against a besieged city's walls. Caesar's sources for such information may well have been a writer on military engineering such as Vitruvius or one of his contemporaries. Vitruvius' *de architectura*, which was probably only circulated after Caesar's death, certainly contained sections about military engineering and probably would have possessed material about siege towers and their construction. But there were others who were interested in such subjects and Caesar who was constantly on military campaigns from the year after his consulship in 59 may well have carried one or more manuals or treatises with him. Information about Massilia will have been inconsistent and sketchy, which therefore allowed the writer to add such specific material into his own work where it was applicable to a siege but which was also of interest to his reader.[79]

The tower was constructed in stages for at first it was simply a place of refuge from attacks by the enemy ('*hostes*') and therefore just one storey in height but with walls five feet thick. The legionaries then realized that if they made this strongpoint higher it would become useful for an assault on the adjacent city wall. Caesar then goes on to describe how the height of this tower was extended by protecting the labourers on the uppermost level with pitched roofs like the *testudo* and protective roofing for the battering rams he has already noted. A roof for the tower was then constructed but not fastened to the storey that had been completed and then this served as a cover as new stories were added. The building upwards was also protected by a wooden screen hung from this cover or roof while the current top storey was given a firm floor and covered with straw mattresses, which acted as cushions in the event that any missiles penetrated the roof. In this fashion six stories were built (*BC* 2.9) with spaces in the brickwork for the discharge of missiles or arrows. When the tower and its projected height was completed, a bridge was constructed of wood, which Caesar claims was up to sixty feet long (*BC* 2.10) and that this, once suitably fortified against all manner of missiles or flames hurled down from the defenders, was launched from the tower's topmost level and connected at the same height to the city's wall.[80] Naturally enough, it seems the defenders hurried to find effective countermeasures, but the text here is also a little mysterious since it appears to rather refer back to the defeat in the last sea battle rather than to the building of a particularly large siege tower. The defenders can hardly have been astonished and 'terrified' by this construction for it must have taken several days of even weeks to complete. The recent loss at sea, however, will have reinforced a general feeling of despondency. The defensive actions against the attackers are precisely those which the bridge and roof of the tower had been strengthened to withstand (*BC* 2.11). The Romans then apparently under cover began to dislodge foundation stones from the defence wall on which their target – a bastion or tower – was situated while the bridge that was now linking these towers was keenly defended by the attacking soldiers. It was this excavation work rather than the elaborately constructed siege-tower that started to cause the city walls and the tower on these to crash down. The defenders immediately ceased fighting and instead crowded outside their walls as suppliants seeking a peace. The Roman commanders listen to the appeals for a truce to await the arrival of Caesar to whom they would surrender because it was argued that if they continued to fight with their walls crumbling around them there was nothing to prevent the complete destruction of their city.

Trebonius agreed to give a truce (*BC* 2.23) in which the Roman troops except for sentries were withdrawn to their camp because he was under instructions from Caesar not to sack the city. Caesar claims that the legionaries were unhappy with this arrangement and only very unwillingly did they obey orders blaming Trebonius with poor generalship in not allowing them what they considered to be their reward for bringing the siege to a successful conclusion. Caesar perhaps reflects on the lack of civilized behaviour among the rank and file of the army, which was plainly at times barely under control without his presence, but also, as events showed, the perspicacity of these common soldiers. The Massiliotes, probably persuaded by Domitius, whose position at that time is not noted but who must certainly have been afraid for his life, evidently had no intention of keeping the terms of a truce and when the moment was right for them they launched a strong sortie (*BC* 2.14).[81] The time was the middle of the day when the on–duty guards were least attentive, some had gone for food and others were simply dozing. The Massiliotes were intent on firing as much of the enemy's siege works as they could. They were helped because there were strong winds, as can be expected in this part of the Mediterranean, especially when they blow down from the Pyrenees. These aided the spread of the fires, which rapidly consumed the sheds protecting the battering rams, the *testudo* and even the great tower. The Romans quickly organized a counterattack but the Massiliotes just as quickly retreated under cover of missiles from the walls through their gates and to safety. Caesar summed up the disaster with this comment:

> *Ita multorum mensium labor hostium perfidia et vi tempestatis puncto temporis interiithostes.*
> Thus the work of many months perished in an instant because of the treachery of the enemy and the forces of the weather (*BC* 2.14).

Following this salutary experience, Trebonius was keen to redouble efforts to conclude the siege and actually utilized the disgust of his soldiers not only at the breaking of a truce but also at the total loss of their previous labours. Now another puzzling item of information, or lack of it intrudes into the narrative, for Caesar is at pains to describe how a new form of ramp was constructed against the city wall that did not have to rely on timber, which was in very short supply since most trees even at some distance from Massilia had been cut down either for use in building siege machines or for the Roman camp. The ramp seems to have constructed with a brick framework (*BC* 2.15) rather than of wood but again hardly seems specifically placed at Massilia and appears to have, anyway, contained a great deal of timber either as filling with rocks and soil and also for roofing. This section is arguably another place where Caesar short of reliable material about what was precisely happening outside the city chose to fill out his account using a more general source about siege practice. The Massiliotes watched this rapid turnabout in the fortunes of the besiegers with dismay and must surely have realized that now there was little room for further manoeuvre. Moreover, by now news must have filtered through of Caesar's victory over Afranius and Petreius and following that the surrender of *Hispania Ulterior* by Varro. There must have been public meetings in the city to come to some agreement about what to do next although the options were few and far between; they evidently decided to sue for peace.

Caesar came to supervise the siege immediately after leaving Tarraco, his pacification of the whole of Iberia now complete. He states (*BC* 2.22) that the Massiliotes were worn out by the desperate nature of the siege and had no hope of success following their defeats on sea and on land but also notes that the city had been in the grip of disease probably caused by overcrowding and a paucity of supplies. Domitius was informed that the city was about to surrender to Caesar and so he and his closest followers commandeered three vessels, which were not necessarily warships since he managed to slip out of the harbour during a storm. The Roman ships enforcing the embargo reacted as quickly as they could in the circumstances and pursued the enemy. Domitius escaped but the two ships with him returned to the city rather than fall into the hands of Brutus' fleet. Caesar ordered that all arms and siege equipment employed by the Massiliotes be handed over together with any surviving warships. They were also instructed to produce any money ('*pecunia*') either in the form of coin or in silver or gold bullion from the public treasury to pay for the costs of the siege against them. Caesar did, however, spare the city any further destruction and allowed it to keep its form of government, but imposed on its citizens a garrison of two legions.[82] He next set out for Rome with the rest of his army and continuation of the fight with Pompey beckoned.

The main and remarkable achievement in the Ilerda campaign here was the elimination of a Pompeian army of over thirty thousand with very little cost to human life on either side and without a major land battle having been fought. The speed by which Caesar obtained the result he wanted must have been dispiriting to those senators who had sided with Pompey. Caesar with an army comprising a high percentage of veterans of up to ten years' experience in the field and no recent or major defeats must have appeared a daunting prospect. Caesar's success at Ilerda resulted in a major shift in the balance of power and whereas before the spring of 49 the outcome of the civil war remained highly uncertain, after the removal of Iberia from the equation there were probably only a few who truly believed that Pompey could emerge victorious from the future conflict. It is well worth noting that whereas Herodotus (Chapter 2) makes all too little of the problem of supplying Xerxes' army and navy as they advanced from the Hellespont into Greece, Caesar dwells, possibly to an inordinate degree on the logistical problems both he and his adversaries faced in the campaign around Ilerda. The world had clearly changed in that the focus of the writing and the audience for which it was intended had become one of specialists. Caesar's audience was not the citizen body that happened upon a story-telling historian in an agora but the senior military corps that dominated political life in Rome during the first century BC. Caesar would not have commented at length about the difficulties of supplying his troops if he thought this was not of interest to those who would read his circulated work. Hence the prominence devoted to food and other supplies for armies on the march or indeed siege equipment for besieging cities and assault techniques as those employed at Massilia. In the manoeuvring around Ilerda the problem of supplying large armies was clearly of particular concern to both commands and the text of Caesar provides one of those rare pieces of literary evidence for exposing the difficulties that affected armies in the field and the logistical issues in supplying them. The weather too played an important role in the outcome of the events, which is again a unique aspect of the record for whereas sudden downpours or other natural phenomena are mentioned in affecting battles such as that of the wind at Vercellae in 101 BC, the snow at Tauromenium in 394 BC, the wind and ice at the Frigidus River in AD 394, it is only at Ilerda that a river in flood is noted as being a vital factor affecting both supplies and movement of the contending military groups. Even at the less well documented account of the siege at Massilia, storms and especially high winds are noted by the writer as affecting the outcome of the episode.

Moreover, the military event that has become known as the battle of Ilerda was in fact a series of skirmishes and assaults on a retreating column over a period of perhaps three weeks in the spring of 49 BC. During that entire episode there was no occasion when the opposing armies fully engaged in a set–piece battle. Their commanders certainly drew up the ranks in battle preparedness, but invariably withdrew after what seems to have been a spell of static martial display. Also noteworthy is the use of the cavalry in several engagements that was employed without the infantry as independent units in much the same way as the Syracusan cavalry had been deployed against the Athenian infantry in the siege of Syracuse in 414/13 BC. And indeed there is certainly a memory in Caesar's account which harks back to Thucydides (Book 7) either a deliberate reuse of the essential material about an army in retreat with obvious differences in local detail but nonetheless a distinct connection between the two compositions. There may also be some reminiscence of Xenophon's *Anabasis* in Caesar's approach to the writing up of this campaign where Caesar becomes the Persian followers and Afranius the Xenophon figure. In both of these earlier accounts the weather had a role as did the problem of logistics, but neither have as much detail regarding these aspects as Caesar's account of Ilerda. The siege of Massilia has all the necessary detail expected from a writer experienced in handling this type of warfare. Unlike the campaign at Ilerda, Caesar was not present for most of the time and therefore relied on eyewitness accounts or dispatches sent to him during the siege. But for episodes such as sea fights there is certainly an element of invention mixed with the use of topical material suitable for incorporation in such descriptive passages. Military treatises, which had become a common enough genre by this time, also provided basic information about how an army might conduct a siege and how the besieged might react.[83] The course of events was probably less dramatic than is portrayed and when the detailed account of the construction of siege towers is removed then the account becomes almost skeletal in comparison to the coverage of Ilerda. The chance to attack the character of Domitius is clearly evident at the start of the siege but thereafter Caesar loses interest in that and almost consigns one of his most outspoken critics to obscurity rather than indulge in copycat invective. All in all, placed alongside the account of Ilerda the account of Massilia is unsatisfactory and hardly the standard one might expect from Caesar, but the encounter with the Masiliotes was perhaps in his eyes small fry compared with the greater struggle to come.

Chronology

November 50:	Caesar crossed the Rubicon just north of Ariminum and so began his invasion of Italy.
January 49:	Caesar in Rome.
February 49:	Caesar at Arelate.

Campaign at Ilerda

March 49:	Caesar proceeded via Narbo and the road via Prades across the Pyrenees.
	Caesar arrived two days after Fabius was attacked following the storm and destruction of the bridge.
+ 1 day:	Bridge repaired and Caesar advanced to Afranius' camp.
+ 1 day:	Caesar's new camp was fortified and the old camp abandoned.
+ 1 day:	Camp of Fabius abandoned.
+ 1 day (?):	Caesar attacked the mound (*tumulus*).
+ 1 day (?):	Storms affected the Pyrenees and the area around Ilerda.
+ 7–10 days:	Extensive flooding to the area around Ilerda.
+ 1 day (?):	Reinforcements and supplies for Caesar turned back by Afranius.
+ 5 days (?):	Construction of boats to cross the river.
+ 2 days:	A new bridge built across the river and a legion plus cavalry moved to the south bank.
+ 1–2 days:	Afranius decided to quit Ilerda.

+ 1 day: Pontoon bridge ordered (and completed) at Octogesa. Two legions of Afranius crossed the Segre River.

+ 1 day: Afranius and his army departed from Ilerda.

+ 1 day: Both sides camped on the south bank of the Segre. Afranius' night attempt to escape.

+ 1 day: Both sides contemplated future action.

+ 1 day: Both sides advanced to the hills above the Ebro. Afranius' escape blocked.

+ 1 day: Pompeian army in its previous camp (*BC* 1.73).

+ 1 day: Afranius and Petreius supervised construction of defensive works for securing water.

+ 1 day: The Pompeian army renewed its oath and set off to Ilerda, pitching camp far from water.

+ 4 days: Caesar encircled Pompeians who came out to give battle and then surrender.

Total days of campaign – roughly 37 days a little over a month in March–April 49 BC.

Siege of Massilia
Late February 49 – May: The siege probably occupied a period of 10 weeks.

Appendix: Family Tree of Caesar

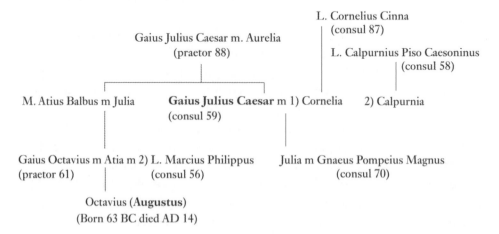

L. Cornelius Cinna (consul 87)

Gaius Julius Caesar m. Aurelia (praetor 88)

L. Calpurnius Piso Caesoninus (consul 58)

M. Atius Balbus m Julia

Gaius Julius Caesar m 1) Cornelia   2) Calpurnia (consul 59)

Gaius Octavius m Atia m 2) L. Marcius Philippus (praetor 61)   (consul 56)

Julia m Gnaeus Pompeius Magnus (consul 70)

Octavius (**Augustus**) (Born 63 BC died AD 14)

Chapter Four

Tacitus on the Battles of Bedriacum and the Deaths of Two Emperors

As with the other campaigns discussed earlier in this work, battlefields are not simply a matter of location, although a successful commander such as Alexander the Great or Gaius Marius, will have taken a great deal of care, when time allowed, to choose the best possible site on which to fight, because logistics, climate and weather all have a significant role in the outcome of the fight. This is particularly notable in the two battles of Bedriacum, related by Tacitus in his *Histories* (Books 1–3), which took place in the troubled year AD 69 when the Roman Empire was, engulfed in an increasingly savage civil war. Besides these various factors affecting battle outcomes there are also a number of interesting threads that not only offer an insight into Tacitus' method of reconstruction of the past but also how the Roman themselves viewed military events and their chief players. Particularly noticeable, for example, is the constant contrast between cautious and lethargic old age and vigorous and headstrong youth, which is a pervasive theme in these books of the *Histories*. Otho, no military figure like his opponent Vitellius, is given youthful vigour as opposed to the laziness of his older contender for power. Moreover, among the important subordinates, yet key-players, a similar dichotomy is evident and will be explored for the impact it has on the events as they unfold. Finally, it is the portrayal of heroism and tragedy by Tacitus not only in the battles but also for the deaths of Otho and Vitellius which, while historical events, are clearly embellished by the historian to add further drama to his narrative. Tacitus was familiar with the history of 69 and had some experience of warfare, although there is no evidence for a senior military command either during major campaigns launched by Domitian in the 80s or by Trajan after 98 both focussing on the Danubian frontier. Tacitus did, nonetheless, employ a fairly varied body of evidence drawn from both written and orally transmitted sources, but these alone do not explain all the nuances present in the text. The elder Pliny wrote a history of this time but Tacitus clearly drew on the recollections of senatorial colleagues who were actively involved in the events on 69, some of whom held senior commands and were close to the contenders for power in the Roman Empire.

The battles themselves took place in that central part of the Po Valley, now modern Lombardy between the cities of Cremona and Verona, as Tacitus duly notes:

> The village [of Bedriacum] is situated between Verona and Cremona, and because of the two Roman disasters is now notorious as being an unlucky spot. (Tacitus, *Histories*, 2.23)

> *HistoriesInter Veronam Cremonamque situs est vicus, duabus iam Romanis cladibus notus infaustusqueHistories.*

The River Po is one of the great rivers of Europe, not in length perhaps when compared to the Rhone, the Ebro or the Danube, but certainly in terms of the effect it has had, and continues to have, on the local landscape. In this respect the Po ranks as probably one of the most significant of waterways. The gradient of the river's course from its origins in the Alpine ranges above Lake Geneva and close to the Great St Bernard Pass to the sea a little to the south of modern Venice is at first naturally steep but then very rapidly plateaus out so that the river meanders in a sluggish fashion along much of its course to its mouth on the Adriatic Sea. This is at least what can be seen when the weather is dry, which even in what the Romans knew as Cisalpine Gaul is for a long periods of each year. However, since the river is joined by numerous large tributaries such as the Taro and Oglio (the latter had its own part to play at Bedriacum), and all are fed by the snow melt from not just the Alps but also the northern parts of the Apennines, when these water sources are combined with the intense storms which characterize the climate in this region of Italy the slow-moving channel of the Po becomes a formidable torrent, which reaches out far beyond its banks. Since the overall height of the land is also low-lying, in places lower than the river's bed (much like the land adjacent to the Mississippi River of North America) the surrounding countryside easily becomes inundated. To counteract the danger from flooding, dykes have been constructed since ancient times. The area is therefore crisscrossed with manmade hillocks that often carry the routes of communication, but their very existence can also make the movement especially of armed forces rather difficult. A cursory glance at the landscape might well indicate a flat and broad plain seemingly ideal for the rapid deployment of troops and especially of cavalry units, on closer inspection, however the dykes actually impede movement forcing any commander to utilize the small number of roads or pathways that lie either on the dykes or on lower levels bounded on both sides by deep-sided ditches. These ditches everywhere act as drainage channels for this damp locality. Tacitus gives some prominence to this factor in his account of the first battle of Bedriacum and shows that the difficulty of advancing along these narrow stretches contributed to the defeat of Otho's army, while the skilled use of the waterways by some of the auxiliary troops of Vitellius gave his army an undoubted advantage. The timing of the battle in mid–April may also have worked against Otho's army, since advancing from the south it encountered the rivers and especially the Po at high levels as should have been anticipated in the early spring and which would have been taken account of by any general of experience. Otho had commanders with many years' training in the field but these were, says Tacitus, overruled by others in the emperor's entourage who were not well acquainted with military logistics or tactics.

On the other hand, the second battle of Bedriacum fought in late October does not appear to have been unduly affected by the seasonal fluctuations of the river's height and extent. Still, in the aftermath of the defeat of Vitellius' troops it was the weather that then influenced the course of the next six to seven weeks and allowed the emperor an unexpected breathing space, although Tacitus shows that the time was frittered away and gave the supporters of Vespasian time to put a conclusive end to the strife. Tacitus clearly shows that the winter of AD 69 was harsh and it arrived earlier than usual. In late November 50 BC Caesar had encountered no problem at all in forcing the Apennine passes in his march from Ariminum against the government at Rome and after successfully laying siege to Corfinium arriving in the city by the end of January or at the beginning of February. The reason why he crossed the Rubicon was precisely to make all speed for Rome, which he was able to do because he knew that the winter snows had not yet arrived. In AD 69 it was completely different since the snow arrived by early November and blocked the passes making them perhaps not impassable to infantry troops carrying their arms and packs, but certainly making the movement of cavalry, wagons and any other supplies very difficult. Antonius Primus who was leading the vanguard of the Flavian invasion at that juncture arrived outside Rome on 19 December, more than seven weeks after he had overcome the opposition of Vitellius' army at Bedriacum. Unlike Caesar there was no siege on the advance route and just one minor engagement near Interamna. A journey that a single courier might accomplish in one to two days took Primus' legions nearly two months. As has been shown earlier here, the role and effect of the weather is considerably underestimated by modern scholars in their coverage of ancient battles. Now as then Nature's complex hold on the planet can throw the plans and aspirations of its inhabitants into untold chaos. In late 69 the weather delayed an end to the civil war, which caused immeasurable harm to the economy and society of Italy and elsewhere in the empire and a loss of life and livelihood to its citizens not witnessed since the civil war between Sulla and the supporters of his opponents such as the younger Marius who controlled the government in Rome in the late 80s BC.[1]

Tacitus' senatorial career was promoted and further advanced (*Hist.* 1.1) by the Flavian rulers Vespasian, Titus and Domitian (AD 69–96). Although he reached the consulship during the rule of Nerva (97) this position had probably already been designated for him by Domitian. His proconsulship of Asia about 112 suggests that he was considered a steady hand by the emperor Trajan by then engaged in the initial planning of a campaign against Parthia. Still Tacitus' loyalty towards especially Vespasian is notable in the extant sections of the *Histories* as indeed is his relentless dislike and disdain for both Otho and Vitellius. He clearly regarded both rulers as worthless and a stain on the dignity of the office they held, albeit briefly.[2]

> Indeed before the ruin of both, in which Otho gained exceptional glory Vitellius the greatest disgrace, the stupid pleasures of Vitellius were feared less than the burning desires of Otho. In addition to this was fear and hatred for the murder of Galba, on the other hand nobody ascribed the start of the war to Vitellius. Vitellius by overindulgence and gluttony brought dishonour to himself, Otho brought greater danger to the state by excess, cruelty and pride. (Tacitus, *Hist.* 2.31)

> *Sane ante utriusque exitum, quo egregiam Otho famam, Vitellius flagitiosissimam meruere minus Vitellii ignavae voluptates quam Othonis flagrantissimae libidines timebantur: addiderat huic terrorem atque odium caedes Galbae, contra illi initium belli nemo imputabat. Vitellius ventre et gula sibi inhonestus, Otho luxu saevitia audacia rei publicae exitiosior ducebatur.*

The emperor Nero had committed suicide on 9 June AD 68. There was no heir to the Principate from Nero's family and his death therefore left the avenue open for the establishment of a new dynasty. The rebellion of the Gallic aristocrat Julius Vindex quickly followed by the declaration of insurrection by Servius Sulpicius Galba in *Hispania Tarraconensis* had so unnerved the last Julio-Claudian that when he was declared a public enemy by the senate he took his own life rather than fight for his rule. Vindex was quickly suppressed by the governor of *Germania Superior*, Lucius Verginius Rufus, who when acclaimed emperor by his troops refused what he obviously regarded as a poisoned chalice, and instead offered his allegiance to Galba who had already received senatorial support and recognition as the new *princeps*. Galba's rule lasted just seven months and ended with his murder in the Forum,[3] an event graphically described by Tacitus at the start of his *Histories*, which were composed soon after AD 100 and which present to us by far the most detailed account of this turbulent year.[4] Otho may had initially found just twenty-three active supporters when he broke his cover and declared his own bid for power outside the temple of Saturn in the Forum (Tac. *Hist.* 1.27),[5] but once he had arrived at the camp of the Praetorians he found such enthusiastic support that the death of the emperor, his new heir and his closest advisers occurred within an hour or two.[6]

As dramatic as that episode is, and this element of tragic portrayal will mean that the death of Galba and his heir Piso will resurface in the discussion here, it is rather the military campaigns that culminated in two battles both at Bedriacum (near modern Cremona in the Po Valley) and the consequences of the engagements that resulted in the deaths of two further emperors which is the focus here. Otho who was responsible for the death of Galba and who was proclaimed emperor by the Praetorian Guard in their camp at Rome had been the proconsul of *Hispania Baetica* when Galba announced his rebellion against Nero. Otho had quickly offered his support, although militarily he had little to contribute, and with evident eyes on the succession to the new emperor who was elderly and infirm (Tactus, *Hist.* 1.6: '*invalidem senem,*' 1.12; Suetonius, *Galba*, 21; Dio, 63.3.4). Meanwhile, in early November or perhaps late in October of 68 Aulus Vitellius was sent to replace Fonteius Capito as proconsul in *Germania Inferior.*[7] Capito had been assassinated earlier in the autumn while plotting a coup against the new emperor. However, Tacitus (*Hist.* 1.7) suggests another altogether more sinister possibility: that Capito did not possess the drive and ambition to carry out such an undertaking but that when pressed to rebel by his legionary commanders Fabius Valens and Cornelius Aquinus had refused. To save themselves they had then accused their proconsul of treachery and secured his murder and their safety. The prominence at this stage given to Fabius Valens is an indication in Tacitus' account that here was to be one of the major players in the subsequent events of that year.

Verginius Rufus was recalled to Rome by Galba who was suspicious of him and was replaced as proconsul of *Germania Superior* by Hordeonius Flaccus who is described by Tacitus (*Hist.* 1.9) as 'old and unwell'. Moreover, he was a lax commander and was unable to, or lacked the interest in, maintaining or instilling even basic discipline among his troops.[8] These remained very restless after the suppression of the recent Gallic revolt and the suspicious death of Fonteius Capito. This was accentuated by a general unease caused by reports of the new emperor's lack of control and unpopularity.[9] What precisely caused the mutiny that would lead to outright rebellion is rather obscured in the ancient accounts, but it appears from Tacitus' brief mention that there was almost a spontaneous rejection of Galba without naming an alternative. The troops were clearly disaffected and Tacitus claims that the reason for this state lay in the recent defeat of Vindex, which had given these legions, for a long time used to just peacetime duties, a taste for war and the prizes that might be obtained from another (*Hist*. 1.51). But there was, moreover, an awakening in various minds of the power that the army held in the empire.[10] A poor impression of central government had emerged and these legionaries were not impressed with the latest scandals in Rome nor of an elderly emperor who suddenly appeared unsuited for the position and realized that it was in their power to enforce change. Yet the reasons that emerge remain rather fuzzy and quite unlike the very real grievances of a lack of regular pay, which caused the mutinies among the Rhine and Danube garrisons after the death of Augustus in AD 14 as is well recounted by Tacitus in the first book of his *Annales*. The underlying impression is that the legions that had subdued Vindex expected greater recognition for this action but because their commanders had been slow to acknowledge Galba as the new ruler they were being penalized in some way. Meanwhile the legions in Iberia that had seen no recent fighting were being advanced since they were the first to salute Galba as emperor. This was the first occasion on which jealousy between the various regional garrisons of the Roman Empire was to be a cause for civil war and instability, a feature that was to become ever more visible in the years to come.

The disquiet had presumably to be channelled through some spokesmen who made these views known and that it was time for a new emperor to be chosen by the senate. At this stage no figure is suggested as being behind the moves, although it is certainly plausible to suggest that both Fabius Valens and Cornelius Aquinus were partly responsible for the tense situation.[11] Aulus Caecina Alienus who was later to achieve joint prominence with Valens has yet to appear in Tacitus' account but his later role as strong advocate and one of the senior commanders of Vitellius' regime suggests that his support began at the beginning of this crisis, which he may well have in some way have engineered. A figurehead was needed. Galba's appointment of Vitellius is said to have been based on the lack of drive and ambition displayed by this senator, a son of the close confidant of Claudius but whose lazy behaviour appeared to make him trustworthy. Furthermore, Vitellius' lack of resources and debts were evidence that he would be more concerned to follow the well–established senatorial tradition of recouping personal financial losses from his provincial command by embezzlement rather than indulging in grander forms of ambition. Galba's trust or contempt for Vitellius was quickly shown to be misplaced for this new proconsul lost no time in accepting his acclamation as emperor.

Directly under Vitellius' command were the legions I *Germania*, V *Alaudae*, XV *Primigenia*, and XVI. Legion I was stationed at Bonna (Bonn), the Fifth and the Fifteenth were garrisoned together at Vetera, while the Sixteenth was at Novaesium (Neuss near Düsseldorf). Under Hordeonius Flaccus' command in Upper Germany were IV *Macedonica* and XXII *Primigenia*, both at Moguntiacum (Mainz), and the XXI *Rapax* at Vindonissa (Windisch). Vitellius could also count on the support of the garrison in Britain, which then comprised a further three legions: II *Augusta*, IX *Hispana*, and XX *Valeria*, and the legions in Gaul, I *Italica* in Lugdunum (Lyons), and in Iberia legions VI *Victrix* and X *Gemina*. Altogether, this accounts for thirteen legions out of a total of thirty then under commission.[12] On the other hand, the seven legions of the Danube garrison posted in Moesia (Legion III *Gallica*, VII *Claudia*, VIII *Augusta*), Pannonia (VII *Galbiana*, XIII *Gemina*, XIV *Gemina Victrix*) and Dalmatia (XI *Claudia*) had declared for Otho. Although these appear to represent roughly an equal number of troops as the Rhine army, when the contingents from other legions were added to Vitellius' total they were rather fewer in number.[13] They were also not summoned to defend Italy as soon as Vitellius was proclaimed emperor in early January and only when his armies were already on the march. The collection of an army in support of Otho was therefore a more haphazard and protracted process than the concerted action taken by Vitellius' generals Valens and Caecina. Moreover, in Rome and throughout Italy although Otho had access to some troops these were neither as seasoned nor in anything like the quantity as those committed to Vitellius. Of course Otho had the complete loyalty of the Praetorian Guard numbering roughly ten to twelve thousand men. These had thrown in their lot with Otho having joined en masse the conspiracy to overthrow Galba.[14] As such they could expect very few favours from Vitellius and if they survived at all they would certainly face demotion and service in a legion far from Rome and all its evident attractions. In theory these cohorts represented a sort of esprit de corps but in fact they were recruited in Italy and stayed close to Rome and rarely took part in military campaigns. They had become the emperor's ceremonial household guard and participated in festive and formal occasions and less frequently in policing duties. Less reliance could be placed on the other units stationed in Rome, however. The Urban Cohorts were under the command of the Prefect of the City, an appointment of the emperor. The serving prefect was Flavius Sabinus, elder brother of Vespasian, the proconsul of Judaea. His loyalty was not under doubt having been held in high regard by Nero and a recent appointment of Otho. In early 69 there were six thousand men in these cohorts but were probably meant more for garrison duty than as effective units in the field. Lastly there were the *Vigiles* with units totalling about seven thousand, composed of freedmen, which were primarily designated for the night watch and fire-fighting and so were not expected to fight in battle situations. Altogether, on paper these represented about 23,000 men, some of indifferent military training, and effectively perhaps 15,000 for use in a military campaign. Besides these forces there was one legion (*Legio* I *Adiutrix*) stationed in the city, which had been formed from naval forces and the survivors of the massacre ordered by Galba when he had arrived in Rome the previous autumn. These must have numbered about four thousand. There were also in addition two thousand gladiators whom Tacitus writes disparagingly that such a force was disgraceful ('deforme') but that it was employed in times of civil unrest by even the most correct of generals (*Hist*. 2.11). Some cavalry units and other auxiliary troops were also available. Thus there were possibly as many as 25,000 troops available to Otho but few of these had seen actual combat and those who had served in any campaigns had not done so for several years. Thus notwithstanding Otho's optimistic front on land he had to rely very heavily on the Danubian forces for anything like a real chance of defeating his opponent for power.

This fact becomes clearer when the initial strategy against Vitellius was put into operation since it consisted of no immediate land operations at all. Otho could rely on the fleets stationed at Misenum and Ravenna because their crews were promised promotion to full legionaries in the event of a victory. It was decided to employ the Misenum fleet in attacks on the rear of Vitellius' advance, across the coast of Liguria west to Narbonensis Gaul, in an attempt to hamper his supply routes and encourage communities there to come over to Otho's cause. Devastation was caused in several places, although the end result was hardly of any consequence to the campaign because the fleet could have little impact on the gathering of the forces in the Po Valley. It is also evident that even by the time the fleet was carrying out its instructions Vitellius' forces had already occupied the passes through the western Alps.[15] The naval force were under the command of a freedman named Moschus but who was accompanied by a number of seasoned centurions and military tribunes of whom Suedius Clemens was the most influential and, says Tacitus, 'ambitious' (*ambitiosus*),[16] while the rowers were supplemented by infantry detachments from the city's watch and some units of the Praetorian Guard (Tac. *Hist*. 1.87). Tacitus' account of this campaign (*Hist*. 2.12) shows its lack of importance, and the unruly nature of the command made it become more of a piratical raid than an organized strategy and part of an overall military campaign. Little planning went into this move even if the resources of the fleet were substantial. Such joint land and sea operations had been employed to good effect in the past but in this instance the makeshift approach reveals stark inexperience among the senior figures holding the reins of power. In order to provide this force with the capability of moving inland to cause damage and mayhem this reduced the pool and quality of troops on which to draw in Rome for the inevitable march north.

The chain of command under Otho was complex. The senior generals he appointed were Suetonius Paulinus, Marius Celsus and Annius Gallus, all distinguished senators with the order to defend Italy initially by holding both north and south banks of the River Po. Tacitus states that the emperor recognized their competence in pursuing a military campaign (*Hist.* 1.90).[17] Gaius Suetonius Paulinus had been a highly competent proconsul of the province of Britannia for three years where he had suppressed the uprising of the Iceni in AD 61.[18] Marius Celsus had been consul in 61 and was consul for a second time in 69 under Vitellius who overlooked this influential figure's role under Otho.[19] Appius Annius Gallus had been a consul in 67 and so probably had the experience of a legionary command and although he was a little junior to the other two ex-consuls it also means that he was slightly older than either of Vitellius's generals Valens and Caecina and had probably spent more time in military duties. An important commander is named as Titus Vestricius Spurinna (*Hist.* 2.11) who appears to have acted as a second in command to Gallus. He must surely be the Vestricius Spurinna who was to be awarded a consulship in 73 and who in later life almost certainly was acquainted with Tacitus since they were both friends of the younger Pliny.[20] Tacitus describes all three senior senators as possessing the experience to manage an important campaign, but that they were also cautious in their tactics. This was in contrast to Salvius Titianus, Otho's brother and also an ex-consul, and Licinius Proculus, Prefect of the Guard, both of whom like their emperor wanted immediate engagement with the Vitellians. The other Praetorian Prefect was Plotius Firmus and like Licinius Proculus he had neither seen nor commanded a war-time campaign or indeed ventured further than Italy in any military capacity.[21] Proculus together with Otho's brother Titianus who also lacked any military experience were effectively in control of strategy and the emperor who also had no experience of warfare left everything to this pair about whom Tacitus also has nothing good to say (*Hist.* 2.33 and 39).[22] Thus an acute observer might well have considered that with far fewer immediate resources Otho seemed likely to fail catastrophically if his forces came under attack before the bulk of the regular legions from the Danube army were brought into play.[23] This fact was clearly compounded by poor intelligence work about the strength of his opponents if Otho's determination to give battle at the earliest opportunity is a good indication.

Whereas Galba had had the luxury of no opposition and had been able to travel from Tarraco to Rome in relative comfort, probably some part of that journey by sea, Vitellius who had not long before travelled up from Rome now proposed to march south with a sufficiently large force to mount a campaign for sole rule consisting of two armies drawn from the two Germanic commands.[24] Each of these armies was under a commander appointed by Vitellius and it should come as no surprise that Caecina Alienus and Fabius Valens should have been in the forefront of the enterprise and be given these two vital positions. In terms of experience they were hardly in the forefront of the Roman imperial command structure but where there may have been a desideratum here this was more than compensated by the force of personality both men possessed, and presumably also the acumen to rely on senior commanders even among their centurions. Caecina was not much more than thirty years of age and his youth is particularly emphasized by Tacitus (*Hist.* 1.53) who describes him twice in successive sentences as *iuvenis* or a 'young man.'

> *At in superiore Germania Caecina, decorus iuventa, corpore ingens, animi immodicus, scito sermone, erecto incessu, studia militum inlexerat. Hunc iuvenem Galba, quaestorem in Baetica impigre in partis suas transgressum, legioni praeposuit ...*

> In Upper Germany Caecina, a young man of unblemished looks, a commanding presence but excessively high spirits had subverted the allegiance of the soldiers through skilful speeches and putting on a dignified manner. Galba had placed this young man in charge of a legion, who when quaestor in Baetica had enthusiastically joined his cause.

Therefore Caecina had been quaestor only in 67 or 68 when he had been assigned to Otho who was then governing *Hispania Baetica* as his second-in-command and like his superior he had rapidly joined the ranks of supporters of Galba.[25] Fabius Valens was a little older but not by much since he and Caecina were clearly meant to act together neither holding a senior place over the other and both answerable directly to Vitellius.[26]

What is interesting is the age of both of the senior commanders. They were much closer in age to Otho or to Titus, Vespasian's son, than to either Vitellius or to Galba. In the narrative they appear to be cast in the nature of Alexander the Great, young, impetuous, and unscrupulous, nevertheless accomplished generals. Still where were other more senior figures? Hordeonius Flaccus had been ignored and it is surprising that this nominee of Galba's who replaced the popular Verginius Rufus was not murdered.[27] But there were still six other legionary commanders, none of whom are named, and they cannot all have been as young as Valens and Caecina. However, there were no other senior senators in the vicinity who could have joined Vitellius at this stage, a fact that illustrates the lack of experience among the high command of the Roman forces in the field and that the legionary garrisons relied heavily on the professional middle range officers – the centurions – rather than on leading figures who may well have been at Rome, as can be shown by the support given to Otho but who were not allowed to hold provincial commands except when absolutely necessary. Nero had employed senior figures such as Domitius Corbulo and Suetonius Paulinus earlier in his rule and in AD 68 had maintained C. Licinius Mucianus (cos. 65) and Flavius Vespasianus in their field commands in the East. But by and large specific appointments were made in response to particular crises and the sole general of equivalent stature of Caecina and Valens to be found in any of the western provinces in AD 68–69 was M. Antonius Primus commander of *Legio* VII (*Galbiana*), stationed in Pannonia. Although he was rather older than Vitellius' generals he was just as ambitious and, in Tacitus' opinion, 'a dangerous figure in time of peace'.[28]

Once it was decided what the plan of advance would be Vitellius appointed Valens and Caecina jointly to the command of an army that Tacitus numbers as 70,000. Vitellius advancing behind these was accompanied probably by as many as another 30,000 troops. The plans for the campaign were clearly championed by Valens and Caecina and they constructed a competent plan of campaign in which it can almost certainly be assumed Vitellius acquiesced rather than involved himself too deeply. Vitellius' character was the particular subject of ancient invective and denigration to an inordinate degree and so some caution must be exercised when dealing with this figure. He was clearly not a military specialist yet must have spent some time in the army before reaching the consulship in 48 and a provincial command in Africa in about 60–61. By the time of his appointment he was in his early fifties and rather younger than his fellow proconsular colleague in Upper Germany.[29] The invasion force from the Rhine frontier was an extraordinary show of Roman military manpower (Tac. *Hist.* 1.60), and the basic strategy was to be one consisting of two advancing columns that were to gain possession of the Alpine passes and Italy north of the Apennines or that region which had been Cisalpine Gaul. This was no pincer movement as had been planned by the Cimbri and Teutones in the planned Germanic invasion of Italy in 102 BC. The two divisions were to march south in fairly close proximity but at a sufficient distance to allow them reasonable access to sources of supplies. A single advancing column in mid-winter might well have exhausted local resources and be forced to slow or even halt its movement. The division of the army therefore made sound sense under the circumstances and illustrates some tactical expertise among the commanders upon whom Vitellius relied heavily.

Valens and Caecina appear to have departed from their respective camps at Bonna and Vindonissa shortly before their commander–in–chief.[30] Vitellius must have set out from Colonia Agrippina where he had been in residence in early January but to whom he entrusted effective command of the forces with him is not disclosed by Tacitus. The fact that it was mid–January was not regarded as a deterrent and possibly indicates that this particular winter was not yet severe enough to confine troops to their barracks or prevent normal traffic moving from north to south.[31] Tacitus makes the point (*Hist.* 1.62) that the troops were impatient and that they would not be delayed either by the weather or the time of the year. Unlike Vitellius who is said to have passed his days in idle celebration of his newly elevated position the soldiers or at least their commanders realized that speed was essential if they were to be victorious.[32]

Caecina had been assigned or had chosen an army of 30 000 composed mainly of vexillations from the garrison of *Germania Superior* (Tac. *Hist.* 1.61), and was directed or chose to head for the *Alpes Poeninae* and the Great St Bernard Pass.[33] Caecina's advance was swift since the distance involved was not that great and if he had marched without interruption he could probably have commanded the entire Po Valley up to the passes of the Apennines before Otho could have made any response.[34] As it turned out Caecina encountered some opposition when he advanced through the territory of the Helvetii. Tacitus claims that the Helvetii had yet to hear about the murder of Galba, which is perhaps unlikely unless Caecina was already in this region by 15 January and the tribe very understandably refused to acknowledge Vitellius as emperor. Troops from Caecina's own legion XXI *Rapax* increased the tension by seizing Helvetian funds intended for an auxiliary fort that this tribe financed and presumably garrisoned in the neighbourhood. The Helvetii then very unwisely for they lacked any recent experience in warfare detained some of Caecina's couriers who were taking despatches to the legions in Pannonia. In reply Caecina ordered a town that possessed a popular spa to be sacked and the land around plundered. He also sent orders for auxiliary troops posted in the nearby province of Rhaetia (roughly modern Bavaria) to join his forces. The Helvetian chiefs called up their tribesmen but were obviously no match for the regular Roman divisions especially since the Rhaetian troops surprised the enemy by attacking them from the rear.[35] Caught as they were between a double assault the Helvetians whom Tacitus described as having been full of hot air beforehand now in the midst of a real battle were terrified out of their wits (*Hist.* 1.68). They rapidly broke ranks and fled some hoping for safety on *Mons Vocetius*, the mountainus area around the Bözberg Pass between the modern cities of Basel and Zurich, but Caecina ordered in Thracian auxiliary troops who were well acquainted with such terrain and few escaped. Thousands are said to have been killed and as many sold as slaves.[36] The fortifications of their city Aventicum (modern Avenches) were decrepit, states Tacitus, and could easily be stormed by the rampaging legionaries. However, a deputation sent by the townspeople to Caecina managed to avert total disaster, although it might be assumed that some form of bribery was also needed. Caecina ordered the execution of one of the Helvetian chiefs and the rest he sent to Vitellius who after some delay granted an amnesty.

There are some problems with Tacitus' geography in his description since *Mons Vocetius* sought as refuge by some after the Helvetian rout is one hundred and twenty kilometres (70 miles) north of Aventicum and it would have taken at least two to three days for Caecina's army to arrive there following the battle. Tacitus states that the army moved on Aventicum (*Hist.* 1.68) but it is certainly plausible to suggest that the engagement actually took place near the town of Augusta Raurica (modern Augst) and this should be understood from the historian's account. As it is the battle, the rout, the survivors and then a promised destruction of a town cover too wide an area to have taken place in the brief time that seems to be allocated to it in the narrative. Furthermore, with a permanent legionary camp in Helvetian territory the people living in the area will have been all too familiar with the Roman presence and the dangers this meant in the event of any rebellion. There is perhaps something missing from Tacitus' account here and the details he presents must to some extent be his invention. Caecina would also have known Helvetia well. If the advance began at Vindonissa then it had hardly begun and it was still early in the month and this might suggest a deliberate provocation by the commander or by his troops to show not only that they were not to be trifled with but also that the devastation of the Helvetian lands was to be a grim message to any others who might wish to emulate them, or even more importantly not to consider any reckless activity once they had departed. It is hardly remarkable therefore that Caecina made rapid progress through the mountains even in the middle of January and he arrived in Transpadane Gaul (*Gallia Transpadana*) meeting no resistance at all.

In fact, while he was still in Helvetia waiting for Vitellius' decision regarding the tribe Caecina received news that a cavalry unit stationed in *Transpadana* described as an *ala Siliana*, perhaps one thousand strong, had offered its allegiance to Vitellius.[37] These troopers or their officers remembered Vitellius from his time as governor in Africa where they had been stationed and still held him in some regard while they knew nothing about Otho.[38] These were the sole troops posted in this region of Italy and were evidently being employed in garrison duty in a number of local towns, which followed their lead in declaring themselves subject to the rule of Vitellius. These included the cities of Mediolanum, Eporedia, Vercellae and Novaria. Realistically, of course, their citizens had no choice since there was as yet no sight of any pro-Otho forces north of the Po and if they had decided to support Vitellius' enemy this would certainly have incurred his anger and the anger of his troops. The meagre policing forces at the disposal of local communities meant that they would be quickly overwhelmed and destroyed by forces composed of regular and professional soldiers.

Caecina had moved down from the Alpine foothills to take possession of *Transpadana* (the area between the Po and the Alps) and sent on ahead of his main column some auxiliary infantry cohorts from Gaul, Iberia and Britain with Germanic and Arab cavalry, in total perhaps a force of four thousand.[39] At this stage Tacitus says that Caecina considered his options, which were either to march directly to the Po or to march east to Noricum since the proconsul of that province appeared to favour Otho and had made no move to join Vitellius. He decided on the second course since Noricum possessed few resources or a real threat to his advance, while a dash to secure the north bank of the Po would be a major success.

In the meantime, it had been decided that Valens would cross the Cottian Alps, which form the border between the modern French region of Provence and the Italian province of Savoy. The mountains rise to four thousand metres above sea level but with several negotiable passes that were clearly open to Valens' men and their supply trains. The region is small but was strategically important because of its numerous entries into Italy. The inhabitants consisted of Ligurian tribes, formidable fighters in their own right, but long loyal to Rome. One of their chiefs named Cottius had ruled the area as a king subject to Roman rule, but Nero had this client kingdom converted into a *provincia* under the jurisdiction of a Roman official with equestrian status. Valens' line of march was therefore the less direct and would take a longer time. His route lay through the lands of the Treveri (capital Trier) and the Mediomatrici where the first hostile incident occurred where the nervous and undisciplined legionaries supposed a local plot against them and massacred four thousand inhabitants. Any future uncertainty about where loyalties lay among the municipalities along the chosen route were to be dispelled by abject submission and offers of supplies, probably far beyond the means of the affected communities. Tacitus (*Hist.* 1.63) may well be correct to assign just erratic behaviour as the cause for excessive force at Divodurum (Metz) but there must be some suspicion that this was an action sanctioned by Valens and which considerably eased the pressure on him regarding the supply of the army.[40] Valens was already in southern Loraine perhaps at Nancy when the news arrived of Galba's murder and Otho's succession. The date must have been no later than 20 January 69.[41] From there Valens marched into the territory of the Lingones who were loyal to Vitellius but even here fighting broke out not between the local people and the army but between Batavian auxiliaries and legionaries.[42] Valens restored order by punishing some of the Batavian ringleaders thus emphasizing the superior status of the legionaries, but at the same time perhaps causing ill-feeling, which could soon be exploited by others.[43] From there he marched through the lands of the Aedui where the tribe was purposely intimidated but offered no resistance and so was left untouched. Its urban centre at Augustodunum (Auton) had been established by the emperor Augustus and this fact probably saved it from being pillaged. The people of Lugdunum (Lyons) welcomed the invading force. Its garrison of a legion and a cavalry brigade had already sworn allegiance to Vitellius. The legate of Legion I *Italica* Manlius Valens was side-lined by Fabius Valens who claimed he could not be trusted.[44] The citizens of Lugdunum took the opportunity to slander their closest neighbours at Vienne (Vienna). There had long been rivalry between the two cities. Lugdunum had been slow to proclaim support for Galba since it had been a favourite city of Nero. As a result Galba had imposed financial sanctions on its citizens and granted additional benefits to Vienna. The people of Lugdunum worked on the feelings of Valens' troops who were stirred up enough to demand that Vienna be sacked and began to advance against this city while their commanders had completely lost control and discipline vanished. The citizens of Vienna were in great danger and came out to meet the invaders and threw themselves at the mercy of these troops. The anger of the soldiers abated but it was a gift from Valens amounting to three hundred sestertii says Tacitus (*Hist*. 1.66) that managed to calm the situation. The city was, however, left undefended and probably financially ruined but at least it escaped a worse fate. The Vitellian army then marched on through the lands of the Allobroges and Vocontii until it reached the Alps.[45]

Since Vitellius played no role in the entire campaign his rate of advance was much slower and at some distance behind Valens, although probably along much the same route. It is possible that Tacitus thought that there was a siege train with Vitellius but as the events unfolded rapidly this was not required (*Hist*. 1.61). Vitellius' clemency towards the Helvetians and to Vienna, his time in Lugdunum and his avoidance of the Mediterranean coast where the fleet from Misenum, acting on Otho's orders was active, all made his progress quite pedestrian compared to that of his commanders.

Caecina was well ahead and advanced with his main forces towards Placentia, which was situated on the south bank of the river Po. This seems to be dated by Tacitus to late February or early March (*Hist.* 2.11, 2.17) and well before Otho had gathered any forces in defence. Caecina was careful not to alienate the communities, which had so recently joined Vitellius' cause, although Tacitus states (*Hist.* 2. 20) that he caused offence by appearing in Germanic dress rather than using the customary toga. Still, the march was uneventful – the prize must have seemed almost within grasp. Moreover, all that was posted at Placentia was a section of the advance guard sent from Rome. The overall command had fallen to Annius Gallus who had assigned the town to Vestricius Spurinna. On the north bank of the Po some of Gallus' forces were defeated at Cremona and near Ticinum and many of these troops were taken captive or had surrendered. A great swathe of Italy from the Alpine foothills in the northwest to Cremona in the east had fallen to Caecina with hardly a casualty. There was no opposition north of the river and this was easily crossed at Placentia by some of the German and Batavian auxiliary troops whose origins were along the banks of the Rhine. Spurinna had just four thousand in the garrison of the town drawn from the Praetorian Guard and a detachment from *Legio* I *Adiutrix* (Tac. *Hist.* 2.18).[46] Spurinna recognized that the Vitellian troops were unsupported but that his own were untried so he decided to remain within the fortifications. His troops would not accept his orders, however, and ignoring centurions and tribunes they ran off to engage their enemy convinced that their commander was in cahoots with the opposition. He was taken along but then made it appear that he was in agreement with his men in order to take control of the situation once the mutiny lost steam. This indeed happened once daylight faded and the troops were obliged to dig in for the night. The physical exercise associated with encamping came as a shock to troops used to the easy duties of the Praetorian Camp and soon enough the enthusiasm to engage an enemy that might well be far superior in number to their own small force had a sobering effect. The centurions and tribunes worked on this new uncertainty and soon the wisdom of holding Placentia with all its resources and defences seemed now a very reasonable alternative to charging about in search of an enemy. Respect for Spurinna returned and he was able to lead most of the troops back to the town and order a strengthening of the defensive walls. A small force was left behind to watch out for and to report any enemy movement.

Caecina proceeded to cross the Po following his auxiliary troops and moved closer to Placentia where his troops, perhaps remembering the poorly fortified defences of the Helvetii, approached the walls without good cover, and lacking any order. The walls were well defended and clearly in good repair. Attempts to fire the fortifications resulted only in the destruction of the amphitheatre that was situated outside the town. Each side blamed the other for this needless loss but the defenders clearly had the upper hand and Caecina had to withdraw with unexpected heavy casualties (Tac. *Hist.* 2.21). He recognized that siege equipment was necessary, although this seems to have consisted mainly of screens to protect engineers undermining the walls while the defenders in their turn in expectation of this action prepared stakes and rocks to throw down on the besiegers.

With day scarcely begun, the walls were filled with defenders, while the plains glittered with armed men ...

Vixdum orto die plena propugnatoribus moenia, fulgentes armis viris campi ... (Tac. *Hist.* 2.22)

Tacitus surely knew that such preparations could not have occurred overnight and so the narrative that follows here is, like Caesar's description of the siege of Massilia (see above) a series of topical elements made to apply to the scene more for the benefit of the reader than for any concern to retrieve the real historical event. Thus the German auxiliaries attacked in a haphazard fashion more in keeping with their tribal customs than fulfilling the requirements of light armed troops on left and right wings of the more densely packed legionaries. The legions were employed to undermine the walls and attack the gates but in each case they were outwitted by the defenders. These caused havoc among the attackers by discharging missiles onto the protective screens of the besiegers below and an attempt to construct a ramp towards one of the gates seems to have been foiled by the Praetorians who hurled down milestones. Caecina ordered a withdrawal when it became obvious that the siege could not be concluded quickly and there were probably reports that Spurinna was about to be relieved by Annius Gallus. Caecina's retreat across the river and then a march to occupy Cremona is regarded by Tacitus as a great victory for the Othonian forces but it is likely that the narrative here has also been constructed in such a way that it was meant to enhance the reputation of the historian's friend Spurinna. Caecina did not possess a full siege train, Placentia was clearly much better defended than the towns of the Helvetii, and Caecina had probably been instructed or had agreed to delay and wait for the arrival of Valens. This much may be inferred from Tacitus' account later when he accuses Caecina of reckless behaviour and that it was in keeping with his character (*Hist.* 2.24). Caecina's apparent reverse may actually have been prompted by the desire to press on to Cremona and prevent Annius Gallus who was either then coming up from central Italy or was operating near the Adriatic coast.[47] Gallus who is said to have been on his way to relieve Placentia received news from Spurinna regarding Caecina's latest move then took up a position at the village of Bedriacum (*Hist.* 2.23) about thirty-six kilometres (23 miles) from Caecina, now in Cremona.[48] Both sides in the conflict were now on the north bank of the Po but south of what is now the River Oglio.

Gallus' troops then scored a signal success some days later. Tacitus (*Hist.* 2.23) has the two thousand gladiators commanded on this occasion by Martius Macer transported across the river where they put some auxiliary troops of Caecina to flight and inflicted heavy casualties. The victory was not followed up, however, since Gallus knew he was heavily outnumbered yet his troops rather than accepting the obvious were suspicious of treachery among their commanding officers and so what should have had a positive effect actually caused the opposite. There is also a problem here with Tacitus' account since he had claimed that Gallus was already in Bedriacum, which is actually further northeast of Cremona, which is situated on the north bank of the River Po. Bedriacum is actually situated close to the River Oglio and so the details in the narrative make little or no sense. It is possible that Tacitus has made an error here and that Gallus was actually at Brixellum, which later became Otho's command centre. Brixellum now modern Brescello is on the south bank of the Po, which would allow Martius Macer to cross the river and encounter Caecina's auxiliaries perhaps out on reconnaissance east of Cremona.

As a result of these two defeats Caecina's reputation as the dashing young commander was considerably dented and knowing that Valens was soon to arrive in the area decided to try and retrieve some of the respect he had lost. He was more driven by his audacity than by any notion of good generalship, says Tacitus (*Hist.* 2.24). He decided to try and draw the full Othonian army towards him at a cross-roads shrine dedicated to Castor and Pollux about twelve Roman miles due east of Cremona.[49] He ordered his cavalry to find the enemy and then retreat towards 'Castores' where he stationed auxiliary troops in hiding, perhaps in a small wood or copse. Large forested areas were probably not that common here. Once the enemy passed these hidden troops they were to emerge and attack from the rear while the cavalry would wheel about and face their opponents. The tactic was hardly novel but might have been effective had the plan not been leaked to the opposing side. By this time Suetonius Paulinus and Marius Celsus had arrived from Rome. Otho seems not yet to have been close at hand, although Tacitus reports that he left Rome soon after his generals with at least five cohorts or roughly half of the Praetorian Guard (*Hist*. 2.11). So Paulinus and Celsus took command of the forces available to Annius Gallus and which had now been augmented by some of the forces from the Danube garrison. Tacitus is again careless in his narrative for he states that the vexillation from Legion XIII (*Gemina*), four cohorts of auxiliaries and five hundred cavalry, in total about three thousand five hundred men occupied the right wing, three Praetorian cohorts advanced along a high road in the centre, about three thousand troops, and *Legio* I (*Adiutrix*) with two auxiliary cohorts and one cavalry *ala* were stationed on the left wing, perhaps another three thousand five hundred troops. This represents a force of about ten thousand against which Caecina had proposed to employ only auxiliary units and not his regular legionaries.[50] This means that he was probably already outnumbered even if his tactics were to go according to plan. His cavalry made contact and withdrew but Celsus ordered his men to hold back. Caecina's auxiliary troops attacked before the trap was sprung and fell into the trap prepared for them for they were now faced with the extended lines of their opponents which outflanked them on both sides, while the cavalry sealed the trap. However, there seems to have been some lull in the fighting, according to Tacitus, because he says that Paulinus was by nature an astute tactician who wanted to ensure victory by tackling all possible avenues before ordering an attack.[51] He therefore ordered his men to fill in the drainage ditches in order to remove this obstacle preventing unhampered and rapid movement especially of his cavalry units. This allowed Caecina's men to escape the trap and seek safety in a nearby vineyard and coppice, which offered protection from airborne missiles and would hamper any attacking force. These now made a counterattack and killed some of the troops from the Praetorian Guard who were leading the assault, but once the regular legionaries advanced they routed their enemy consisting entirely of auxiliaries.[52] Caecina did not immediately send up reinforcements from his camp, which must have been situated fairly close by and not at Cremona. Instead, he sent individual cohorts and these in turn were thrown back by Paulinus' legionaries and confusion reigned since troops arriving from Caecina to offer support were caught up in a rout. Moreover, in his camp the *Praefectus Castrorum* (prefect in charge of the camp) was arrested since he was believed to be plotting to turn the camp over to Paulinus. This supposed treachery was based on the apparent fact that his brother was a tribune serving under Paulinus, although he too had been arrested by equally suspicious troops. Caecina's entire army was in great danger but Paulinus did not follow up his advantage and ordered a retreat which was again viewed with much distrust. He claimed that his soldiers were tired and needed a respite but there were many who thought that he wavered in his loyalty towards Otho.

There are a number of issues in the narrative here since many of the details do not fit well with the terrain. Tacitus plainly knew that although the land was level it was almost certainly waterlogged at this time of the year as he indicates in the actions of Paulinus and so an army drawn up for battle in the manner he describes initially would simply have not been possible. The Praetorians notably occupied a road on a raised bank ('*aggerem viae tres praetoriae cohortes altis ordinibus obtinuere*') as is still commonly found today in the area (see plate), and they advanced in close order or, in other words, as a column. To their right and left the other troops fanned out as best they could, probably not in close formation at all, and they may well have lagged behind the centre. Indeed, they may have marched behind the centre on the same raised bank. Advancing in such an order made it highly unlikely that on a flood plain they could actually be outwitted by the tactic of an ambush. Moreover, Caecina's cohorts were also apparently trapped by a manoeuvre of Paulinus' cavalry yet this would have been clearly seen. Indeed it must have been in order to allow a retreat to occur and therefore the trap could never be fully closed as Tacitus claims and readily illustrates.

Still this new disaster further undermined Caecina's reputation even if he tried to throw the blame on his unruly troops. Valens leading the second column of the invasion force now made his appearance in the vicinity. Caecina's position was saved by the huge numbers of additional troops and in both forces a measure of discipline was restored since the troops now perceived that the fight was to be a more difficult and bitter one than many had anticipated. Among the Batavian auxiliary cavalry units, nevertheless, there remained a show of indifference to commands and several of the troopers went out to hurl insults at Othonian units positioned nearby. Valens was concerned about this blatant act of insubordination and decided to send some of the Batavians back to Gaul to help deal with the fleet, which was causing widespread disruption along the coast and had defeated some of the resident garrisons there (Tac. *Hist*. 2.28). His decision was greeted with loud complaints from his own legionaries who argued that these veteran fighters could not be spared with a major battle imminent. Matters again quickly spiralled out of control and Valens was faced with a full-scale mutiny and was forced to hide to save his life after he was stoned by the mutineers in his own camp. His tent and belongings were plundered since there was a widespread belief that he had pilfered much gold on the march, especially from the citizens of Vienna. The situation seemed about to degenerate into chaos when Alfenus Varus, the *Praefectus Castrorum*, ordered the centurions to ignore their troops and not to give the usual trumpet calls to duty. The unexpected silence had a profound effect on the legionaries who were so accustomed to a strict daily routine and common sense soon prevailed.

At that point Valens was still encamped at Ticinum (modern Pavia) some ninety kilometres (52 miles) from Cremona and when news arrived of Caecina's failure against Paulinus the troops almost mutinied again since they claimed that they were being denied an opportunity of engaging with the enemy. The army departed at once but the new arrivals were not greeted with as much enthusiasm as they might have expected since Caecina's troops for the most part appear not to have had a high regard for either Valens or his army (Tac. *Hist*. 2.29).[53] These complained that no help had been forthcoming when they needed it, which was irrational and probably not a reflection of the view of commanders but of rank and file. It is also used in the narrative to reinforce the picture of the disorder and indiscipline which predominated among armed forces during wars between citizens of the same state. Valens was also not as well liked as Caecina who for all his faults and recent failures remained charismatic, charming and approachable. Valens commanded the larger force but he was disliked especially by his fellow general who thought him too fond of money.[54] Both wrote abusive letters to Otho and therefore very openly aligned their futures with that of Vitellius. Otho's generals were altogether more secretive in their responses and were careful not to enter the propaganda war plainly in case they were on the defeated side.

The union of the two invasion columns at Cremona now meant that there was no need to delay any further a major engagement with their opponents who were close by both at Bedriacum and Brixellum.[55] Otho was present with his forces and convened and chaired a meeting of his senior generals and advisers. Paulinus, Gallus and Celsus were unanimous in thinking that it was unwise to risk an immediate fight and that they should wait for the arrival of *Legio* XIV, which was soon to arrive from Moesia (*Hist*. 2.32). Otho was in no mood to wait nor were his closest advisers, his brother Titianus and the Prefect Licinius Proculus. Yet Paulinus, the most experienced general on either side, was at pains to show how a delay would play to Otho's strengths while at the same time their reinforcements were still ten to fourteen days' march away.[56] During the interim the forces of Caecina and Vitellius would face shortages, a crisis in Gaul and uncertain support from the provinces further west and south. His argument was to some extent incorrect since Vitellius' column was also moving south and the resources of Gaul and Gallia *Transpadana* were considerable and the fleet operating along the coast was not that effective. Still, it is clear that Otho's forces were inferior in numbers and quality while his more enthusiastic advisers obviously believed mistakenly that such units as the Praetorians would be more effective than veterans from the Rhine legions. Titianus and Proculus overruled the more cautious advocates and the decision was taken for an engagement in the field. It was also decided that Otho should not lead his army in person but remain at Brixellum where his field headquarters were situated probably in a farmhouse or in the villa of some unnamed estate.[57] Once again Tacitus makes it clear (*Hist.* 2.33) that neither Paulinus nor Celsus were in favour of this move, which was perhaps meant to place the emperor in a more secure physical location. But it also denied the troops ease of access to their leader and kept him isolated from the events as they unfolded.[58] Moreover Otho was to be guarded by a strong force drawn from the Praetorian Guard and the cavalry, which further reduced the numbers available to his generals already outnumbered by the opposing side. The troops who were to fight were already in a despondent mood and did not trust their commanders. Otho also left unclear the chain of command, whereas his presence and popularity with the rank and file would have bolstered spirits and shown exactly who was at the apex of the complicated command structure.[59] Tacitus or his source was certain that the result of the battle was already sealed by this stage: 'this first day damaged the Othonian cause' (*is primus dies Othonianas partis adflixit*).

On the other side of the River Po, Valens and Caecina were kept fully informed about Otho's decision to give battle by, says Tacitus, the constant stream of deserters to their side, although their plans do not appear to have been blighted by the same phenomenon. The extent of the information available to Valens and Caecina suggests that there may have been some high level desertions from Otho at this stage or, just as significantly, that messages were sent by influential figures to their opposite numbers.[60] Scouts sent out by the commanders of Otho's army were also not that skilful in their assignments and their presence was observed by their opposition as was their intended strategy. Valens and Caecina seem to have acted in unison and complete agreement. A joint command was both feasible and strong, while the lack of organization in their enemy's senior hierarchy was a visible and defining difference between the two opposing armies. The generals of Vitellius approached the imminent hostilities calmly and knew that if they waited long enough the enemy was sure to make a rash move. Instead of searching for a fight they ordered a bridge to be constructed over the river and made a show of apparently aiming to deal with the two thousand gladiators still stationed on the south bank. The bridge was the usual construction of pontoons with a timber superstructure. The bows of the boats faced the flowing and apparently rising waters, with their anchors above the bows to prevent any movement downstream.[61] The pontoon closest to the south bank had a fortified tower, which was manned to provide protection to the legionaries extending the bridge behind it. On the opposite bank the gladiators also had a tower from which they launched missiles against the bridge builders. Tacitus then proceeds to detail a skirmish between the two sides, which he claims took place on an island in the river about midway in its course some distance possibly downstream from where the bridge was being built. The gladiators went across by boats, perhaps to launch a counterattack, but found some of the German auxiliary troops had already swum there and a fight between the two ensued but the gladiators even with their individual training were no match for these battle-hardened troops. They were unsteady on their lurching boats and so arrows or javelins failed to find their victims while the troops on dry land had a surer stance and more easily inflicted casualties. The gladiators seem to have been gripped by panic and fell among the rowers and the various boats lost any momentum. The Germans, however, plunged into the waters, grabbed hold of the boats, either jumping into them and causing mayhem or killing their opponents in close combat. In the end the gladiators and many of the boats seem to have broken away and returned but the rout had been witnessed by both armies, which had collected along the banks.

Some points need analysis here since this episode is unlikely to have been entirely historical. The Po is a great river but it is not so broad that many pontoons would be needed to bridge it. This was no Hellespont. Even in AD 69 when the river probably meandered with changing banks according to flood and drought it was never more than perhaps one hundred metres across. The scene of numerous pontoons and a nearby island is therefore drawn from the sort of topical elements needed to illustrate a river battle. The idea that the 'naves' or ships in Tacitus' text (*Hist*. 2.35) can have been larger than dinghies with two to four rowers seems highly unlikely. Moreover, where would the Othonians have obtained full size galleys at such short notice? The answer is these were local fishing vessels. The engagement was a minor affair. The gladiators whose calibre Tacitus had already denigrated were inevitable losers in the fight. But even a small scale affair could have important consequences for those watching would either have been encouraged or become more fearful of the future. The troops of Valens and Caecina would have gained much by this victory which corrected recent defeats.[62] The gladiators on the south bank were immediately mutinous and their commander, Martius Macer, was injured when a javelin was thrown in the fracas that occurred afterwards, although he was rescued by his fellow officers. At that moment Vestricius Spurinna arrived from Placentia with most of his force to bolster Otho's army.[63] Macer was replaced by Flavius Sabinus, another senior senator among Otho's entourage, a move that pleased the gladiators but not the commanders, none of whom were anxious to obtain leadership roles in such volatile circumstances.

Tacitus pauses in his account (*Hist.* 2.37–38) to reflect on information he had evidently obtained from one of his sources, which claimed that because neither contender for power was particularly well liked the armies and their commanders were considering a truce before any major hostilities took place. The historian doubts the evidence since he considers that while a small number of men including senior officers such as Paulinus might have given some thought to such a possibility, even Paulinus would have recognized that the vast majority would rather be carried along by the prospects of plunder and service under a lenient ruler.[64] And indeed Tacitus then briefly reviews the way that personal ambition and a desire for power had played an important role in the history of Rome and in its evolution from city state to imperial power, with mention of Marius, Sulla and Pompey, Caesar and Augustus whose armies never once turned aside from war for peace. Therefore, the armies of greatly inferior leaders like Vitellius and Otho were most unlikely to buck that trend.

After Otho went to Brixellum to wait for the outcome of the forthcoming battle nominal charge of his army fell by default to those most keen to open hostilities while the opinions of seasoned commanders were ignored. The army advanced four Roman miles (*Hist.* 2.39) from Bedriacum in the direction of Cremona, but the basic logistics of supplying the marching column was disregarded with the result that the soldiers went thirsty in an area where there was abundance of water.[65] Once the objective had been accomplished the army paused, its commanders unsure of what to do next. Messengers from Otho urged immediate action but the troops were less enthusiastic without the presence of the emperor. They were also keen that the forces that had been withdrawn to guard Otho return to join them, but to this request there was no response.

The next objective appears to have been to strike for the pontoon bridge that Caecina was still in the process of constructing. This meant a march of a further sixteen Roman miles to where the Po was joined by a small stream now known as the Arda, about nine kilometres (6 miles) east of Cremona and surely the place where Caecina's men were still busy bridge building.[66] A march of sixteen Roman miles would occupy the whole day for an army on the march and so it is likely that the intention was to camp and then attack both Caecina and the enemy camp outside Cremona on the following day, which would have been 15 April AD 69. Yet, the Othonian plan never reached fruition. Tacitus describes an advancing column accompanied by its baggage train, yet any experienced general would have known that this was a recipe for disaster when the enemy was so close and had its own camp and so could march out quickly with a minimum of equipment and supplies.[67] Paulinus and Celsus are said to have raised objections to this advance, although this may not have been at the time but in later recollections when it would have been expedient to be seen to have been more outspoken in their opposition to this foolhardy strategy. Tacitus claims that they realized that weary troops fight less effectively than those well rested and these troops were mostly little tested in opposition to an entire force of veteran legionaries and auxiliary troops. Otho's army possessed just a single regular legion, the army of Vitellius detachments from at least eight: the concern of Paulinus and Celsus given the numerical inferiority and lack of battle experience is fully understandable. However, these concerns were overruled by Titianus and Proculus. Another courier from Otho containing orders for an immediate engagement could also not be ignored.[68] Tacitus claims (*Hist*. 2.40) that the delay was painful and unbearable for Otho's hopes and fears ('*aeger mora spei impatiens*').

As this column advanced in a southwesterly direction two tribunes from the Praetorian Guard sought a meeting with Caecina who was still supervising the bridge building.[69] But just as the interview was about to start more couriers arrived with the news that the enemy column was approaching, and the conference was terminated. Tacitus (*Hist*. 2.41) is precise about the number of Othonian tribunes but cannot give the reason that brought them to Caecina: some unknown strategy to outwit their opponents, their desertion alone or with their troops, or some official business.[70] They were dismissed and Caecina went immediately to the Vitellian camp and found Valens and the whole army in readiness for battle. As the legions were drawing lots for their places in the line of battle ('*de ordine agminis sortiuntur*') the cavalry moved out of the camp to intercept the approaching enemy column.[71] These unexpectedly came off worse in their first encounter with their enemy who was clearly by now very close to their camp since Tacitus states that the cavalry were about to be caught under their own fortifications. The situation was saved by the intervention of the infantry from the legion which had been stationed at Lugdunum (*Legio* I *Italica*) who seem to have driven the cavalry back into combat by using the flat sides of their swords against their own horsemen. The legions then drew up quietly and efficiently and were not intimidated by the sight of their opponents because these were hidden from view behind some vineyards.

If the Othonians had been in sight that view would simply have lifted the spirits of the Vitellians. Those on the march from Bedriacum had generals who were afraid and troops under their titular command who were suspicious of every move and order that was given out. Wagons, baggage carriers and servants intermingled with the infantry and cavalry, all moving slowly along a narrow raised road with steep sides into drainage ditches either side. The road could barely have accommodated an advancing column in good order but the circus-like movement of this army showed its lack of training and an absence of any command.

> Some of the troops grouped around their standards others were looking for theirs, everywhere there was uncertainty and the shouting of men running and calling out. The result was that for each one fear or temerity drove them firstly to the front of the line or then they fell back to the rear.

> *Circumsistere alii signa sua, quaerere alii; incertus undique clamor adcurrentium, vocantium: ut cuique audacia vel formido, in primam postremamve aciem prorumpebant aut relabebantur.* (Tac. *Hist.* 2.41)

The Othonian army plainly did not realize it was so close to their enemy and their objective and the suddenness of the cavalry attack took them by surprise. Then a rumour circulated that their enemy was about to desert Vitellius' cause en masse and the earlier desire to fight drained away. If the Vitellians began this rumour then it was well judged, but it may equally have come from individuals in Otho's army who were less loyal. Whatever its origins it served the purpose of causing the marching side to lose impetus and some even cheered their opponents. There were, however, no cheers in response, which only made matters worse since further along the column other troops became afraid of further treachery. The Vitellian army now advanced in good order and both in experience and in numbers vastly superior.

Otho's army went into action, although it had been marching all day and its commanders had probably wanted a night's rest before challenging Valens and Caecina. The fighting took place on low lying ground but there was no field of battle as such since the countryside was broken up with its drainage channels between which were vineyards and other cultivated fields divided by walls, hedges, wooded areas. Therefore the opposing lines as such engaged where they met each other. On some more open ground near the river legions XXI (*Rapax*) and I (*Adiutrix*) clashed. Otho's *Legio* I (*Adiutrix*) had never seen combat in battle before and its legionaries, former naval crews, were itching to come to grips with their enemy and earn some glory.[72] Their opponents were veterans and the *Rapax* famous but initially the troops were surprised by an enthusiastic onrush, which cost them their legionary standard – the Aquila or Eagle. Stunned by this embarrassment the XXI quickly replied with a charge that carried through the opposition lines and the legate of *Legio*

I, Orfidius Benignus, was killed. Elsewhere, the Fifth Legion (*Alaudae*) drove back *Legio* XIII while a *vexillatio* from *Legio* XIV was also overrun.[73] By this stage the senior generals of Otho had already disappeared (Tac. *Hist*. 2.44).[74] The daylight must have been starting to fade by this time as well since the conflict cannot have begun until late in the afternoon if Otho's army had already marched from close to Bedriacum. Still Valens and Caecina were still sending out orders for further troops to be sent into combat in order to ensure that the rout was complete. The arrival of the Batavian auxiliaries who had very recently defeated the gladiators at the river and had also possibly received their surrender with any other units at that place who were under the command of Flavius Sabinus.[75] These completed the rout probably on the left wing of Otho's army perhaps *Legio* I *Adiutrix*, which had already been under pressure from the Legion XXI. These Batavian cohorts were then able to attack the centre composed largely of the Praetorian Guard probably still occupying the high road but vulnerable now to a flanking attack by cavalry. It seems that these troops withdrew in disorder along a road that was soon filled with dead and dying before they reached their camp during the night. There the surviving Praetorians turned on their Camp Prefect, Vedius Aquila, who was roughly handled and verbally abused but not murdered. He appears to have been saved by Annius Gallus who was still respected – he had recently been injured after falling from his horse and had taken no part in the battle – and sentries were posted in an attempt to restore some sort of order. Gallus urged the troops not to use any remaining energy against each other but to rest and conserve what they had since the fight might not yet have ended.

In the aftermath of defeat few soldiers still possessed the spirit to carry on. The Praetorians according to Tacitus (*Hist*. 2.44) were angry and put it about that they had been defeated by treachery and not by better opponents.[76] Some argued that the campaign should continue since the Vitellians had also suffered casualties and reinforcements could be summoned from Brixellum and even further afield. The untried troops at Brixellum would have made little difference and the legions from the Danube were still too far off to be of much comfort. If these were still ten days marching time away, how was Otho to defend himself in the meantime with his army having already sustained serious losses in manpower? The details of the whereabouts of Otho's army after the battle are particularly suspect. This marching column had appeared close to the Vitellian camp having probably spent much of the day on the road. An army with a baggage train, and this is specified by Tacitus, would not have marched much more than the sixteen Roman miles before camping for the night. Therefore the battle occurred late in the day, perhaps lasted an hour, and then there was a stampede by the Othonians back to their camp near Bedriacum, another gruelling sixteen miles. The events described in the camp by Tacitus and the recriminations that followed the defeat therefore must have occurred very late in the course of the night or more likely at dawn next morning (15 April). The arguments attributed to the Praetorians after the battle look very much an act of desperation since they had the most to lose. The number of casualties given by the sources cannot apply only to the combatants who probably lost far fewer than those unarmed servants and camp followers who were in the Othonian baggage train. These probably accounted for as many if not more. Otho's army can hardly have been composed of more than twenty-five thousand, but the marching column from Bedriacum could easily have been double that number. This then would account for the heaps of dead bodies that are said to have been left unburied, unclaimed and unknown whereas fallen soldiers will probably have been sought by comrades in arms. Thus the forty thousand dead in total that is given in the epitome of Cassio Dio (64.10.3 = Xiphilinus) is probably not far from being an accurate figure.[77] This would allow minimal losses to the armies of Valens and Caecina, perhaps ten thousand lass than or roughly a half of Otho's army, the rest non-combatants.

By next morning level heads won the day and the argument for continuing the fight was no longer seen as feasible. Valens and Caecina had moved their forces overnight to within five Roman miles of Bedriacum, which means that they were in fact a mere thousand paces from their enemy's camp. They had slept rough, states Tacitus, but with victory in sight the troops were happy to rest under arms. A deputation was sent to Valens and Caecina and although there was some delay, which caused fears to resurface, there was soon news of a formal surrender.[78] The camp gates were thrown open and the troops from both sides intermingled quickly with the usual shows of warmth and sympathy from the winning side contrition and relief on those who had lost this battle. A few of the dead were sought by family members and friends but it is said that the vast majority lay where they had fallen. Some of the bodies remained piled high along the road from Cremona to Bedriacum.[79]

Some points related to the strategy of each side is worth noting. The fact that it was Caecina's force alone that engaged the first elements of Otho's army newly arrived at the Po may indicate in part the latter's strategy of fighting the two advancing columns in turn and attempting not to allow them to unite and so gain a numerical superiority. Paulinus' timidity in the aftermath of his victory over Caecina allowed this strategy, if it indeed existed, to fall apart and allowed the opposition to assemble its greater strength at Cremona. It does seem possible that Paulinus' intention may have had the purpose of scuttling Otho's chances. For at that stage the forces of Otho had not yet been gathered together at Bedriacum. It is clear that it was imperative for Vitellius' army to strike as soon as it could while Otho, to make the best use of his resources, should have delayed for at least another two weeks. The leadership of Otho's army was also much less committed than that of Vitellius. Valens and Caecina stood to lose everything if they were to fail but the senators with Otho maintained a sensible detachment allowing them the opportunity to switch allegiance should the need arise. Tacitus graphically illustrates the troubled leadership among Otho's senior commanders, which meant that success at Bedriacum was always going to be elusive. It is also plain from the close reading of the narrative that the battle of Bedriacum, which hardly qualifies to be called such an event – it followed a series of skirmishes – is contained in barely two sections of Tacitus' narrative and in terms of time probably occupied no more than an hour, much less than some of the other fighting that had taken place earlier.

Meanwhile, Otho waited anxiously for a result, which he is almost certain to have received on the morning of 15 April. His suicide, which followed within eighteen or so hours, was in Tacitus' opinion the closest Otho, whose entire life and career had consisted of cronyism and deceit, came to obtaining glory. The death of Otho after the first battle of Bedriacum on 16th April AD 69 is surprisingly well attested for what must surely be regarded as a rather minor event in the history of the Roman Empire. With the battle lost and although defeat not yet a certainty Otho chose to end his life in order, state the sources, to prevent further fruitless death in this disastrous civil war. He is therefore given a hero's suicide. Yet how accurate are these sources and does Otho's death really deserve to be described as heroic? Is suicide in any form or fashion truly heroic for in most instances it is or was a way to escape from either a current or forthcoming unheroic situation? Until quite recent times suicide was not regarded as heroic at all. In Greek history suicide is uncommon and, when resorted to, poison appears to be the preferred course, at least as far as Themistocles and Demosthenes are concerned. Neither is remembered for their heroic deaths, while even less heroic appears to have been the failed attempt by another Athenian Demosthenes at Syracuse in 413. No details are recorded but he may have tried to fall on his sword but was foiled and was later executed instead. In the Roman world it is a rare phenomenon overall and really only becomes evident for a brief time in the late Roman Republic and in the first century AD. During the rule of the Julio-Claudians suicide became a manner of death chosen by members of the governing elite as a way of avoiding damnation of a name and confiscation of property, which would have occurred following an execution after conviction for any serious crime. Yet the literary sources – Martial, Plutarch, Tacitus, Suetonius and Cassius Dio – are unanimous in affording Otho a quite glorious end, whereas less than a year beforehand Nero the last of the Julio-Claudians had committed an undignified suicide.[80]

The details of Otho's last hours are worth some detailed examination. His suicide seems to have taken place behind a door or some sort of solid screen and so the actual event went unwitnessed. Tacitus' notice is interesting therefore for its mix of what might have been verifiable and what was possibly plausible. He is said to have talked with his nephew Salvius Cocceianus and reassured the young man or boy about the future and that his supreme sacrifice would prove beneficial for his supporters and family members (*Hist.* 2.48).

With evening approaching he satisfied his thirst with a drink of cold water. Then after two knives had been brought and when he had carefully tested them he placed one beneath his head. And after he ensured that his friends had now set out, he spent a quiet night, and as is confirmed, not without sleep. At dawn he threw his chest against the iron. Following the sigh of one in the process of dying, Plotius Firmus, the Praetorian Prefect, the freedmen and slaves entered and discovered a single wound.

Vesperascente die sitim haustu gelidae aquae sedavit. Et explorato iam profectos amicos, noctem quietam, utque adfirmatur, non insomnem egit: luce prima in ferrum pectore incubuit. Ad gemitum morientis ingress liberti servique et Plotius Firmus praetorii praefectus unum vulnus invenere. (*Hist.* 2.49)

Some points need to be analysed. The sound of death is a curious phrase for how can a single sound bring the entry of such a crowd unless they were waiting outside and had not slept? And there is also the claim that 'a single wound' caused death. The two phrases are juxtaposed but some interval must surely have occurred between the two if Tacitus is not to be accused of omission through brevity. A single wound to the chest by even the sharpest knife could not have done the ultimate damage immediately unless a surgeon was the doer of the deed. So Otho must either have been a really clever individual or very lucky and while Tacitus grants him a degree of recklessness he does not make any note of intellect (*Hist.* 1.21–23).[81]

Plutarch (*Otho*, 17.1–3) also refers to Otho drinking water, but examining not knives but two swords, one of which he chose and kept by his side. He sent his servants away and then slept so deeply that his breathing (perhaps snoring is meant) could be heard by those nearby. In the early morning he summoned one of his freedmen to learn whether or not the senators who had accompanied him and whom he had helped leave his camp in the aftermath of the defeat had in fact departed. When he was informed that this was so, he ordered the freedman to leave in case he was accused of helping his ruler to die. Once alone again he held the sword by two hands facing upwards and propelled himself down on the point. As he felt the pain he gave out a single sound which was loud enough for his servants to hear and these responded with the type of ululation associated with death and funerals. Plutarch's account is much more dramatic and detailed than the others and one has to suspect with more dramatic embellishment especially in the manner by which death was accomplished.

Suetonius provides a rather fuller account than Tacitus but less than Plutarch. With many of the same details as Tacitus it is possible to suggest the same or a similar source. The cold water introduces the episode in all three accounts and perhaps points to sobriety before a decisive action rather than being befuddled by wine or even allowing oneself some courage from drinking the alcohol.

> After he satisfied his thirst with a drink of cold water he snatched up two knives and when he had examined the sharp edge of both of these he placed one underneath his pillow, and after he had closed the folding doors he slept a deep sleep. And just around dawn he woke up and he stabbed himself with a single blow under the left nipple and to those who burst in at his first sigh one minute concealing the wound the next minute displaying it he died.

> *Post hoc sedata siti gelidae aquae potione arripuit duos pugiones et explorata utriusque acie cum alterum pulvino subdidisset, foribus adopertis artissimo somno quievit. Et circa lucem demum expergefactus uno se traiecit ictu infra laevam papillam irrumpentibusque ad primum gemitum modo celans modo detegens plagam exanimatus ....* (Suet. *Otho*, 11.2)

The display of such an honourable wound might have an appropriate place and be worthy of praise but it also has an element of farce. As indeed is the theatrical nature of the whole episode of testing for the better of two sharp implements. Otho should not need to have done such a thing in a society in which arms were an integral part of being a citizen in the community. A soldier might check his weapon but would not need to decide between weapons. Otho is therefore surely meant to be seen as never having owned or been familiar with a sword or knife.[82] This account, however, is perhaps a little more credible than Tacitus' brief and neutral notice because it suggests that there was some delay between the blow and actual death since Otho was neither an expert in martial arts nor of human anatomy. It would be difficult to obtain a guaranteed result from a single thrust. The delay is therefore indicated by Suetonius even if it was not as lengthy a time as would appear to have occurred in the case of the younger Cato after the cause of Pompey had been lost at the battle of Thapsus in 47 BC.

Plutarch has the fullest account. After bathing, Cato dined with friends and drank wine and the talk focussed on philosophical questions, including one of the Stoic 'paradoxes' that the good man alone was free while bad men were all slaves (Plut. *Cat. Min.* 67.1–2). The party broke up and Cato went to his room and read Plato. He saw that his sword was not where he had left it and called a slave to bring it to him. Plutarch says that since the sword was not brought Cato lost his temper and hit the slave at which point his son and other friends arrived and these are said to have pleaded with Cato not to take the course he obviously now intended. Cato responded mostly to his son whom he gently scolded for treating his father as a madman and that hiding the sword merely left him no weapon to defend himself against Caesar but that with or without a sword he had chosen suicide (*Cat. Min.* 68.1–5).[83] The young man left in tears but two close associates of Cato, named as Demetrius and Apollonides, remained and these three continued their discussions in which Cato justified and affirmed the action he was about to take. The Greeks also left in tears having no argument to advance against his decision (*Cat. Min.* 70.1). A child, probably a slave, finally brought Cato his sword and he drew it out of its sheath and tested the point, which was still sharp, perhaps from recent use. But he continued his reading and then slept sufficiently deeply for his breathing to be heard by those outside his room. But at around midnight he summoned two of his freedmen, Cleanthes his doctor so that his fist that he had damaged when he earlier struck the slave could be bandaged and Butas his agent to check whether all those seeking to escape from Caesar had set sail. When he was told that nearly everyone had by then departed but that there was a storm brewing that might force them back Cato sent again for further news. As the dawn chorus broke he fell asleep again (*Cat. Min.* 70.4) until Butas returned to inform him that none of those escaping from the port had returned. Cato ordered Butas to leave closing the door after him, unsheathed his sword, and stabbed himself under the chest. Because of his damaged hand he did not possess the strength to inflict a mortal wound and in his agony he fell from the couch and overturned what Plutarch describes as a geometrical abacus (an adding machine). The slaves ran, in followed by his son and other friends, and the physician Cleanthes was summoned who sewed up the wound. Cato seems to have fainted but then came to and seeing the bandages ripped them off and reopened the wound and then died. For a military man his aim was less sure than that of the unmilitary Otho but then he had hurt his hand hitting his slave!

Dio also covered the death of Cato but to a much lesser extent although he states (43.11.6) that he considered him to be the 'most democratic and strongest minded of all men of his day'. This judgement follows a brief notice about the manner of his suicide which is really rather underplayed: that on the chosen evening he hid a knife under his pillow and then read Plato's *Phaedo*, and that when he had finished this work about midnight he took out the knife and ripped open his stomach. He should have died at once from loss of blood but he fell from a low couch on which he had been reclining. In doing so he alerted those keeping guard including his son who rushed in and who successfully patched up the wound. These took away the knife and locked the door to his room where he lay unconscious but once he came round he tore open the wound again and so died (Dio, 43.11.6). Other than the reference to the philosophical interest of the subject and that he reopened the self-inflicted wound there is little in common with Plutarch's account and may well indicate another less interested source. On the other hand, Plutarch's account of Cato's last hours is detailed and is contained in one of the longer parallel lives hence there must have been a great deal of extant literary material on which to draw, yet this seemingly passed Dio's notice.[84] The death of Cato and the portrayal of this event is clearly of some importance here since his reputation is compared to that of Otho by Martial. Hence some details from the earlier episode may well have transferred themselves to the later. However, it should be recognized that many such self-inflicted deaths had occurred among the famous in the interim; and the death of Nero is perhaps another and more obvious comparable suicide on which to draw.

The suicide of Nero lacks the coverage of Tacitus who may not even have narrated this event and was covered by Plutarch, although his life is lost. Still the episode is found in the life of Suetonius and in the Zonaras epitome of Cassius Dio (63.27.3–28.5). Suetonius relates that the revolt of Vindex had been suppressed but that there was widespread rebellion against Nero (*Nero*, 66–67) and Galba and been recognized by the senate as ruler. The Praetorian Guard deserted Nero (*Nero*, 67.1–2) but no attempt initially was made to assassinate him nor was there any order for his execution. And so after some considerable hesitation he left Rome for a villa belonging to his freedman Phaeon between the Via Nomentana and Via Salaria at the fourth milestone.[85] Nero was accompanied by this freedman and just three other loyal servants including his secretary Epaphroditus and companion Sporus (*Nero*, 68.1). As he set out on horseback an earthquake occurred and he also heard shouts from the Praetorian Camp for his death and the acclamation of Galba. As this group neared the villa they left the horses behind and made their way on foot by an overgrown path and came to the wall at the rear of the villa.

Phaeon suggested that Nero hide in a sandpit while the others could organize an unobtrusive entry. Nero is supposed to have declared that he 'would not go underground while he still lived' (*Nero*, 68.3). Suetonius gives some explicit details at this moment stating that while waiting for the right moment to go into the villa unnoticed the emperor kneeled down to take up some water in his hand from a nearby pool and when he had finished drinking he said 'This is Nero's cold drink.'

> *Dum clandestinus ad villam introitus pararetur, aquam ex subiecta lacuna poturus manu hausit et: 'Haec est' inquit 'Neronis decocta.'*

To enter the villa Nero had to crawl through a narrow passage and dishevelled and exhausted he collapsed on a makeshift bed in a small room in the servants' quarters. Although hungry and again thirsty he refused some offered bread but drank some tepid water.

> *Fameque et iterum siti interpellante panem quidem sordidum oblatum aspernatus est, aquae autem tepidae aliquantum bibit.*

> Disturbed by hunger and again by thirst, he rejected certain low quality bread that had been offered to him, but he drank some (a great deal of) warm water. (Suet. *Nero*, 68.3–4)

Those with him urged Nero to take the obvious course in case he was arrested and executed publicly and so he ordered that a grave (*scrobis*) be prepared with the correct measurements. It was during these preparations and after water for cleaning the body and wood for the cremation had been brought that Suetonius writes that Nero constantly recited the famous phrase (reiterated in Dio) '*Qualis artifex pereo!*' or 'Such a master as I perish!' But death was further delayed when a messenger arrived with the news that Nero was to be arrested and publicly executed (*Nero*, 69.1) which prompted him to snatch up two knives and test their points and discard both. He was still not prepared to take the final step until he heard the arrival of horsemen. Like Otho he carried no sword and seems unfamiliar with weapons. But again it is a theatrical element and an addition to the scene. With the help of Epaphroditus he drove one of knives into his neck but was still alive when a centurion entered and put his cloak on the wound as if to bandage up the wound. Nero's last words were apparently 'too late' and 'this is loyalty'. A single blow therefore to the neck accomplished the suicide, and in fact within the vacillating and theatrical character of Nero hardly a death to be ashamed of. Still, a knife wound to the front (or indeed back) of the throat was likely to lead to instantaneous death severing the wind pipe and the voice box. Nero could hardly have uttered the words given to him by the biographer. A wound to the side of the neck might conceivably have allowed him to retain his speech as he bled to death if an artery was severed. But the blood is more likely to have drained internally rather than to the outside and so his throat would have been blocked. Nero would have choked to death and therefore the chances of speaking after he had inflicted the wound (especially if Epaphroditus had to finish the task) are remote. Descriptions of Nero universally suggest that he possessed a thick probably muscular neck so more than one thrust from a knife like a stiletto in that area might be needed to prove fatal.

The epitome of Dio's description of Nero's death (63.27.2–29.2) begins with identical material to that presented by Suetonius.[86] Nero bereft of guards decided to flee on horseback accompanied by Phaeon, Epaphroditus and Sporus and an earthquake occurred, but here the narrative becomes much more embellished since this natural phenomenon is described as if all his victims were re-emerging zombie-like to take their revenge. The epitome then has Nero lying low in some marsh to avoid being apprehended and wallowing in self-pity. Finally he went to some cave where he ate bread of a quality – presumably poor – that he had never before eaten, and since he was thirsty also drank water that was possibly not clean but is credited with the comment that this was 'his special drink'. Quite why this should have taken place inside a cave is not mentioned and perhaps indicates that he received food and water from someone living there. The text has therefore departed from the material given by Suetonius yet retains similar essential elements especially the water. Soon after this as a result of the senate decree ordering his capture and sending horsemen in pursuit Nero demanded that his companions kill him but they refused, and with the pursuers close by he killed himself first uttering the famous phrase 'Oh Zeus what an artist dies in me!' The blow was clearly not fatal and the epitome states that Epaphroditus had to finish him off. He must therefore have been dead before the horsemen arrived. It is notable that the death of Nero seems more reliable in this account and less dramatic but Zonaras may well have shortened a more elaborate original narrative. The drinking water has remained although it seems to add little to the account, and there is no detail of the method of death nor of comparing the knives, and no last conversation with a centurion. All these may have existed in Dio's history which, if the initial identical material is any indication, accessed the same source as Suetonius.

An epigram of Martial is the earliest evidence for Otho's heroic suicide and probably circulated in the early 90s. It predates Plutarch's biography of the same emperor by as much as half a decade.

Cum dubitaret adhuc belli civilis Enyo,
Forsitan et posset vincere mollis Otho
Damnavit multo staturum sanguine Martem
Et fodit certa pectura tota manu
Sit Cato, dum vivit, sane vel Caesare maior:
Dum moritur, numquid maior Othone fuit?

When Enyo, the goddess of civil war, still hesitated
And perhaps tender Otho might be victorious
He damned a war that should be filled with so much blood
And with a steady hand fully pierced his chest
It may be that while he was alive Cato was greater even than Caesar,
But in the way he died was he at all greater than Otho? (Martial 6.32.5–6)

Martial is alone in linking Otho directly with Cato or rather Cato with Otho. In an epigram the joke or message of the poem usually satirical or ironic lies in the last line so where is it? The connection between the two surely has an ironic or humorous twist rather than simply being delivered as an item of historical interest. The text is therefore perhaps not as straightforward as it first appears. Is there really praise for Otho here or denigration of Cato or is there indeed another figure in the background? The point that was being made had to have some resonance with the audience.[87] Surely the underlying point therefore is a joke about Cato's lack of impact on history since. unlike Caesar, he was nothing more than a quasi-legend. The same lack of impact applied to Otho, a ruler of no importance whose miniscule claim to fame lay in a sharp knife.

If one tackles the descriptions of the two suicides alongside one another the differences emerge. Cato drank wine, talked on philosophical topics, talked with his son and closest friends mainly on topics concerned with self-determination and a desire not to surrender to Caesar. As a soldier he examined the point of his sword, he slept so deeply that he was heard by those outside his room, asked whether his friends had departed safely, then as the sun rose with the dawn chorus killed himself. Otho drank water, had no particular discussions, did not possess the intellect to do so, probably did not know how to use a sword so called instead for knives. He is said to have asked after the welfare of his friends, and he had declared an intention to spare his troops of further losses of life just as Cato was concerned to spare the people of Utica further suffering. Yet the main features of Otho's suicide: drinking water, choosing the appropriate weapon, point of death not witnessed, and a single wound are not modelled on the death of Cato at all. Thus there are one or two overlaps but nothing that indicates that writers thought explicitly of Cato when they wrote about Otho. And it is arguable whether Martial's joke was taken up by any of the later sources who palpably draw no connection between Otho's private suicide and that of the younger Cato.

Still, Otho died a more honourable death than his friend and mentor Nero and that is possibly is what is meant by this mention in the sources from Tacitus to Dio or is what the audience most appreciated. Suetonius (*Otho*, 12.1–2) refers to 'unexpected spirit' and that some of his own troops thought him the 'bravest of men.' Plutarch (*Otho*, 18.2) makes almost precisely that point when he says that Otho while he lived was no better than Nero but that his death was more honourable. It is as well to note that Nero's death is also liberally accompanied with water both cold and tepid, the testing of the knives by a man unacquainted with military affairs, but that a single wound apparently accomplished the deed but that there was a delay of some minutes at least between the blow and death. Cassius Dio (Xiphilinus/Zonaras, 63.15) states that Otho seized power through a ruthless coup but died honourably. He, or rather the epitome of the original, gives no details other than he seized a knife and killed himself. Dio may well have devoted greater coverage to Otho's death.

The positive comments about Otho that pervade the sources, with the exception of Dio who was more distant in chronological terms, all date to the Flavian dynasty (Martial; Plutarch) or the period of Trajan and Hadrian (Tacitus; Suetonius). Flavian propaganda and deference to Domitian, for example, must partly explain the praise and the invention of a heroic suicide. But why Cato when he was an enemy of *Divus Iulius*? The characters of the rulers Trajan and Hadrian add an additional aspect to this discussion. Trajan was closely connected with the Flavian dynasty and a trusted general of Domitian in the 90s, with a consulship in 91. Trajan's father had served with Vespasian in the East and had been rewarded with a consulship in 70. Since Vespasian took his legitimacy from being the heir of Otho and Trajan and Hadrian had no cause to denigrate their predecessors, even if Domitian's memory might have been damned, it is therefore hardly remarkable that Otho's brief reign became somewhat protected and the manner of his death be made heroic when, it fact, it was not comparable to that of Cato.

Yet if a heroic suicide is to be sought then a good example may be found in the death of Lucius Sergius Catilina (Catiline) in 62 BC. This event may no longer have resonated with an audience of the second century AD but the manner in which he died more clearly has the elements of a heroic suicide than any discussed so far (Sall. *Cat.* 60–61). Catiline's conspiracy to seize power in Rome had been revealed in late 63 by informers who had alerted the consul Cicero and the protagonist had fled Rome to join his forces in Etruria. His fellow conspirators in Rome had been arrested and executed, and early in 62 an army commanded by the C. Antonius, Cicero's colleague in 63, and his legate Marcus Petreius caught up with the rebels who had been making their way north with the intention of withdrawing into southern Gaul at Pistoia. Catiline and his army were forced to give battle since with a second army commanded by the ex-praetor Q. Caecilius Metellus Celer guarding the approaches to the Po Valley there was no way of escape. Petreius was effectively the commander of the army out of Rome since Antonius, suspected of sympathies with Catiline, declared that on account of an attack of gout he was not well enough to be present on the battlefield. The two armies faced one another and before they engaged Catiline gave a stirring speech to his followers. Catiline was probably heavily outnumbered but many of his troops were disgruntled veterans from the civil wars in the 80s and so seasoned fighters whereas the army of Petreius was probably recently levied and fresh from training. The clash between the two sides was severe and long drawn out. Catiline commanded the centre while his second in command Manlius took the right wing and an unnamed officer from Fiesole was on the left. Wherever he saw his line in difficulty Catiline raced to support his troops bringing with him fresh replacements, and while in the front line killed many opponents so that he was at one and the same time 'an exemplary soldier and a fine general' (Sall. *Cat.* 60). Petreius proved to be equal to any defence put up by his enemy and after fierce fighting routed the opposite's right and left wing. Catiline saw that he was now surrounded with just a small number of followers, but states Sallust, 'he remembered the nobility of his birth and the high public office he had held and so immediately charged into the seething mass of his enemies until he was killed from multiple wounds.' The ferocity of the engagement could easily be gauged later when it was seen that many of Catiline's troops had died where they were originally stationed while their general was found far to the front of his line of battle among the opposing dead. Sallust claims that he was discovered still breathing and that his face still had that look of arrogant pride that had been such an aspect of his character throughout his life.

Catiline could easily be said to have died a really heroic death and that it was a sort of suicide or at least his actions were positively suicidal. However, the reader or audience of Sallust's *Bellum Catilinae* ('The War of Catiline') might well have expressed some surprise at the concluding comments regarding the protagonist seeing that initially he had been described as having:

... a powerful intellect and great physical strength, but a vicious and depraved mind. From his youth he had delighted in civil war, bloodshed, robbery, and political strife, and as a young adult he spent his time in such pursuits. His mind was daring, cunning and adaptable and he was adept at disguising all his actions. He was highly passionate and longed for the possessions of others and was careless of his own, he spoke eloquently but lacked wisdom. His ambition knew no bounds as he constantly sought after things which were financially beyond his reach. After the rule of Sulla, Catiline had an overwhelming desire to do the same thing and to achieve this he was prepared to go to any lengths. (Sall. *Cat.* 5.1–2)

So in the end should Otho be compared with Nero or Cato or even Catiline? For many, Nero was as great as Caesar when he lived. In death Otho was actually no better than his friend Nero. There are too many differences between the suicide of Otho and Cato for the latter to be the model. Cato like Catiline before him and Antony after him were military men and they did not need to test the implement with which they intended to end their lives. Otho, on the other hand, like Nero had no experience in war and both perhaps did not even own a sword. The water imagery surely contrasts with the soldier's death as well, and also links Otho to Nero rather than to any real hero. The lack of philosophical discussion is evident with both Otho and Nero, but the former like Cato asks after the well-being of his friends while Nero was obsessed about only himself. Otho and Nero evidently took longer to die than is related by the sources, but both Cato and Antony lingered. Yet it is clear that Nero too took longer to die than Suetonius recounts, and although Otho is allowed a rapid demise that is probably not historical and was perhaps meant to fit with his brief period as ruler. A grandiloquent death scene was not to be wasted on such an insignificant person as Otho, even if grudgingly his death might be described as noble. Overall there is more material for Otho's suicide than could be expected for so slight an individual. The emphasis on regard for him by his troops occupies an inordinate space in the accounts, yet he was no philosopher and seems to have possessed little intellect. He was, in fact, a common man, which possibly made him likeable just as Nero had, in fact, been popular with the general population. This is arguably why Tacitus presents him as by far a greater threat to the state had he lived than Vitellius. Otho was remembered as being no friend of the senatorial elite, a perception that has moulded the tradition but that it was probably historical rather than fiction.[88] Otho was not even a pale imitation of Cato and any attempt to compare the former favourably with the latter was surely only to be a gross insult to the enemy of Caesar and indeed any Caesar.

Vitellius, meanwhile, arrived in Cremona via Ticinum forty days after the battle, on approximately 25 May AD 69, which indicates a slower rate of advance preferred by his suite and its accompanying guard. Just how far behind Valens these had marched is less easy to adduce. For Tacitus this slow progress was simply in keeping with Vitellius' character and his addiction to idleness and overindulgence.[89] The main army groups had made good time to occupy the Alpine passes and *Transpadana* and there was no obvious need for Vitellius to hurry. But it stretches credulity to believe that Vitellius was loitering so far behind his senior generals, and it is probably safer to assume that he was actually quite close to Lugdunum on 14 April and that after his future had been decided that he then went on at a slower rate. After all, Valens and Caecina reported in person to Vitellius at Lugdunum where with them he celebrated the victory with parades and speeches. Valens and Caecina and their escorts would have made Lugdunum from Cremona in a few days.

Also at Lugdunum, but probably some days later, the senior centurions of Otho's troops were executed, an act that did Vitellius no credit and for which he was not forgiven. Yet senior figures such as Suetonius Paulinus and Licinius Proculus who also came to Lugdunum were pardoned. Tacitus states that they claimed that they had conspired to give Vitellius victory in the recent battle. This seems at least plausible, but it is also apparent that neither is mentioned again. Proculus certainly lost his post as Prefect of the Guard, while Suetonius Paulinus may have died soon after.[90] Other senior figures such as Marius Celsus and even Salvius Titianus were treated with courtesy and respect.[91] And in general there were less punitive actions taken against Otho's supporters than might have been expected. But Vitellius' clemency was not a policy expected to endure especially once his brother Lucius arrived and became a highly influential figure in the new regime. Tacitus is especially hostile towards Lucius Vitellius for while the historian evidently believed that the emperor had few saving graces his brother had none at all. Perhaps advised by his brother who had travelled from Rome and seen the chaos in northern Italy Vitellius now sought to rid himself of individual soldiers or units that had fought for Otho and, unlike their commanders, were less inclined to be accommodated by the new ruler. Thus the main elements of Othos' army were dispersed. *Legio* XIV was ordered to relocate to Britain (*Hist.* 2.66), while the Batavian auxiliaries were to return to Lower Germany (*Hist.* 2.69 and 2.97), Gallic auxiliary troops to Gaul, *Legio* I *Adiutrix* was sent to Spain, while those contingents from the Eleventh Legion and the Seventh Legion, which had probably arrived at Bedriacum only after the battle had been lost, were sent back to their homes in Dalmatia and Pannonia.[92] The existing Praetorian Guard was largely cashiered but many of these ex-guardsmen later re-joined the forces supporting Vespasian and took part in the later invasion of Italy (*Hist*. 2.67).[93] Tacitus claims that these seriously strengthened the Flavian army, although previously he has had little positive to say about their contribution to Otho's army, and it is possible that this view has crept into the narrative from a source he consulted. Vitellius replaced this entire section of the army with a new Praetorian Guard drawn from detachments of the Rhine legions and the German auxiliaries. The troops who remained behind, specifically those from the defeated *Legio* XIII, were ordered to construct amphitheatres at Cremona and Bononia where Caecina and Valens proposed to hold victory games.[94]

At Cremona following Caecina's games Vitellius viewed the battlefield then moved on to Bononia when Valens produced his games for the emperor. In response, Vitellius honoured Valens and Caecina with consulships, and then moved slowly on to Rome, a progress made even more sedate says Tacitus because of the crowds from all walks of life that arrived at the now imperial court, and by the emperor's addiction to endless celebrations.[95] Nonetheless, Vitellius arrived in the city probably towards the end of June where further celebrations occurred after an elaborate parade (*Hist*. 2.89) before the rebellion of Vespasian was announced. This must have become known in Rome by 18 July when Vitellius unwisely issued a decree about public worship on a *dies nefasti* or 'unlucky day,' that being the anniversary of the infamous Roman defeats at the Cremera River by the army of Etruscan Veii in 477 and the Allia River by the Gauls in 387 BC. The *faux pas* is said to have been regarded as a bad omen for the future (Tac. *Hist*. 91), although such sensational items tend to enter a text with the benefit of hindsight.

On a more practical level the declaration of Vespasian as heir of Galba (Tac. *Hist*. 3.7) at the beginning of July meant that Vitellius was faced immediately with a serious threat to his position but not one that was necessarily as grave as that faced by his predecessor.[96] At this stage Vitellius retained the loyalty of the Rhine army and all those forces that had supported Otho and so in numerical terms this represented a command far in excess of 100,000 troops. Moreover, many of these units were battle hardened veterans. Why then was his position so quickly undermined and why did another single battle bring about the end of his rule? In the first place Vitellius or his inner circle of advisers chose to ignore the reports of widespread rebellion not only in the eastern provinces but also closer to home along the Danube frontier. This was a fundamental error on the part of the new regime in Rome and Vitellius himself who did not take seriously the announcement in a despatch of the defection to Vespasian of the Third Legion (*Gallica*) and its legate Aponius Saturninus. It is said that Vitellius was convinced by his household that there was just a single mutinous legion and that elsewhere all was well. This show of complacency caused a serious delay in organizing essential countermeasures and preparations for another bout of fighting.

For example, Tacitus describes (*Hist*. 2.97) initial calls for reinforcements for the army sent to the garrisons in Britain and Germany but which were greeted with caution by their proconsuls. Hordeonius Flaccus in Germany suspected that a revolt was being planned by the Batavians, and Vettius Bolanus in Britain considered the island to be too unstable to spare troops. In Spain there was no senior official since Cluvius Rufus who had been appointed to govern *Hispania Tarraconensis* by Galba had been ordered to remain with Vitellius' entourage.[97] In other provinces such as Africa the resident garrisons were not substantial enough to warrant their transportation to Italy. In the end it was only when the first Flavian legions had already penetrated the defences of northern Italy that Vitellius became sufficiently alarmed to urge Valens and Caecina to lead their forces north. However, the few months of the summer of 69 had witnessed a growing tension between these mainstays of the regime and this increasing rivalry between Caecina and Valens for primacy was to be fatal to Vitellius' cause. Valens is said to have been recovering from some illness and so Caecina was sent ahead but he was apparently already conspiring to switch his allegiance since his fellow general seemed in the ascendancy. Caecina had discussions with Lucilius Bassus Prefect of the Fleets stationed at Misenum and Ravenna. Bassus was disgruntled because he had not been chosen as Prefect of the Guard and the crews of both fleets had been firm supporters of Otho so here there was a fertile ground for treachery. Caecina was more influential but also faced an uphill task with the legionaries who overwhelmingly still backed Vitellius for all the favours he had allowed them.[98]

Meanwhile, in Pannonia the Thirteenth Legion, which had not recovered from the insult of amphitheatre building, and the Seventh Legion raised by Galba made common cause with *Legio* III. The commander of *Legio* VII was Antonius Primus to whom Tacitus devotes considerable attention. This fascinating individual was somewhat older than either Valens or Caecina, but his incredible energy is palpable in the narrative.[99] Like Caecina in January of that year Primus did not act alone but had as a strong ally in the procurator of Dalmatia or Pannonia a certain Cornelius Fuscus who Tacitus regarded as dynamic and like Primus as delighting in the dangers offered by the moment.[100] It was these two who were as much the architects of Vespasian's victory as Valens and Caecina had been the successful managers of Vitellius' ambitions. Primus and Fuscus immediately sent out couriers to those forces that were likely to have remained hostile towards Vitellius, especially the

Fourteenth Legion banished to Britain after Bedriacum and the *Legio* I (*Adiutrix*) removed to *Hispania Tarraconensis*.

Caecina departed from Rome in command of what on paper at least was an impressive force of arms (Tac. *Hist.* 2.100) consisting of detachments from Legions I (*Germania*), IV, XV, and XVI followed closely by units from the Fifth (*Alaudae*), Twenty-Second. A rear guard, whose commander is not named, was made up of troops drawn from *Legio* XXI (*Rapax*), and *Legio* I (*Italica*), together with auxiliaries and some vexillations from the legions garrisoned in Britain. A cavalry force was sent on ahead to secure Cremona before any Flavian forces arrived in that vicinity. The numbers in this army even if all units were under strength after a long spell of inactivity must have numbered between fifty and sixty thousand; and if less than that which had marched down from the Rhine earlier in the year only because some units had been returned to garrison duty. The problem for Caecina was the lack of discipline and fitness of both men and horses, while at the same time his intention to desert Vitellius had hardened. Valens had not fully regained his health but he was either aware that Caecina was contemplating a change in his allegiance or was anxious that his position might be undermined by his rival unless he was present in person. He announced his intention of hurrying north to catch up with the army, although in fact he did no such thing. Caecina, meanwhile, had divided the army into two sections, one to go to Cremona to join the cavalry the other to Hostilia on the River Tartaro to cover the coastal road to Ariminum. Caecina himself went to Ravenna to consult with Bassus.

The supporters of Vespasian had met at Poetovio, modern Ptuj on the Drava River, in Pannonia, the camp of *Legio* XIII, about 270 kilometres (165 miles) from Aquileia and roughly a two-week march from a confrontation with the legions of Vitellius' army. Here the inevitable discussions took place (Tac. *Hist.* 3.1–4) about the best strategy to pursue: either to wait for the collection of all their forces and Vespasian's closest ally Licinius Mucianus who was on his way from Syria to join them or to strike quickly before Vitellius could gather all the troops at his disposal. Antonius Primus was most in favour of a rapid strike mainly because he realized that a victory would serve his ambitions well while a delay until the arrival of Mucianus would mean that he would immediately be eclipsed and reduced to a subordinate position under the latter's acknowledged leadership. Yet his advice made some sense in that it was self-evident that Vitellius' troops were lacking in recent combat training and that Valens' absence would cause some insecurity since Caecina had not been a particularly successful commander in his own right. Furthermore, if there was some inkling that Caecina meant to change sides then this would also have a deleterious effect on his troops and create a crisis in the command structure of the Vitellian army. His view was supported by his ally Cornelius Fuscus and another commander Arrius Varus who was to prove to be almost as energetic as Primus. *Legio* III under Aponius Saturninus was summoned from Moesia and the Flavian forces seized Aquileia by mid-September (Tac. *Hist*. 3.6).

A small force of Vitellius' army was defeated at Forum Alieni, which opened the way for the occupation of Patavium (modern Padua) by *Legio* VII (*Galbiana*) and *Legio* XIII (*Gemina*).[101] After some days at Patavium it was decided to make for Verona taking Vicetia first, birthplace of Caecina. Verona was chosen because it was one of the great cities of the Po Valley and was on level land that was suitable for exercising the cavalry. Once occupied any aid to Vitellius' army was now forced to use the passes further west, while Noricum and Rhaetia were effectively neutralized as bases for pro-Vitellius forces.

Tacitus states (*Hist*. 3.8) that this latest move had not been sanctioned by Vespasian who believed that with his occupation of all the eastern provinces and control of much of the food supply to Italy he would be able to force the surrender of Vitellius' army. Therefore the order was not to advance beyond Aquileia, which was forcefully reiterated by despatches from Mucianus, but he had yet to arrive in the area. Thus Primus and the other commanders on the ground, including Fuscus, could claim afterwards that instructions sent from Alexandria or from Mucianus still in the Balkans arrived after events had taken precedence and which were beyond their control. To an extent this attitude was justified but those with ambition such as Antonius Primus and Cornelius Fuscus knew that to obtain maximum prestige and to be at the top of the queue jostling for power and influence under a new ruler they needed to keep up the momentum.

At Ravenna Lucilius Bassus had no problem subverting the loyalty of the crews of the fleet but for Caecina subversion of his own troops proved to be a much more arduous task. The rapid movement of Flavian forces west of the Veneto forced the Vitellian forces at Hostilia (Ostiglia) to dig in behind the Tartaro River with the River Po behind. The Flavian forces consisting of the two legions (VII and XIII) were outnumbered and had Caecina attacked rather than chosen to take defensive measures Tacitus is sure (*Hist*. 3.9) that he would have caused the invaders to withdraw from Italy. Howeyer, by delaying an attack – his forces were probably also not in battle readiness so Tacitus is somewhat economical with the truth here – and by sending messages regarding his own desertion and that of his troops he allowed time for reinforcements for the enemy to arrive from Moesia commanded by Aponius Saturninius, and *Legio* VII (*Claudia*) with its legate Vipstanus Messalla.[102] The Flavian commanders urged Caecina to declare openly for Vespasian and join them. He may well have been hesitating since his position among the numerous generals in Vespasian's armies would reduce his stature greatly. By reading Caecina's letters aloud to their assembled troops the Flavian leadership was able to instil greater confidence while knowledge of their general's impending treachery was bound to reach the Vitellian ranks and cause dismay and uncertainty.

The Flavians were waiting for more troops which duly came in the shape of two more legions from the Danube army, *Legio* III commanded by Dillius Aponianus and *Legio* VIII the legate of which was Numisius Lupus. The numerical balance was beginning to tilt in favour of the invaders who could now count on five legions and probably at least an equal number of auxiliary and allied troops, probably roughly forty thousand in total.[103] It was decided to fortify Verona, which had expanded beyond its original walls, and while the construction work was taking place a mutiny occurred, which resulted in two of the legionary commanders – Tampius Flavianus of *Legio* VII, actually working on the new defensive walls, and Saturninus, the proconsul of Moesia – being deprived of their posts and fleeing either to Mucianus or Vespasian. Both were more senior figures to Primus and Fuscus and the influence of this pair in engineering this coup is surely to be identified since it was these two and especially the former who gained almost absolute control of the army with the departure of these two senior and older generals.[104]

At Ravenna the fleet staged a mutiny led initially by the captains of the warships but the crews were happy to join this revolt since many had their origins in the Balkan provinces, which had all declared their allegiance to Vespasian (Tac. *Hist.* 3.12). If Lucilius Bassus had hoped to profit from this move to the Flavian side he was to be disappointed since the captains of the fleet offered the command to Cornelius Fuscus who, having no military post with the Flavian army, willingly took up this command and appears to have been sufficiently close at hand to arrive promptly.[105] As for Caecina, when news of the fleet's desertion became common knowledge he summoned a meeting of his officers and centurions. He put the case for abandoning the cause of Vitellius and supporting Vespasian, specifically because most of the provinces had chosen the latter whose control of the sea meant that Italy could be starved into submission. Those present who knew what Caecina intended followed him in swearing an oath to Vespasian and the rest were pressured to do likewise. When the rank and file realized what their officers proposed at first they were stunned into silence but then hostility quickly grew since it was commonly felt that this move could only result in a degrading spectacle for the Rhine legions whose troops regarded themselves as far better soldiers than those in the Danubian army. They regarded Antonius Primus no better than a bandit and Caecina and Bassus thieves and turncoats. Caecina was arrested, the legate of *Legio* V (*Alaudae*) Fabius Fabullus and the Prefect of the Camp Cassius Longus were chosen to lead the army.[106] The crews of three warships from the Ravenna fleet – perhaps as many as six hundred rowers – who were discovered on land were massacred and it was then decided to make for Cremona to join the other legions sent there by Caecina.[107]

When Primus heard this news he decided to act at once and try to prevent the two forces in Vitellius' army from uniting at Cremona and to engage each one in battle and hence if possible maintain his superiority in numbers. He also believed that Valens had by now departed from Rome and if he was allowed to take sole command of Vitellius' army the Flavian legions would be faced with a general of considerable skill and who commanded the loyalty of the troops under his command.[108] So taking the initiative Primus marched his army in a mere two days from Verona to Bedriacum where a camp was constructed. On the next day he sent out auxiliary troops to forage in the direction of Cremona. He also set out with four thousand cavalry to establish another vantage spot eight Roman miles west of Bedriacum. This represents the midway point between the outskirts of Cremona and Bedriacum. About mid-morning (Tac. *Hist*. 3.16) reports came to Primus that Vitellian forces – probably a mixture of auxiliary cavalry and infantry cohorts – were advancing towards him in large numbers. Although Primus was inclined to avoid an encounter before he could summon his legions Arrius Varus ignored any order and led a detachment under his command to intercept the advancing enemy. He had some early success but as the Vitellian troops gathered in greater strength the attackers were forced into a disorderly retreat. This could easily have turned into a rout and meant a serious setback for Vespasian's ambitions had not Primus intervened in person confronting troops who were scrambling back towards Bedriacum. Through pleas, gestures and finally actually killing a tribune who was running away and seizing a standard he managed to rally just a small number of men but these became the nucleus of a fight-back. As chance would have it these congregated in a reasonably strong place where the road was narrow, had steep sides into drainage ditches and where a bridge over a stream had been demolished so making an attack difficult especially for the cavalry units arranged against them. Their enemy could not easily close the distance between them and Primus' small group and when they did were easily thrown back by the defenders above. Somehow the troops of Vitellius lost heart and were repulsed while at the same time Primus must have received additional support to mount a full counterattack. Tacitus' record of this skirmish is left incomplete since it seems plain that Primus was able to win a victory here either because of lacklustre command from those attacking him or because he suddenly obtained more troops.[109] Yet quite close by and advancing from Cremona a distance of four Roman miles were *Legio* XXI (*Rapax*) and *Legio* I (*Italica*) intent on providing support to their cavalry. However, when these arrived there seems to have been a great deal of confusion, which resulted in neither offensive action nor defensive measures. Primus' troops were now making rapid progress and overran whatever lines the Vitellian legions had established and these too now retreated towards Cremona to take refuge inside the city. Tacitus comments (*Hist.* 3.18) that in victory Vitellius' army felt no need for a commander but faced with defeat they became a leaderless mob.

As dusk fell Primus' army gathered and regrouped outside Cremona where many of the troops, although just arrived after the march of sixteen Roman miles, demanded an immediate assault on the city, which had been in the forefront of support for Vitellius. An immediate attack offered the reward of plunder, a delay until morning would bring pleas for clemency and no material gains for the troops, only their commanders. Primus is said to have delivered a conciliatory speech promising that the army would reap the benefits of a successful campaign but that without siege equipment gaining an entry to the city without suffering heavy casualties looked remote and even if the gates were open there was still the unfamiliarity of what lay inside the walls. Primus sent the slaves and servants to collect the baggage train from Bedriacum – although Tacitus claims that these were as eager for plunder as the soldiers – but the troops were unimpressed with his arguments. Another mutinous situation was only avoided when some captured citizens from Cremona reported that the two elements of Vitellius' army had now reunited and that the forces from Hostilia had marched thirty Roman miles in a single day.[110] The troops came to their senses and again took orders from their officers. An engagement at night, that most risky of all battlefields in antiquity, was about to commence.

Primus drew up the various groups of his army facing west towards Cremona. He may have given detailed instructions of where each unit should position itself but since it was after dark there could be no confirmation that the troops were where they were supposed to be. Thus *Legio* XIII is said to have occupied crossroads on the Via Postumia, which at that point ran along a high embankment, on the left of the main road on lower, level and open ground was the Seventh Legion (*Galbiana*) and then completing the left wing was the Seventh (*Claudia*), which had a drainage ditch before its front line. On the right of the crossroads was the Eighth Legion drawn up where the road had a steep incline in front but no other cover. Next to *Legio* VIII completing the right wing was the Third Legion, which gained some protection from vineyards and other cultivated lands at its front. Auxiliary infantry and cavalry covered both wings with some light armed allied troops from the Danubian provinces acting as skirmishers ahead of the front line.[111] The army of Vitellius in the meantime seems to have re-gathered outside and, remarkably for an army about to give battle, no single commander is identified by Tacitus. The individual legionary commanders seem to have taken it upon themselves to present a cohesive military presence, although without the presence of a senior general any overall strategy for a hostile engagement did not exist and the fight was all about survival or destruction. Tacitus provides the order of the main units in the line of battle, which he says that he has obtained from others – probably Vipstanus Mesalla or possibly even Vestricius Spurinna if he fought in this conflict – but that he cannot vouch for complete accuracy because of the darkness.[112] On the right wing was *Legio* IV (*Macedonica*), in the centre the Fifth (*Alaudae*) and Fifteenth (*Primigenia*) where there were also some contingents from the British garrison from the Second, Ninth and Twentieth, and positioned on the left wing were *Legio* XVI and *Legio* I (*Germania*). The troops from XXI (*Rapax*) and I (*Italica*) who had come only from Cremona appear to have placed themselves wherever they chose as did any cavalry and auxiliary infantry cohorts. A single commander might well have retained some of these troops as a reserve.

With dusk a little after 6.00 pm Tacitus very precisely states that the Vitellian ranks attacked en masse towards the end of the third hour of the night ('*tertia ferme noctis hora*') and so fairly close to 9.00 pm. To be so categorical suggests the reminiscences of a source who had actually been present in the battle and in some position to know the hour since the night was not accurately timed in antiquity.[113] Night battles were a rare phenomenon and the outcome highly unpredictable. Tacitus makes it clear that the Vitellian forces that had arrived from Hostilia should have waited and recovered from their thirty-mile hike until the following morning when they could have then attacked an enemy that had spent the night awake in the lines. The terrible desire of both sides to fight not only has its origin in civil strife in which all norms and good practices are forgotten but also probably owed something to the rivalry between the Rhine and Danube armies. They could not wait to see who would be the victor in the struggle, which is said to have been fought out throughout the hours of darkness where first one side and then the other gained some success or suffered some reverse. Tacitus' precision unfortunately gives way to a more general and vague account, which could apply to any night battle, such as Thucydides' account of the night battle at Syracuse in 413 BC. Still he does claim that the Primus' Legion VII (*Galbiana*) became the focus of the fiercest struggle (*Hist*. 3.22). This is perhaps because it occupied the weakest point in the Flavian line, although the Vitellians cannot have really known this in the darkness since they were nearly as unfamiliar with the landscape as was their enemy. It appears that the Seventh Legion would have been routed were it not for the heroic leadership of its legate Atilius Varus who was killed.[114] Primus too was present wherever there was a need for reinforcing the line and he rushed fresh troops here and these organized a counterattack only later to be driven back. Tacitus states that the Vitellian ranks employed catapults to good effect, especially a large model belonging to *Legio* XVI. Tacitus describes a scene of carnage when this artillery equipment found its mark, although a certain scepticism about its value should also be raised. There was no light and these catapults are supposed to have travelled all the way from Hostilia on wagons and then were set up after nightfall. The text is dramatic, and it may have been reported to Tacitus but it seems rather unlikely to have been an accurate picture of events.

There was a clear sky and the moon started to have an effect on the battlefield probably around midnight. Since it rose behind the ranks of Primus' troops it caused their shadows to be exaggerated, which affected the aim of the catapult engineers who began to miss their targets, although how they could see these in total darkness is not explained. The light from the moon also made the Vitellian troops easier targets for their opponents since there was what might be described as a spotlight effect on their bodies.[115] Primus used this advantage fully and spurred on his legions and gave particular attention to *Legio* III, which was on the right and therefore the offensive wing. The legion had been protected by the nature of the land around its position and so had time to recover from the exertions of the march from Bedriacum. Yet these troops did not advance until sunrise, which suggests that the moon, in fact, had little real impact on the fighting, which continued in a sporadic fashion over several hours.[116] This legion had previously been stationed in Syria where it was common practice to salute the rising of the sun and as the troops went through this habitual custom their opponents thought that the Flavian army was cheering the arrival of further reinforcements.[117] This encouraged Primus' troops to make yet more effort while the Vitellian forces, which were already struggling with a lack of command structure, were plunged into greater insecurity. The Vitellian line had become quite disorganized in the dark and in some places gaps had opened up, which were exposed in the daylight. Primus ordered columns of troops to charge these gaps knowing that once inside the enemy's line there was a good chance of forcing a retreat and rout (Tac. *Hist.* 3.25). Everything went according to this plan and while fierce fighting took place the Vitellian army fled for safety to its camp, which was situated close to walls of Cremona on the Via Postumia.[118]

Both sides were exhausted but Primus knew that unless he took the camp quickly there was no safe place for his own troops while his enemy had the time to recoup their energies. The camp was well fortified so the legions were each assigned a section to assault, the Third and Seventh (*Galbiana*) were assigned the section facing south east towards Bedriacum, the Eighth and Seventh (*Claudia*) the section facing to the east, and *Legio* XIII the northern rampart that lay towards the town of Brixia (Tac. *Hist*. 3.27). There was a brief lull in the fighting as the besiegers went in search of implements that could be used to undermine the fortifications and then legionaries employed their shields as a *testudo*. The defenders responded with rocks that were thrown down on the enemy in the hope of opening up the *testudo*, which then allowed soldiers with pikes and javelins to aim for the heads and shoulders of the men below. Without specialist siege equipment and a good period of rest the efforts of the besieging forces were bound to fail, at which point the Flavian troops were promised Cremona as the prize for victory.[119] The besieging troops redoubled their efforts and the fight became a gruelling test of stamina and it was the forces inside the camp that began to give way. Some began to try to escape from the camp into Cremona as the Flavian Third Legion broke in through the Brixia Gate. The Vitellian forces now suffered heavy casualties but the citizens of Cremona closed their gates and manned the walls in anticipation of a further siege. In the Vitellian camp there was panic as the officers took down the portraits of the emperor and the Prefect of the Camp released Caecina who was begged to try to intervene with Primus in the hope of preventing further deaths. He reluctantly agreed and when troops there displayed the signs for a surrender from the walls ('*velamenta et infulas pro muris ostentant*', *Hist*. 3.31) he and the forces previously under his command marched out between lines of the triumphant Flavian forces.[120]

A truce appears to have been negotiated while the Vitellian troops were disarmed and placed in some holding area since there must have been about forty thousand of these and the authorities of Cremona were evidently persuaded to open their gates and participate in a parade in celebration of Primus' victory. No mention was made of the deal that Primus had promised his soldiers and when some fights broke out between the Flavian troops and the citizens, and when Primus is believed to have given his assent, the victors, also about forty thousand in number, entered the city in force. It was four days before the Flavian legions pulled out of a city they had all but destroyed and where thousands of unarmed people were presumably killed. Primus wanted to advance on Rome. Vitellius' army had been destroyed and support for the emperor was slipping away very rapidly. The second battle outside

Cremona sealed his fate just as surely as it had brought on the suicide of Otho six months earlier.

The successful general of the first battle of Bedriacum, Fabius Valens, was at last persuaded by Vitellius to go north to join Caecina (Tac. *Hist.* 3.36).[121] He was somewhere in the Apennines when he heard of the desertion of the Ravenna fleet and in Tacitus' opinion had the time to reach Hostilia in order to persuade Caecina not to switch allegiance to Vespasian, or failing that would have been present to command the army against Primus. Those closest to him were not unanimous in their advice, some were for him making immediately for Hostilia or Cremona by back roads others thought he should summon the Praetorian Guard from Rome so that he would have the manpower to force his way through to join the army. This suggests that substantial Flavian forces were already operating just north of the Apennines but this is not reported by Tacitus and so may not be accurate. But Valens did nothing and wasted several days in apparent inactivity, which Tacitus happily censures. What is not clear is whether Valens had really recovered from his recent illness and certainly his actions in the next few weeks does not accord well with the ebullient and capable general found earlier in the account. Tacitus naturally portrays a man who was made incapable by the effects of a luxurious lifestyle when it is more likely that ill health was the cause of the change apparent in Valens' character. In response to his request for additional troops Vitellius sent three cohorts and a cavalry unit, perhaps four thousand in total, but these were already in two minds about where their loyalty lay.[122] In Valens' presence they remained faithful but he realized that these were too weak in number and resolve to be able to fight a way through to Cremona. Valens therefore sent them ahead to garrison Ariminum while he set out with a small group of friends intending to find a ship to take them to the coast of Gaul where, it is claimed, he would be able to incite the local population to rise in rebellion and seek reinforcements from Germany for an attack on Italy.[123] Tacitus gives this account as if it were feasible, although it is obviously the last desperate attempt by Valens to remain free as he does not appear to have contemplated switching his support to Vespasian. He found and perhaps commandeered a ship from Portus Pisanus (Livorno) and put in at Portus Herculis Monoeci (Monte Carlo) where he met with Marius Maturus, the proconsul of *Alpes Maritimae*. Maturus had remained loyal to Vitellius but had no troops in this small province and the procurator of neighbouring *Gallia Narbonensis* Valerius Paulinus was a friend of Vespasian and had been levying troops in order to secure the region for the Flavian cause. Maturus advised an immediate departure and with the support for Vitellius crumbling could not suggest a safe haven.[124] Valens and his small group of followers were driven in a westerly direction and beached on one of the small islands close to Massilia where he was arrested by Valerius Paulinus. Outside Italy Vitellius' cause was lost and the provinces almost unanimously swore allegiance to a new ruler, Flavius Vespasianus.[125] While Caecina was able to achieve some rehabilitation under Vespasian's rule, Valens was very clearly the object of abusive sentiment. Tacitus' coverage of Valens' last days is almost as negative as his account of Vitellius' death. Valens is said to have dawdled on his way north from Rome, moving just like Vitellius had done moving south from Germany, almost like an oriental monarch accompanied by the worst dregs of society.

Unlike Otho's death in a dark place or at least in a dim light and in a situation where there were no witnesses, Vitellius' death on the face of it should cause no anxiety because of the entirely public nature of the event. Indeed, the execution of Vitellius has much in common with the death of his predecessor Galba since both occurred in a crowded place, the centre of power, the Roman Forum. However, it is entirely reasonable to treat the events that are described in the literature with some critical analysis since some if not all are equally the product of literary invention or creation. Vitellius died in the Forum itself or possibly on the Gemonian Steps and this must have been witnessed by hundreds or even thousands. Therefore the problem of mass or crowd manipulation may be evident not to mention the intrusion or topical or generic elements demanded of writers of history.

Take, for example, from opposite ends of the chronological spectrum: first Ammianus Marcellinus (14.7.5–8) and his account of the emperors Constantius II's Caesar Gallus in AD 353.

> After this when Gallus was on the point of leaving for Hierapolis, ostensibly to take part in the campaign, and the people of Antioch came as suppliants to beseech him to save them from the fear of famine, which … was then believed imminent, he did not, following the way of rulers whose great powers sometimes cures local problems, organise any provisions or command that supplies be brought in from nearby provinces; but to the crowd, which was fearful of extreme needs, he delivered up Theophilus, the consular governor of Syria, who was standing close by and constantly reiterating the statement that no one could be without food if the governor did not wish it. These words stirred up the recklessness of the lowest elements among the crowd and when the lack of food supplies became more acute, impelled by hunger and fury they set alight the grand house of a certain Eubulus, a distinguished citizen in his community. Then as if the governor had been given to them by an imperial decree they assaulted him with kicks and blows and trampled him underfoot when he was half

dead (*conculcans seminecem laniatu miserando discerpsit*) and with terrible mutilation tore him to shreds. After his terrible death each one saw in the other an image of his own peril and dreaded a fate like that which he had just witnessed. (Ammianus, 14.7.5–8)

Next a passage from Polybius (15.33.1–12) concerned with events in Alexandria in 206 BC and the downfall of Ptolemy VI's guardian and regent Agathocles and his family and closest supporters at the climax of a brief but violent episode of civil unrest.

The bloodshed and murders which followed occurred because of the following. One of Agathocles' followers and sycophants Philo came into the stadium worse for wear because of the wine he had consumed. When he saw the popular agitation he said to those nearby that if Agathocles came out they would regret their actions as they had done some days before. When these heard Philo's comment some began to verbally abuse him, others to actually attack him physically and he tried to defend himself some soon ripped his cloak off and others ran him through with their spears. Then he was dragged still alive into the centre of the stadium where he was finished off and the crowd now turned its attention to the arrival of others. Not much later Agathocles was led in chains, and immediately following his entry certain individuals ran up and stabbed him out of kindness not hatred for they saved him from enduring the fate he really deserved. After him Nico was brought in and after him Agathoclea who had been stripped naked and her sisters were also brought in alongside her and all the members of her family. Finally, Oenanthe was dragged from the Thesmophorion and was led into the stadium naked on horseback. All of these were delivered into the mob's hands. Some began to bite them with their teeth, others stabbed them and again others tried to dig out their eyes. Whenever one of them fell they tore their bodies apart until in the end they had mutilated them all. The cruelty of the Egyptian people is infamous when they are angry. (Pol. 15.33.1–11)

Neither Ammianus nor Polybius nor anyone they knew witnessed the events which they obtained from other sources and they both composed their narratives based on a familiar code: that of death in a crowd. The victims were famous yet the record of their death was almost entirely constructed rather than a historical re-enactment. Similarly Tacitus, Suetonius and Dio, all of whom relate the death of Vitellius, faced this historical event from a chronological distance and without much or any accurate source. Each one drew on generalities and inserted appropriate detail with elaboration to suit the temperament of the writer.

In the aftermath of the second battle at Bedriacum the supporters of Vespasian made slow progress towards Rome because early and severe snow storms had blocked the Apennine passes (*Hist.* 3.59). Primus was able to cross through the mountains but the advance was much slower than it would usually have been in November. The accumulations of snow in the mountains would usually have made contact with central Italy difficult by January but this unexpected intervention by the weather extended Vitellius' time as emperor and contributed to his hopes of extracting something positive from the recent defeat. It is possible that, like Otho, Vitellius wanted to avoid further bloodshed since at that point he still had sufficient troops to mount a last stand against his opponents. But that support rapidly dwindled as the emperor vacillated between organizing a defence of Rome and the resignation of his powers for safe retirement. Abdication was not allowed him, however, by his garrison in the city that had the most to lose.

Primus led the Flavian army's advance guard to Saxa Rubra which is no more than 16 kilometres (10 miles) north of the city along the Via Flaminia, while in the city itself all order broke down following the murder of Vespasian's brother and city prefect Flavius Sabinus. Domitian Vespasian's younger son was in hiding and as his safety was in jeopardy Vitellius was persuaded to leave the palace and was carried by sedan chair to the Aventine Hill (*Hist.* 2.84), a situation that allowed the possibility of an escape south. Galba had also been taken in a sedan chair on his last journey before his assassination. This is hardly more than coincidence perhaps since most wealthy men were carried rather than choosing to walk, but is an interesting doublet nonetheless. There was fighting between the troops supporting Vitellius and Vespasian along the northern approaches to the city by the Milvian Bridge and the Praetorian Camp. There were heavy casualties especially among the defenders who had little to lose, but on the other hand, the emperor is described as being in a sort of shell shock, befuddled and in a world of his own. While the home of his wife allowed some protection for a short time his companions and entourage appear to have deserted him since he is then said to have wandered alone back to the *Domus Aurea*, the palace (*Palatium*) of Nero that he had only recently vacated. The problem with the narrative at this point is that there can have been no witnesses to Vitellius' movements in these hours and certainly no motive for his wanderings other than he was more alone than even Nero had been in his last hours. Finding no one about, the silence of the place and the solitude in which Vitellius found himself terrified him (*Hist.* 3.84: *terret solitudo et tacentes loci*). He opened doors to closed rooms and shuddered at their emptiness (*temptat clausa, inhorrescit vacuis*) and finally tired or worn out ('*fessus*') by his wandering he found a shameful hiding place (*pudenda latebra*). There he was discovered by a tribune of a cohort a certain Julius Placidus who dragged him out. This is highly dramatic but of course almost entirely invention except if a Julius Placidus later claimed to have discovered Vitellius and that this was recorded by a writer whose composition was available to Tacitus. Arguably, such a notion is implausible and the entire episode thus far was therefore one created by Tacitus. It may be entertaining but is tragedy in a narrative rather than history. Tacitus says he was led away with his arms bound up and his clothes torn. He was subjected to verbal abuse and no one pitied him (*multis increpantibus, nullo inlacrimante*) because Vitellius was held responsible for the sacking of the city, which was taking place as he was dragged away (*deformitas exitus misericordiam abstulerat* – 'the shameful ruin had driven away pity'). One of the soldiers from the Rhine legions struck at him in anger but, claims Tacitus, possibly to kill him before he was subject to further humiliation out of some memory of kindness. Instead, he sliced off the tribune's ear and was himself killed. The translation of *obvius e Germanicis militibus Vitellium infesto ictu per iram* should more likely mean a soldier from one of the German legions rather than a German soldier, although Tacitus has earlier emphasized (*Hist.* 2.32, 2.35) the formidable nature of the Batavian troops whom he terms 'German'. This definition may well also act as a sign of what is to come with the rebellion of the Batavians under the leadership of Julius Civilis. If the tribune was the same Julius Placidus then perhaps he survived and his story was indeed circulated. Vitellius was forced to raise his face since the point of a sword was placed under his chin and so look at those insulting him and also to watch while his statues were demolished and to pass by the *Lacus Curtius* where Galba had been murdered just eleven months before. The procession of Vitellius along the entire *Via Sacra* is surely meant to remind the reader of that recent occasion when Galba took exactly the route on the way to his own death, which was another public execution. It should be noted that although both might have been reviled by their eventual killers both retrieved some dignity at the point of death. When he was dragged to the Gemonian Steps, where the body of Vespasian's brother had recently been left exposed and abused, the emperor was further insulted by the tribune. Tacitus notes that Vitellius responded with the noble remark that nevertheless he had been his tormentors' ruler. He was then killed as the result of several blows and his body was left to the savage attention of a mob. (*Hist.* 2.85). Vitellius therefore might be said to have suffered the very public death that many no doubt, especially among the wealthy elite, should have wished to inflict on Nero. Yet Vitellius was much more distant from the last

Julio-Claudian than Otho, whose death while accompanied with many of the same props to the event as his former friend is related as being much more dignified. Tacitus' account of Vitellius' death represents the earliest existing commentary (*Hist.* 3.84–86) and is almost identical in length to that of his coverage of Otho's suicide (*Hist.* 2.48–50). Vitellius wandered alone through the palace not long before vacated by the man who ordered its construction and so again there is a pervasive presence of Nero in the last hours of this latest ruler of Rome.[126] Tacitus concludes this book of his *Histories* with the telling statement that there was chaos in the city but that Domitian, Vespasian's son, had come out of hiding and been greeted enthusiastically by the victorious troops of Antonius Primus.

Suetonius' account is much less extensive than that of Tacitus, yet is more specific in some of its details. Vitellius' place of refuge is named as a janitor's room where he tied a dog to the doors perhaps to sound an alarm, and barricaded these with a bed and a mattress. Soon enough soldiers dragged the unfortunate Vitellius from his hiding place and when they asked him who he was, since they did not know him, and whether or not he knew where Vitellius was, the emperor tried to escape by lying. Then when he was recognized he kept asking that he be placed under guard in some prison or other so that he could relate to Vespasian certain things concerning his rival's safety. But they tied his arms behind his back and placed a noose around his neck, tore up his clothes and dragged him half naked into the Forum and all along the *Via Sacra* among a great verbal onslaught with mocking abuse, his head pulled back by his hair, as was the custom for criminals, and also the point of a sword was placed under his chin so that he could not look down but that his face was on view to all. Some of the onlookers pelted him with mud and filth, others called him an arsonist and glutton, still others made fun of his defective body. Finally at the Gemonian Steps he was tortured for a long time and then killed and from there his body was dragged by a hook to the Tiber (Suet. *Vitellius*, 16–17). Suetonius seems to have lost interest in his subject and concludes his account of Vitellius' death and indeed the entire work, which is one of the shortest lives, quite abruptly.

Dio's epitome (64.20–21) includes some interesting elements of farce mixed in with the public performance of tragedy. The narrative follows Tacitus in essential details but seems to give Vitellius a more scheming nature. He disguised himself and hid in a kennel, which perhaps is a reference to the philosopher Diogenes the Cynic, and intended trying to escape to the river and then take a ship south to Tarracina, which was still held by his brother. It is worth noting here Dio appears to have followed Suetonius with the dog connection and embellished it and not Tacitus who may rather have had a toilet or lavatory in mind. If Dio used Tacitus he might have wanted to translate *pudendus* or shameful as *canis*, which could also have a similar meaning but that still does not explain Suetonius' use of a real live *canis*. Vitellius was soon discovered after the palace was occupied by the troops of Antonius Primus and dragged out covered in filth and blood since Dio claims that he had been bitten by the dogs. This was perhaps his first torment with worse to come since the soldiers stripped him and placed the noose around his neck and then dragged him out of the palace and along the *Via Sacra*. The procession towards the Forum follows Tacitus in that Vitellius became the butt of crude jokes and the violence of his captors. Then the German, probably to be identified as one of his bodyguard attempted to do Vitellius a favour by killing him but only manages to wound him and then kills himself in something approaching a heroic suicide. At the *Tullianum* at the foot of the Capitoline Vitellius is supposed to have said, 'And yet I was once your ruler.' From there he was dragged to the Gemonian Steps, killed and beheaded. His head was paraded around the city. The text has been embellished compared to the accounts of Tacitus and Suetonius.

The problem with the historicity of a procession through the Forum is that there was widespread fighting and looting taking place across the city so the average citizen would surely not have had the time or the inclination to participate in this latest death of a ruler. The mob referred to may therefore have been mostly enemy troops or there was not such a great crowd or the people encountered along the *Via Sacra* were from the lower sections of the social hierarchy, mostly slaves. The greater the crowd the less easy it becomes to find more than the bare outline of an event since most witnesses will have seen just a snapshot of the event. However, too few witnesses produce the same problem as is encountered in the account of a solitary suicide. The tribune Julius Placidus seems to play a large role in the events as described by Tacitus and there may be some cause here to see in this person some personal source available to the historian. Interestingly, he is absent from the accounts of Suetonius or Dio, which while taking the same general route have probably more invented elements to suit the tragedy unfolding around Vitellius.

The accounts of the suicide of Otho and the execution of Vitellius are equally difficult to accept as they appear in the sources. The private suicide is made public on the one hand and the public actually becomes private. There were supposedly no witnesses to Otho's actions yet a whole assemblage of detail is constructed. There were apparently many witnesses to Vitellius' death yet the details cannot have been easily available and the elements would fit other such public death episodes. In the end this is all about the inventiveness of the writer who employed fundamental props to enliven the narrative. How could one have a year of four emperors if there was no gruesome death to describe and AD 69 is particularly rich in that aspect? The events of this year provided Tacitus, one of the great practitioners of the art of writing history, with the perfect subject for his composition and for his genius. Otho's whole approach to his battle at Bedriacum was fatalistic and his suicide on reflection seems the natural denouement since his involvement in the military side was negligible. The murder of Vitellius follows almost an identical pattern in that he too had no military role and the drama of his death is constructed in much the same way and was as inevitable as that of Otho.

In conclusion, Tacitus' *Histories* provides by far the fullest account of the battles at Bedriacum and as a source this work provides much of the relevant information for the hostilities between the supporting armies of Otho and Vitellius and also more generally for the events in 69 leading to the accession of Vespasian. The narrative is, however, not impeccably accurate for the historian relied on the information of other sources, some written some oral and some in the tradition of the genre. A multiplicity of earlier sources is indicated, for example, between *Histories*, between 1.87 and 2.12, where there seems to be mostly a repetition of the earlier notice of the decision to launch assaults along the coast of Liguria and Narbonensis Gaul. Written material may have been extracted from the history of the elder Pliny, although he is not named, while the prominence given to Vestricius Spurinna indicates another type of source, mostly oral. Then in the death of Vitellius the looming presence of the tribune Julius Placidus in the narrative an otherwise unknown figure suggests yet another source, the tribune himself, his descendants or another writer concerned with this episode possibly Pliny. Tacitus was a master of providing the dramatic or tragic backdrop to the events he covers. The tragedy of war and unnecessary death casts a gloom over the narrative as is promised at the start of the work but that there were small shafts of light in this darkness so that the agony of civil strife is not entirely relentless. In this respect the death of Otho, not by any means really heroic and not quite modelled on the death of Cato, provides that alleviation. Vitellius, too, while his fate may have been utterly pathetic, is allowed some dignity at the end and so even in the death of this most hopeless of rulers there is allowed some spark in the darkness. The later writers make less use of the tragedy or are incapable of surpassing Tacitus, if they read him, and so fall back on minutiae (Suetonius) and even some farcical elements (Dio or Xiphilinus/Zonaras) to raise the emotional content of the text and make it more real for the audience.

Antonius Primus had entered northern Italy by the beginning of September a little more than six weeks after Vitellius had been first informed of trouble. The exposure of Caecina's duplicity only become fully appreciated by his troops on 18 October, a further six weeks in which the two sides had spent most of the time avoiding contact in an attempt on the Flavian side to establish numerical superiority, on the Vitellian to recover some of its army's expertise in battle. Once Vitellius lost his battle at Bedriacum the way to Rome lay open. The delay was caused by the weather and so a further six weeks was spent in advancing through the mountains. Once the supporters of Vespasian were across the Apennines, Rome fell to the invaders within a single day. The garrison was small, perhaps as little as three thousand troops, which was all that remained of Vitellius' Praetorian Guard while the Urban Cohorts formerly under the command of Sabinus may well have gone over to Antonius Primus before he entered the city. Rome was also not well fortified. The ancient walls attributed to one of its early kings, Servius Tullius, but more likely belonging to the third century BC served little purpose for an urban area that had long extended beyond these fortifications, which had also long before fallen into disrepair. It is therefore remarkable that the capital of an empire ranging from one end of the Mediterranean to the other was virtually defenceless. After the death of Vitellius the city was pillaged by the triumphant troops loyal now to Vespasian. Tacitus (*Hist.* 3.86) concludes his usual terse coverage of events with the comment that the day hurried to its close ('*praecipiti in occasum die*'), a day on which another emperor was murdered and a new autocrat took power.

Chronology

9 June AD 68	Suicide of Nero.
Summer AD 68	Galba made slow progress from Tarraco to Rome.
1 December 68	Vitellius arrived in Lower Germany.
1 January 69	Vitellius informed of unrest in the legions in Upper Germany.
2 January	Fabius Valens saluted Vitellius as ruler in Colonia Agrippina.
3 January	Vitellius acclaimed emperor by all the Rhine legions.
15 January	Murder of Galba and Piso in the Forum. Otho recognized as emperor by the senate.
15 January	Caecina already in Helvetia, Valens progressed towards Lugdunum.
28 February	Caecina in the Po Valley.
1 March	Annius Gallus in the Po Valley, Vestricius Spurinna in command at Placentia.
14 March	Otho left Rome with a force of between ten and fifteen thousand.
14 April	Othos's army advanced and was intercepted, resulting in the first battle at Bedriacum.
16 April	Otho committed suicide.
18 April	Otho's death announced at Rome.
24 May	Vitellius at Cremona.
18 October	Treachery of Caecina (*Hist*. 3.13). Lunar eclipse at 9.50 pm.
24 October	Second battle at Bedriacum began after dusk.
25 October	Second battle at Bedriacum concluded in the morning followed by the sack of Cremona.
28 October	Cremona destroyed and abandoned by Flavian forces.
November	Snow blocked the passes of the Apennines and slowed Primus' advance.
18 December	Surrender of last forces loyal to Vitellius at Narnia and Interamna.
19 December	Siege of the Capitoline and murder of Flavius Sabinus.
20 December	Antonius Primus arrived at Saxa Rubra. Vitellius went to the Aventine Hill.
21 December	Vitellius discovered in the palace (Nero's *Domus Aurea*) and killed in the Forum or on the Gemonian Steps.

Appendix 1: A comparison of the Details Concerning Otho's suicide in the relevant sources with that of Cato the Younger's suicide in Plutarch's biography

Martial	Plutarch	Tacitus	Suetonius	Cassius Dio
Cato and Otho	–	–	–	–
	Quelled mutiny Gave away money	*Burned letters, gave away some money. Mutiny quelled*	*Burned letters, gave away money, quelled disturbance*	*Burned letters, gave away money, quelled mutiny*
	Spoke with nephew	*Talked to Salvius Cocceianus*	*Spoke to all who came*	
	Drank a little water	*Drank water*	*Drank water*	
	Tested two swords	*Tested two daggers*	*Grabbed two knives*	
	Slept heavily and heard	*Said to have slept*	*Slept very heavily*	
With steady hand he pierced his chest	*Spoke with anonymous freedman*			
	Fell on sword and single sigh as sword cut in	*Stabbed himself*	*Stabbed himself under left nipple*	*Seized a knife and killed himself*
		Dying groans heard		
	Lamentation by servants then troops	*A single wound attested*	*Exhibited wound to those who came in*	

Plutarch's coverage of the death of Cato the Younger
Talked to son and friends
Talked with Demetrius and Apollonides
Sword sent in carried by small child
Took out sword from sheath
Tested point of sword
Finished reading Plato's *Phaedo* twice
Fell into deep sleep heard outside his room
About midnight summoned his doctor and agent

Cleanthes bandaged inflamed hand, Butas sent to enquire after safety of friends
Butas returned, heavy storm brewing
Dawn chorus
Butas came again with news of calm harbour. Ordered to leave and close the door
Stabbed himself with sword
Thrust feeble on account of injured hand
Fell and overturned counting machine
Friends, son and servants ran in
Covered in blood but bloody wound and fainted
Cleanthes pushed intestines back in and sewed up wound
Regained consciousness, pushed doctor away and reopened wound and died

Appendix 2: A Comparison of the Details in the Accounts of Vitellius' Public Execution

Tacitus	Suetonius	Cassius Dio
Taken to wife's house on Aventine Hill	Taken to father's house on Aventine, then taken back to palace	No mention of Vitellius' actions before:
Wandered back alone to the palace		
Opened empty rooms	Hid in janitor's room	Purposely went into hiding
So unnerved that he hid in a sordid place		
	Tied dog to doors	Bitten by dogs
	Used bed and mattress to block up doors	
Discovered by a tribune named Julius Placidus		
	Denied being Vitellius	Tried to lie his way out
	Asked to be imprisoned – information for Vespasian	
	Dragged along Via Sacra	Dragged along the Via Sacra
Attacked by soldier – one of his own – who was killed		A German tried to help Vitellius but wounded him then killed himself
Last words and killed at Gemonian Steps	Tortured at Gemonian Steps	Last words at the Tullianum but killed at the Gemonian Steps
	Body dragged by hook to Tiber	Beheaded
		Head paraded around city

Notes

Chapter 1

1. The coast of Ionia is therefore roughly 640 kilometres in length (400 miles), but from Ephesus to Smyrna just 58 kilometres (36 miles) in a straight line – perhaps Strabo had a Roman road in mind – but by sea 400 kilometres (250 miles). Shipping from Ephesus to Smyrna had to negotiate the broad peninsula on which Erythrae and Clazomenae were situated, Strabo, 14.1.31.

2. There were originally twelve Ionian cities that formed a socio-religious Ionian League: Miletus, Priene, Myus, Erythrae, Clazomenae, Teos, Lebedos, Colophon, Phocaea, Ephesus, and the islands of Chios and Samos (Herodt. 1.142; Strabo, 14.1.3). Smyrna was a later addition to the original twelve (Herodt. 1.143, 1.150; Strabo, 14.1.4). However, all the cities along the eastern Aegean coastal strip and the near hinterland from the Bosphorus to at least Halicarnassus were highly Hellenized, but not all were regarded formally as Greek by mainland Greeks. There were other urban settlements in Ionia, including towns such Heraclea ad Latmos but these were clearly regarded as being insufficient in size or wealth to warrant full status among the other Ionian cities.

3. For a discussion of Darius' relations with individual rulers of Greek or Hellenized cities in western Asia Minor see Austin (1990: 298–305).

4. For further discussion of the events between 490 and 480 see Chapter 2. The role and influence of Athenian or pro-Athenian literary sources for this dominant perception cannot be overlooked.

5. A strong show of force in the east before undertaking a more difficult and ambitious campaign was an understandable move by the new monarch and had been intended to ensure as much as possible that the eastern satrapies were left in a pacified condition and to reduce any chance of a rebellion while the king was absent elsewhere. Neither the satrap of Egypt nor Oroetes, satrap of Lydia, had been quick to recognize Darius as king in 522 (Herrodt. 3.126–128; Austin, 1990: 299–300). Besides these there was always a high risk of revolt in this far-flung rule.

6. At Salamis twenty years later the Persian fleet consisted of Egyptian, Phoenician, Cypriote and Cilician contingents (Herodt. 8100). There was also a Carian contingent, and ships from Samothrace, but also a substantial number of warships drawn from the cities of western Asia Minor, including Ionia and islands such as Samos and Chios.

7. At the battle of Lade in 494 the Ionians had a fleet of three hundred and fifty-three triremes, and by far the greatest number was provided by Chios, Samos and Miletus, and Lesbos (Herodt. 6.8). See further in Chapter 1.

8. The Milesian fleet by this time was, however, probably financed by the king and so de facto a Persian fleet under lease.

9. There is a clue in Herodotus that he actually marched northwest into the Carpathian Mountains and retreated from here. Herodotus (4.125) mentions a tribe he calls the

Agathyrsi who are located in this region rather than towards the Crimea, perhaps Darius' original objective. The Agathyrsi are considered to be related to the Thracians.

10. Herodotus, 4.138, gives an interesting list of the tyrants of western Asia Minor. Besides Histiaeus at Miletus there were the rulers of Abydos and Lampsacus on the Hellespont, Parium, Proconnesus, Cyzicus and Byzantium, and Aeolian Cyme, Herodotus also names the tyrants of Chios, Samos, and Phocaea.

11. Megabazus was the satrap of Hellespontine Phrygia (Herodt. 6.35). The seat of the satrap was at Dascyllium on the eastern shore of the Propontis to the west of Cyzicus.

12. Megabazus was escorting the Paeonians whom he had conquered in recent fighting from their homeland in Thrace to new homes in central Phrygia (Herodt. 5.23. 98). The satrap seems to have been especially concerned about Histiaeus fortifying Myrcinus, although any settlement that might be vulnerable to attack would have possessed some form of defences.

13. Herodotus' narrative here should be treated with some scepticism. It is possible that he had an antipathy towards the inhabitants of Asia Minor, although this was his own background. Perhaps mindful of an Athenian audience made him denigrate both Aristagoras and Scylax. His own account suggests that Megabates was officially in command of the expedition but that there was also a clash of personalities between him and Aristagoras.

14. Herodotus (5.54) gives an additional time of three days for a messenger to reach Sardis by road from Ephesus to Sardis, about one hundred and fifty kilometres (94 miles). Note further below that an army would have taken much longer than this, and the historian has in mind a single courier on horseback.

15. Hecataeus' advice is remarkable since the Greeks did not usually ransack the treasuries of their temples to finance their wars. By the fourth century this had become common practice by leaders such as Dionysius I of Syracuse. However, by leaving the treasures intact at Didyma the Milesians left an irresistible temptation for others and indeed the Persians sacked and plundered the sanctuary at the end of the war in 494. Hecataeus opposed the rebellion in 499 as must others (5.35) but he was still resident in Miletus in 494/3 (Herodt.5.126), and he clearly survived the siege (Diod. 10.25.4) and the supposed destruction of the city.

16. It is puzzling that Aristagoras himself did not go to Myus, especially since the Milesian named Iatragoras is accorded the same character trait 'cunning' that is also applied to the leader of Miletus. Aristagoras/Iatragoras may, in fact, be the same person, even if the beginning of the names differs in meaning from 'best' to 'healer'. This could be a copyist slip in the manuscript or an epithet applied to Aristagoras.

17. These were mostly tyrants just like Histiaeus who had been installed by the Persians to keep the peace in their cities. Those named were Oliatus of Mylasa, Histiaeus of Termera, Aristagoras of Cyme and Cöes of Lesbos, but several others were also imprisoned. Cöes was killed by his fellow citizens when he was returned to Lesbos, but most of these leaders were allowed their freedom. In all probability most sought the protection of Artaphernes or Otanes.

18. This cannot have been the entire two hundred warships provided by Artaphernes but those of the Greeks of Asia Minor since quite clearly by 494 these were not among the list of the allied warships at Lade.

19. The title is commonly found in modern works.

20. Gray and Cary (1926: 220).

21. It would no doubt have resonated with an audience at Athens, which would have remembered the Medizing of Pausanias after the battle of Plataea in 479 (Herodt. 5.32), and later incidents of corruption among Spartan commanders such as Gylippus, Thibron and Dercylidas by the close of the fifth century.

22. Dorieus, brother of the Spartan king Cleomenes, who was said to have participated in the defeat of Sybaris in 510, according to Sybarite survivors of the catastrophe (see Evans 2013, Chapter 1), had before his arrival in Croton supposedly spent time in North Africa and died at Erice in Sicily trying to establish a permanent Spartan colony there (Herodt. 5.42–48). Diodorus (4.23.3) relates that Heraclea Minoa was founded by the same Dorieus, but Strabo, 6.2.5, has no mention of this episode and indeed claims that the entire southern coast of Sicily was deserted in his day.

23. The story in Herodotus, 5.51, of Cleomones' young daughter Gorgo and her role in persuading the king to ignore the bribes of Aristagoras amounting to fifty talents – an immense sum for a Spartan at that time – was meant to entertain and enliven the narrative rather than offering a true episode that the historian cannot have known.

24. Thucydides, 6.59, believed that Hippias' stay in Sigeum was temporary and that he moved to Lampasacus along the coast and then to Susa where he was living in 490 before he accompanied Datis and Artaphernes to Marathon (see Chapter 2).

25. Hippias had ruled Athens for about sixteen years, 527/6 to 510 (Herodt. 5.65), and in about 500 was probably still in early middle-age, perhaps less than fifty years old. He certainly lived on beyond the battle of Marathon at which he was present in 490.

26. It is true that Sigeum is not mentioned either as a rebel or having been lost to the Persians during the conflict. Silence is also evident about cities such as Abydos, but that does not mean that they were unaffected and may simply reflect Herodotus' rather erratic coverage of events.

27. Ironically, Cleisthenes was the grandson of Cleisthenes the tyrant of Sicyon and uncle of Pericles' mother Agariste.

28. The Cyclades were certainly close enough for the Persians to launch an attack on Attica and a much easier route than overland via Thrace.

29. The Ionians traced back their roots to Attica and there was some memory of early settlers from mainland Greece setting up new homes in places such as Miletus according to Strabo, 14.1.3. True or not it was the source of an emotional link between the two communities (Herodt. 6.21).

30. Diodorus' account in Book 10 is mostly lost with just one fragment, 10.25.2–3, related to the Ionian War. Thucydides gives passing mention in Book 1 of his history of the Peloponnesian War while Plutarch has some information in his lives of Themistocles and Aristides. Writers from Asia Minor such as Hecateaus of Miletus and Xanthus of Lydia will probably have recorded many of the events that they may also have witnessed, but these accounts have not survived in part because the later Persian invasion of Greece and its outcome overshadowed the earlier episodes, and also because these writers mark the very start of Greek historical writing and were to be greatly overshadowed by the next generation of recorders especially Herodotus and Thucydides. Gray and Cary (1926: 215) also note works by Charon and Dionysius, both of whom lived at about the time of the war.

31. Oracles appear to have been regularly consulted when the Greeks began to set up new settlements outside Greece from about 750 BC, which was probably connected with Apollo

as the deity of new beginnings (Diod. 8.17.1–2): the foundation of Croton. Oracles themselves appear to be less a less important feature in Homeric society (Johnston 2008: 39), and are hardly noted although oracular sites such as Chryse in the Troad at the start of the *Iliad*, Delphi and the Necromanteion (perhaps in Epirus) in the *Odyssey* were clearly early and important cult centres. For the Trojan Cassandra's 'gift' of prophecy see Johnston (2008: 42).

32. The most famous oracle without any doubt is the advice to the Athenians to trust in their wooden walls, which was interpreted by Themistocles as referring to their fleet and not to wooden fortifications on the Acropolis as some believed.

33. There is little evidence for the operation of a democracy at Miletus during the rebellion against the Persians other than the election of generals. However, the presence of Hecataeus pleading on behalf of the Ionians at the end of the war might indicate that a system involving a wider participation in government (Diod.10.25.4). The problem with this fragment is that it clearly refers to the end of the war and perhaps after Miletus had already been sacked. Robinson (1997) has no discussion about the government of Miletus in this period and there is evidently nothing to draw on in terms of literary material. Moreover, Hecataeus, one of the most prominent philosophers and public figures of his day, may well have been chosen to represent all the Ionian cities in an embassy to the satrap Atarphernes and if he had been expelled from Miletus in 499 then lived in exile in the region.

34. The larger trireme, which became the ubiquitous warship by the end of the 490s, was probably not as much in service by 499 and hence the Athenians and Eretrians probably used smaller vessels for this expedition or perhaps a mix of the newer model and the older biremes and pentekonters.

35. Charopinus was a brother of Aristagoras. That he had influenced their election suggests that democratic institutions were not fully effective in Miletus even if the tyranny had been abolished. The choice of generals must be information Herodotus extracted from earlier recorders of such events such as Hecataeus or Xanthus.

36. It is possible that its gates had been removed as occurred at Athens in 404 BC when the city's walls including the connecting walls with the harbour at the Piraeus were sufficiently dismantled to render the city vulnerable to attack. The walls were restored soon after 394, but there were no fortified gates to the Piraeus until 378 (Xen. *Hell.* 5.4.20), when the Spartan Sphodrias invaded Attica.

37. Gray and Cary (1926: 221).

38. If the causal relationship between Persian attack and Greek offensive is maintained it is possible that the former advancing down the Meander Valley turned about when they heard that the Greeks had attacked Sardis but that would mean that Miletus was never invested.

39. There are clear and frustrating gaps in the narrative here. A shattering defeat might explain an Athenian withdrawal, but it was plainly not a catastrophic rout. The Athenian decision to break off ties remains a mystery.

40. There is clearly something missing from Herodotus' coverage since he has not mentioned Caunus or Caria before. The mention of Caunus is also interesting since it was not the most important city in the region, which was Mylasa. Therefore this may be on account based on a local source used by Herodotus or from personal recollection of a city he may well have known earlier in his life when he was at Halicarnassus.

41. It is interesting to observe how Darius made use of family members – Artaphernes was his brother – in important commands and positions throughout his kingdom on a regular basis.

42. It is also notable that Smyrna, easily as wealthy a city as Ephesus and Miletus is not mentioned at all as having participated in the war and may have remained neutral or loyal to Persia. The Hermus Valley joined Smyrna to Sardis, the most direct route into the interior of Anatolia, and as such its strategic value may have caused the Persians to retain a garrison here. Although it belonged to the league of Ionian cities its ties were perhaps less strong. Neither Herodotus nor a later source explains the absence of Smyrna from involvement.

43. Darius of course knew the Athenians well enough since Hippias their former tyrant had gone into exile in Persia in 510 and had been granted the city of Sigeum in the Troad as a residence (Herodt. 5.65). The historian's embellishment of the truth (5.105) was obviously meant for his then current and presumably a mostly Athenian audience.

44. Histiaeus' ambition was actually fairly limited to restoration of his position in Miletus not to some indefinite larger rule throughout the region and he therefore posed no threat to Darius or his satraps.

45. Herodotus probably means the centre of the line rather than on one of the wings which became the chosen place of commanders such as Philip II or Alexander the Great who invariably commanded the right wing.

46. The mention of Salaminian charioteers suggests that these were the wealthy elite who may well have been less than happy about Onesilas and his rebellion and hence their timely desertion to the Persians (Herodt. 5.113). It is also interesting to note the use of chariots among a Hellenized community whereas in Greece and even Ionia this is not attested by the late Archaic Period and points to a much stronger Persian-Oriental influence on the island than is seen further west.

47. The people of Amathus received an oracle which advised that the head of Onesilas be honoured as a hero if they wanted future prosperity.

48. The siege of Soli was successful after five months; the siege at Naxos lasted four months and resulted in a withdrawal of the besiegers. Both sieges are exceptionally long and were possibly less than Herodotus recounts.

49. The name Pixodarus and his affiliation to a certain Mausolus means that these were ancestors of a family that later became dominant and held the satrapy of Caria as if, certainly by the fourth century, it was an independent kingdom. Artemisia Queen of Halicarnassus during the Persian Wars captained a trireme at Salamis, while a later Mausolus who achieved universal fame through his tomb, the Mausoleum, are the most famous descendants of this Pixodarus.

50. The Meander although a slow moving river is deep with steep banks and is also prone to flooding, which was the primary cause for the silting up of its course through what was then the Gulf of Latmos, which is now simply a broad flood plain. The Marsyas was a smaller stream and posed fewer logistical problems for an army crossing. Strabo, 12.3.27, 12.8.15, writes that the Marsyas was a tributary of the Meander, and that Apamea in Phrygia through which it runs was close to its source. This source is said to have been a lake from which both the Marsyas and Meander flowed (Strabo, 12.8.15).

51. For the Meander River as the boundary between Ionia and Caria see Strabo (12.8.15).

52. Herodotus says that this cult was unique to the Carians, and being Carian himself should be regarded as a secure source of information. However, there may well have been a

long history to the cult since it probably has some relationship with the later Roman cult of Jupiter Stator or the 'Thunderer', which had a temple on the Palatine Hill. The Romans adopted a number of cults from this part of the eastern Mediterranean, notably the Magna Mater from Pessinus in neighbouring Phrygia, but also Ascelpius from Epidaurus in the Peloponnese, and the ideology and practice of the ruler cult, probably from Pergamum. A borrowing from the Romans of Zeus Stratios, a strikingly militaristic cult, would not be at all surprising.

53. Herodotus (5.121), probably from local sources records that a certain citizen of Mylasa named Heraclides was the commander of the Carian forces.

54. Herodotus calls this city Cius of Mysia, Mysia being a vague geographical area that could be applied to much of western Asia Minor or more specifically to that region between Aeolis and Ionia and the valley of the Caicus River. Cius was later renamed Prusias and is modern Bursa.

55. This information may have come from Hecataeus' own history of the revolt and it may also be a false scene designed to dramatize the situation, although it needed little embellishment, to stress the unreliable nature of Aristagoras and the more secure thoughts of a philosopher.

56. The date is not known but was perhaps in 494 rather than earlier but before the Persians reasserted control in Thrace.

57. His actions when seeking support from the Greeks on the mainland and his disdain for hiding on Leros in 494 indicate a figure with at least energy and ambition even if his grandiose plans were ultimately to fail.

58. Herodotus clearly used Hecataeus as his major source for many of the background details to the Persian Wars, although he is unlikely to have known or met him. Hecataeus is considered to have died about 475 BC while Herodotus was still a child.

59. Herodotus as we have seen was not averse to manipulating dates and it seems a little unlikely that Histiaeus' arrival should follow so soon on Aristagoras' departure. There may well be an element of construction in the narrative, bearing in mind that the present form of the entire history and of the Ionian Revolt now found at the end of the fifth book and the beginning of the sixth gives a misleading picture of the historian's original coverage, which may have been intended to be rather more theatrical rather than scientific.

60. The literal translation from the Greek is: 'you stitched the shoe, but Aristagoras wore it.'

61. Fortunately for Histiaeus he used the recent example of the removal of the Paeonians from Thrace to Phrygia (Herodt. 5.15). The mass movement of people was certainly fairly common in antiquity. Perhaps the most famous was that of the Jews to Babylon by Cyrus also within living memory.

62. It is notable that the Mytilenaeans were not prepared evidently to allow their ships to commit hostile acts against their neighbour Miletus.

63. No figures are identified at this stage and Herodotus may simply have not known who the leading commanders were, although some emerge later at the Battle of Lade. See further discussion below.

64. Panionium was a religious site, a *temenos*, containing a shrine to Poseidon of Helicon (Herodt. 1.148). Festivals were regularly held here, probably each year, in which all the Ionian cities participated.

65. Phrynichus' tragedy *The Fall of Miletus* was banned from production in public because of the outburst of emotion it seems to have generated at the Festival of the Dionysia in perhaps 493/2, and far from winning the prize for best play the author was instead fined a thousand drachma, a huge sum for even a successful playwright.

66. From Herodotus (6.9), it certainly looks as if the Persian land forces were already outside Miletus before any engagement at sea.

67. The Hecatomnids do not appear to have been badly affected by this war and remained in control of the region around Mylasa, including Pedasa, and perhaps even extended their control within Caria. On possible concessions granted to the Carians by Artaphernes see Gray and Cary (1926: 226).

68. It is probably significant that the text of Herodotus at the end of Book 5 looks very much like a summarizing of a more detailed source, perhaps again Hecataeus or Xanthus. Herodotus was more concerned about the later Xerxes' invasion of Greece and needed to move his account along and therefore details must have been excluded at this point.

69. For Rhodian opposition but no details see Gray and Cary (1926: 225).

70. Lade is no longer an island but became joined to the mainland with the silting up of the estuary of the Meander River. It is now just a hilly outcrop at the coast some kilometres away, but still easily discernible from the upper sections of the theatre at Miletus, which is now much further inland (see plate).

71. Myus provided three ships. This city was at the mouth of the Meander and surprisingly seems to have been ignored by the Persians who could easily have taken this small settlement en route to Miletus. Perhaps it had already fallen and these were fugitives at Priene. With the silting up of the Meander Myus was later abandoned and its people migrated to Miletus.

72. The presence of so few ships from Phocaea is remarkable seeing that it is remembered as a major colonizing city in the western Mediterranean and founder of Massilia and Velia. It is possible that Phocaean ships had already been lost to the Persians when Daurises campaigned in the area in 499, but the city would have had the resources to rebuild. It may also indicate that elements in Phocaea were against further opposition to the Persians. Phocaea, like Ephesus and Smyrna, does not appear to have suffered unduly in the aftermath of the revolt.

73. It is worth noting the absentees: Lebedos, Colophon, Ephesus and Smyrna. No reason is given for their apparent indifference but they may have already been lost to the Ionian cause. Clazomenae had already been retaken by the Persians. Still this represents nearly half the Ionian confederation. Also of interest are the statistics that show that the harbour cities Myus, Priene, Phocaea, Erythrae and Teos possessed few warships of their own while the islanders – Samians, Chians and Aeolian Lesbos – contributed by far the greater number of vessels and crews. The murder of Chian crews by the Ephesians (Herodt. 6.16) is described as a mistake, but the episode points to Ephesus being again under Persian control.

74. Gray and Cary (1926: 226) perhaps rather commenting on the effectiveness of the Persian fleet than its size; cf. Wallinga (2005: 10), who argues that the overall total of about a thousand ships is confirmation that this represents the number available to the Persian command in Xerxes' later invasion of Greece since the Ionian ships were actually those of the Persian king who had simply deserted.

75. Herodt. 5.30; Wallinga (2005: 13).

76. On the *diekplous* and the Battle of Lade see Wallinga (2005: 110–111).

77. On the relationship between the two movements see Van Wees (2004: 228).

78. Note Gray and Cary (1926: 226) for the possible existence of bias against the Ionians in Herodotus' account. His history was written at a time when these cities were members of the Delian League and allies of Athens where Herodotus was by then living. The apparent

derogatory tone of Herodotus' text may have rather less to do with the intended audience than with his Carian origin. The Carians had been at least, if not more, forceful in their conduct of this war than the Ionians but were less well remembered in the tradition.

79. Common cause is perhaps too strong a phrase since there were tensions within the Ionians and their allies some longstanding. For example, it is interesting that the Milesians and Samians were on opposite wings. In the Lelantine War of the late eighth century each had supported opposing sides, the Milesians Eretria, the Samians Chalchis. These ancient enmities may have resurfaced at this crucial point.

80. Syloson was a brother of Policrates, the tyrant of Samos in the 520s, whom he succeeded (Herodt. 3.149), in about 520 BC, and had been one of those rulers expelled in the general uprising in 499 (Herodt. 6.13). No mention of him appears here, which suggests that he died some time before the battle of Lade.

81. The Samians who remained and fought at Lade were later celebrated on a stele in their home town. Other Samians who were not in favour of a rapprochement with either the Persians or their former tyrant's son sailed off into exile and settled in Sicilian Zancle (Messene).

82. A Chian source seems highly likely given the prominence this *polis* is given in the account (Herodt. 6.15–16). Herodotus also knew Samos (Herodt. 6.14) and so may have picked up another viewpoint from a Samian source. He evidently did not try to synthesize his source material or arrive at a more comprehensive account of the battle.

83. For further discussion of this engagement see Evans (2013: 31–82).

84. The contingents from Miletus, Lesbos and Samos must also have comprised similar numbers if they possessed triremes in their fleets. The overall total in crews and armed infantry was probably in the order of fifty thousand men.

85. Herodotus oddly makes no mention of the Milesian fleet but it must have played its part in the battle for the crews of this city were no strangers to the sea or sea battles. Dionysius apparently settled somewhere in Sicily where he attacked Carthaginian and Etruscan shipping but not fellow Greeks.

86. According to Gray and Cary (1926: 227), the area was devastated, but it is perhaps more likely that in the brief spell that the city was denuded of inhabitants, that the river changed its course and that the reoccupation of the urban area took this change into account.

87. The former Milesians were resettled at Ampe on the Persian Gulf (Herodt. 6.20). Since the city was soon flourishing again many no doubt returned, or that the exiles were those who had been supporters of Aristagoras and that those who had opposed him were allowed to remain. The *chorē* or territory is said to have been assigned to Persians or to the Carians of Pedasa. The latter had clearly reached a new arrangement with the Persians when they concluded a joint peace probably the year before. Herodotus appears to contradict himself (6.25), by stating that Caria was subdued after the sack of Miletus, but this unlikely and it is more probable, given his Carian origin, that he would want his own people to be seen as more formidable enemies to the Persians than the Ionians.

88. On the antiquity of the oracle see Herodotus (1.157) and Strabo, (14.1.5), and its treasures said to have been the gift of the Lydian king Croesus (Herodt. 1.92, 5.36). The sacred spring above which the oracle was delivered reportedly dried up following the destruction of the temple and was probably deliberately blocked by the Persians. It began to flow again only in 334 when Alexander visited the shrine when the precinct was reopened. It is likely that a lack of funds caused the long hiatus in the oracle's history. It is claimed by some writers that Alexander massacred descendants of the Branchidae

whom he encountered in Sogdiana (Curtius, 7.5.28–35); cf. Diod. (17.67.1) who does not give this episode either because it is not historical or showed a negative side of the king's character. Strabo (15.1.36) claims that the precinct was destroyed by Xerxes and that the Branchidae fled with him only when the Greeks regained control of Ionia after 478. Yet Herodotus (6.19) is quite specific in stating that the Persians who were under the direct command of Artaphernes were responsible for this act in 494. There was evidently some confusion among commentators dealing with the history of the oracle at Didyma. See Tarn (1948: 272–273), for example, on Alexander and the historicity of his killing of the Branchidae.

89. Thasos was soon occupied by the Persians who encountered no opposition, says Herodotus (6.44), compared to the resistance that greeted Histiaeus only shortly beforehand. The Thasians clearly preferred the prospect of Persian rule to that of a fellow Greek.

90. Herodotus' chronology is far from precise. The Ephesians had been celebrating the harvest when they killed the Chian refugees from Lade. Then Histiaeus returned and then campaigned against Thasos, all in the space of the autumn of 494. This is a further indication that the Thasian expedition is likely to have been either an earlier episode in Histiaeus' adventures or invented by Herodotus. That Chios was now hostile towards Histiaeus seems likely since Atarneus was a Chian town that the Chians had received from the Persians during the reign of Cyrus (Herodt. 1.160).

91. Herodotus (6.30) states that Histiaeus was impaled, decapitated, and the head preserved, which was sent on to Susa.

92. Tenedos is not mentioned elsewhere as having participated in the war, but was one of the Aeolian *poleis* and so perhaps had an alliance with Aeolian Lesbos.

93. Herodotus, 6.33, mentions that Cyzicus was not attacked yet this city was on the eastern side of the Propontis and close to Dascyllium, the satrapal capital of Hellespontine Phrygia, and that the people of Cyzicus had reached a settlement with the satrap, named as Oebares. This had probably occurred sometime before the battle at Lade when Daurises and Hymaees campaigned here in 499/8. Herodotus' geographical knowledge can be surprisingly vague, but his mention of Cyzicus may also be indicative of a memory that this area too was unstable and that its cities, freed from strict Persian control, went through periods of rebellion between 499/8 and 493. Note too that the island of Proconnesus and the town of Artace on the same peninsula as Cyzicus were also attacked. The general instability may have been connected with Histiaeus' recent acts of piracy.

94. Herodotus uses 'Phoenician' to describe the Persian fleet whereas at Lade contingents from Cilicia, Cyprus and Egypt are noted. It is possible that the Persians were employing just Phoenician warships in these operations or that the historian is using the name 'Phoenician' rather loosely for the entire Persian fleet.

95. If one ignores, of course, such episodes as the Ephesian killing of Chian refugees from Lade or the Samian and Lesbian desertion from the Greek fleet on the same occasion. Local infighting was a commonplace in the region if Xenophon's *Anabasis* (7.8) is any guide to the state of affairs in Mysia, but there the raiding was between Greek and Persian communities not among just the Greeks. Herodotus statement (6.42) looks as if it comes from a source closer to a Persian than Greek tradition.

Chapter 2

1. Herodotus even repeats the tale (Herodt. 6.94) but also adds the more convincing information that the family of Hippias, ex-tyrant of Athens, constantly raised the issue of

the conquest of Athens, which might bring it back to power as vassal of the king. Hippias may by then have been living in Susa rather than in Sigeum especially after Mardonius seems to have replaced many tyrants with more participative forms of government in the cities of western Asia Minor.

2. Mardonius replaced Oebares who was satrap as late as 493 (Herodt. 6.33). Artaphernes was probably still satrap of Lydia but may well have died before Marathon since one of the two Persian commanders of that expedition is categorically named as Artaphernes the son. The younger Artaphernes evidently succeeded his father as satrap since he was in command of a contingent from Lydia and Mysia during Xerxes' invasion (Herodt. 7.74), and so had not been punished for his failure in 490 although he was clearly not among the circle of military commanders closest to the king.

3. Herodotus argues that the installation of democracies proves that his description of a discussion of the ideal constitution in which Otanes spoke in favour of democracy shows that this episode must have had a historical basis and that the Persians were open to the arguments for such a government.

4. That Artaphernes is given no credit is noteworthy, and perhaps indicates his absence or death when Mardonius visited the region.

5. Three hundred ships is perhaps an exaggeration, although the crews of this number of warships of trireme design would total roughly sixty thousand, and twenty thousand dead would not be incompatible with the sort of proportion expected to be lost in such circumstances. The losses probably represent warships and transports, especially the latter, which would have been present to supply the army on the move.

6. It may be that Mardonius lost his place as satrap but that is not specifically noted by Herodotus. The losses incurred under his command had been huge but that would not necessarily have put him in disgrace and his command had lasted barely a full campaigning season, so it is certainly possible that he remained as satrap of Hellespontine Phrygia and Thrace but not in command of the forces to be directed in the future against Athens and Eretria.

7. Herodotus, 6.48, does not specify which cities were expected to contribute ships to a new expedition and it might have been applied to the whole coastal zone of the eastern Mediterranean including Egypt, Phoenicia, Cilicia and Cyprus. However, a particularly heavy burden will again have fallen on the cities recently re-conquered by the Persians.

8. Herodotus, 6.49, does not name the Medizing cities or states and says only that these were numerous. Among them were the cities of Thessaly since the Macedonian king their immediate neighbour to the north already had a treaty with the Persians. The most significant perhaps then but certainly later was Thebes the chief city of Boeotia whose pro-Persian stance in the war against Xerxes was never forgiven or forgotten.

9. Mardonius had no role in the Marathon campaign, but he may still have been satrap with the command over Thrace and hence more involved in the overall strategy than is presented by Herodotus. The ethnic background of Datis is reiterated by Diodorus (10.27.1). Artaphernes was Darius' nephew.

10. A trireme might have held thirty horses comfortably, a bireme perhaps just twenty.

11. While Herodotus explicitly differentiates between 'horse carrying ships' and 'triremes', he claims that the infantry were carried in the warships. The mention of cavalry must mean that mounted troops were not merely a few scouts but were a substantial section of the army.

12. This is the stretch of sea west of Samos to the Cyclades and includes the island of Icaria. The Persians, according to Herodotus (6.98), had received additional forces and supplies from Ionia and Aeolia while they were at Delos.

13. Herodotus (6.97) does not give the reason why Datis should be more sympathetic and generous to the Delians when the cult centre at Didyma had recently been destroyed. Datis may have been instructed to be lenient with the Greek states other than Athens and Eretria while the sack of Naxos was merely an instance of revenge. He may also have made a private pledge to the Delian deities for a successful outcome of the campaign and indeed was conspicuous – perhaps too liberal – in his gifts to the cult. An earthquake soon after his departure should, however, have alerted him to future disaster. Note that unlike in the main episodes of the Ionian War, Herodotus works into his narrative the supernatural and especially the oracular power over the events.

14. Carystus had strategic value at the southern end of Euboea but the Persians were clearly under orders not to cause needless damage where they went and to concentrate their anger on Eretria and Athens.

15. Athens had defeated the Chalcidians in the Lelantine War, which dates to about 550 BC, following which Athenian settlers had been given land near Chalcis on Euboea itself. Herodotus does not say where these troops were mustered from, and whether they came only from Chalcis a mere twenty kilometres (12 miles) north of Eretria. They returned to Oropus, which suggests some inaccuracy in Herodotus' narrative since it would have been easier to return north than go to Attica. These four thousand troops also do not feature later on and it has been argued that this military intervention was either a later invention designed to conceal Athenian reluctance to help its ally or that the four thousand troops mentioned actually represent the Athenian war fleet of twenty triremes, Munro (1926: 237). The Athenian fleet probably numbered about forty warships by this time, but if these were naval rather than infantry personnel it would also mean that they were light armed. In later times such troops, who also rowed the ships, would have been described as peltasts, and not the usual citizen hoplites, and probably an important point to remember in discussing any battle involving Greek troops before the mid-fifth century.

16. Eretria on Euboea is clearly visible from Oropus, the most northerly community of Attica and an important port for the Athenians, which lies directly opposite across the stretch of sea called the Euboeic Channel. At this point the straits, according to Strabo (9.2.6), are 60 stadia wide, about twelve kilometres or roughly 7½ miles, but at Chalcis this narrows to merely two hundred metres, a little more than 200 yards. It would have been useful for the Persians to have occupied Chalcis but under strict orders to attack Athens they evidently ignored this strategically important site entirely.

17. For a more detailed discussion of Gongylus and his family and possessions in Mysia see Evans (2012: 4–22).

18. Interestingly enough, Hippias was given charge of these captured Greeks, whom he transported to a transit camp on the island of Aegilia near Styra. After he had carried out this task he arrived at Marathon where the rest of the assault force was disembarking. He had been troubled by the contents of a dream he had had the previous night in which he had slept with his mother and which he interpreted as a successful outcome to his ambitions to return to Athens. However, on the beach he had a violent fit of sneezing and, says Herodotus, since his teeth were loose on account of his advanced age, he lost one in the sand. All attempts to find the tooth failed and he realized that in fact his tooth held the only part of his ancestral land that he would ever have and hence the dream was a portent for failure.

19. Strabo (10.1.10) says that the city was destroyed and its citizens rounded up by the Persians using the same tactic of a human cordon as they had employed elsewhere on the island. He does not mention the sanctuary of Athena but refers to one of Artemis some 7 stadia (1.5 kilometres, 4000 feet) outside the Eretria of his day.

20. Herodotus duly notes (5.123) that once the Eretrian prisoners had been paraded before Darius he had them resettled near Susa.

21. See Munro (1926) facing 241 for the names of the individual summits of these mountains.

22. Attica had been divided by Cleisthenes into ten tribal divisions, each of which contributed one thousand hoplites to the army and a general to command them, hence the ten generals or *strategoi* and a standing army of ten thousand. The role of the cavalry was important but draws less comment from the sources, which often do not differentiate between infantry and cavalry units.

23. The marathon, an event in today's Olympic Games, is obviously a modern creation and had no ancient equivalent and certainly did not feature in the ancient games held in Olympia, Delphi, Nemea or Athens or indeed anywhere else. The Pan-Hellenic contests of antiquity contained no long distance running events.

24. It is a curious doublet that both Aristagoras of Miletus in 500/499 and Pheidippides in 490 should both have received negative replies and surely illustrates a certain amount of antipathy towards Sparta even if later in the wars it redeemed itself.

25. At this time, each year the Athenians elected three officials entitled archons as the senior figures of the state: the eponymous archon, the basileus archon and the polemarch who was the senior military commander.

26. Miltiades' fall from grace was equally dramatic and he died in exile. Curiously, Herodotus states that he was the tenth general, although he must have been representing one of the tribes. Miltiades' family belonged to the deme Oeneis, which was situated towards Mount Parnes in western Attica.

27. Miltiades' own position was threatened if the Athenians were defeated since he was obviously a well-known figure to the Persians. He is said to have argued that the possibility of the return of Hippias should spur the Greeks on to fight and not risk coming to terms with the invaders.

28. The victory is ascribed to Athens and Plataea alone but it is not impossible that some of the other Greek communities in the region were represented there, in particular survivors from Eretria and Carystus.

29. Some maps confine the battlefield to a rather small area between two streams, although the main river midway in the bay is the Charadra. Munro (1926) notes possible extensive marshland at either end of the bay and which was perhaps visible in the early twentieth century but no longer with modern building developments. In 490 BC the land may have consisted of tidal flats, although in late summer probably quite dry if Hippias considered the bay suitable for cavalry deployment.

30. Aeschylus in his tragedy *The Persians* also describes an attack on the ships reached by the charge of the Athenians, an encounter in which his own brother was killed. It is obviously based on historical fact but this is drama not history and Herodotus may have reused this material in his own account without knowing if it was really accurate. The main Persian force was clearly unaffected by this charge since most of the fleet escaped damage.

31. See, for example, Caesar's description of the interaction between Germany cavalry and infantry in his fight against Ariovistus in Book 1 of *The Gallic Wars*.

32. It is also worth noting that Thucydides in his coverage of the Athenian expedition against Syracuse in 415 up to its catastrophic climax in September/October 413 constantly refers to the lack of cavalry among the invading force and the Syracusan strength in this military arm, Evans (2013: 3181).

33. Munro (1926: 246–248) details the battle but assumes a rapid advance only about two hundred metres (200 yards) from the enemy which would not be correct if large numbers of cavalry were deployed by both sides. Van Wees (2004: 180) raises doubts about the worth of Herodotus' testimony regarding the charge of a supposedly hoplite force but does not purse the obvious conclusion.

34. See Munro (1926: 246) and his useful and detailed map facing 241.

35. Herodotus, 6.112, includes the curious information that this was the first occasion that a Greek army made a running charge against an enemy and also the first time the Greeks fought against men in Persian dress without being afraid even to 'hear the name Mede'. Yet neither comment is credible since the Athenians had sent four thousand citizens to aid the Ionians in 499, joined in the sack of Sardis and been defeated at Ephesus on their retreat to the coast, and charging in battle was hardly an uncommon practice.

36. Munro (1926: 246–248); cf. Lazenby (1993: 67).

37. Van Wees (2004: 180).

38. On this total as an invention see Marincola (1996: 587). It has also been suggested that numerous Persians, probably non-combatants died in marshes to the north and south of the battlefield. The existence of marshland in the Bay of Marathon suggests a higher sea level than today where no salt marshes are evident.

39. The latter was a brother of the playwright Aeschylus who also fought in the battle and provides evidence of the battle in his tragedy *The Persians*, written some years later in Sicily.

40. It was usual whenever a rout occurred for the losing infantry to throw away heavy armour in order to make escape easier but at the same time left them vulnerable to attack by pursuers and explains to a large extent the high casualties on losing sides in battles in antiquity. Camp followers and servants had no armour or weapons so were easily singled out by the victorious side.

41. See Sabin (1996: 59–77) who discusses, in the context of the Second Punic War (218–201 BC) the reasons for the relative extremes in casualties between the victorious side and the vanquished. His arguments are certainly applicable to any period in the Ancient World, although he ignores the additional presence of non-combatants on the battlefield which the ancient sources frequently note.

42. Munro (1926: 249) postulates an early morning assault: 'a brief affair, a morning's work before luncheon', although Herodotus claims a long fight, but is probably correct to attribute to the Athenians a double attacking column rather than a static drawn up line, which would have fallen apart in the attack. A morning attack would also have meant that the Athenians faced into the rising sun and rising temperatures not the soundest of tactics which could easily have been avoided. If the Athenians had been camped in the hills for some days they need not engage until they were ready.

43. For the inscription see Meiggs and Lewis (1969: 35); Tod (1946: 16–17).

44. Excavations of this tumulus apparently yielded evidence of just eleven inhumations.

45. For the fresco see, for example, Neils (2001: 18–19); Meiggs (1972: 276). Cimon's wife was Isodice. The fresco was painted about 460 soon after Pericles became de facto ruler of Athens.

46. Plutarch, *Cimon*, 17–18; *Pericles*, 9, who notes that Cimon's sister Elpinice was instrumental in bringing the two together as allies, although they were probably never comfortable with each other's political stance, Cimon being much more conservative than Pericles.

47. For a discussion of the Callimachus inscription see Tod (1946: 16) who notes that the polemarch appears to have promised a dedication to Athena prior to the battle and that this was fulfilled later perhaps by family members. For the identification of a statue of Nike (Victory) as the dedication see Meiggs and Lewis (1969: 33–34).

48. Plato states that the Spartan forces arrived on the day after the battle, Munro (1926: 251), but whether that means Attica, Athens or Marathon is left uncertain.

49. Based on the figures provided by Herodotus for the battle of Plataea in which 5000 Spartiates were accompanied by 35,000 helots, a force of 2000 Spartiates would indicate an army of around 15,000 and even more if allies such as Tegea, Mantinea and Corinth were requested to send troops as well.

50. Neils (2001) 11-26, notes that the Parthenon was erected as a memorial to the victories at Marathon and Salamis. However, the preponderance of cavalry on the frieze suggests a quite different message and that it has nothing to do with the increase in the number of hippeis or cavalry at Athens in the 430s, contra Neils, 184, but rather reflects the role of this element in the army in the battle in 490.

51. It is fortunate for modern scholars that although Diodorus' account lies in a single fragment and clearly knew his Herodotus, he chose to employ the later Athenian historian Ephorus as his main source. In so doing he gives a glimpse of another interpretation, perhaps much embellished and a more elaborate interpretation, of the wars against Persia.

52. That Rhamnous should have become associated with Marathon is hardly surprising considering its position just north of the plain where the battle took place. The Persians could easily have put into Rhamnous, which is opposite Euboea between Eretria and Carystus (see plate) on their way to Marathon but was equally accessible from their landing site in the bay.

53. Herodotus (6.115) relates that the Persian fleet, or a part of it, collected the Eretrian prisoners from Aegilia on the way to Athens. If accurate it suggests that at that stage the Persian commanders considered an invasion of Attica still possible.

54. The attraction of Phaleron is easily accountable for it is visible from the Acropolis, while the Piraeus is at a lower altitude and out of sight to the south east of the city. However, the Piraeus offered two easily fortified harbours either side of the promontory of Munychia, and with the advent of the trireme fleets, which needed to be berthed and repaired and kept in constant readiness, boat sheds became a necessity, which the flat beach at Phaleron could not provide as securely.

55. Herodotus (6.109) has Miltiades talk of the decay or corruption that might infect the Athenians if there is a further delay in fighting the Persians.

56. Cynosarges was situated between Athens and Phaleron. At Marathon the Athenian camp was also said to have been in or near a shrine dedicated to Heracles.

57. If the battle was late in the afternoon Phaleron one hundred kilometres (70 miles) from Marathon cannot have been reached the following morning or indeed for some days given the size if the fleet and the need to supply crews and animals. The invasion fleet would not have been able to anchor off Phaleron for too long either for exactly the same reasons and Datis must have ordered the fleet to find another beaching place along the coast. He could not simply have sailed back to Euboea. If the Persians took longer than a

single night to sail from Marathon then the question of halts for the fleet becomes even more complicated since rowers did not usually spend the night at sea and certainly not more than one unless absolutely necessary.

58. The history of this image is left untold, whether it was originally brought to Delos or whether it had been stolen from Delium and by whom. The Persians are not known to have reached Delium in this expedition and so Datis may have been intervening in an older dispute.

59. Herodotus notes an oracle given to the Thebans about the return of Apollo's image, which Datis had returned to Delos and which the Delians were supposed to return to Delium. The Thebans duly returned the image to its home (Herodt. 6.118). However, this hardly relates to the Marathon campaign. Strabo (9.2.6) confirms that a cult to Apollo was to be found at Delium that was 'in imitation to that at Delos.'

60. Note the tale of the cause of the blindness of Epizelus who is reported to have said that a phantom giant appeared before him just before he lost his sight in the battle (Herodt. 6.117).

61. Herodotus says that Mandrocles was well rewarded for the task and dedicated a picture of his accomplishment to Hera at the deity's temple on Samos (Herodt. 4.88).

62. The older of the modern bridges (1973) over the Bosphorus has a span of one thousand and seventy-four metres, the newer bridge (1988) has a slightly longer span of one thousand and ninety metres.

63. For a positive view see Barker (2005: 29); Hammond and Roseman (1996: 90–91); cf. Wallinga (2005: 24), who hardly mentions the bridges.

64. Thucydides (7.59–60) has much the same information but does not give the time scale, which Diodorus probably obtained from another source, either Ephorus or the Syracusan Philistus.

65. See Barker (2005: 29) for a detailed discussion of this point.

66. Herodotus (7.36–37), gives an account of the cables, their origin and composition and preparation. The question of the cables said to have joined the ships that composed the two bridges has also come under scrutiny and opinion remains divided between those who consider that this was feasible especially if the cables had been assembled locally and those who consider that such as feat was impossible at this period.

67. The name Harpalus of Tenedos has become attached to the episode but seems to be a modern invention since Herodotus, nor any other ancient source such as Diodorus or Plutarch, mentions a specific figure connected with the design of the Hellespont bridges; cf. Munro (1926: 269) for the name but no source.

68. Shipbuilding and the production of all other necessary war materials including armour will have occupied not only those cities in western Asia Minor, Cyprus, Phoenicia and the recently pacified Egypt.

69. On the total number of Persian warships at Doriscus see Walllinga (2005: 45). The ships used for the bridging of the Hellespont cannot have been reused for the expedition into Greece since the bridges were supposedly left standing until destroyed in a storm at the start of autumn 480.

70. Strabo (fr. 56) refers to a single bridge of Xerxes between Madytus and Sestos and states that this was one hundred and seventy stadia (21.6 kilometres or about 13 miles) from Eleus, which lies at the entrance to the Hellespont. Of course, he may have meant the bridging of the Hellespont rather than specifically one construction. For a map of the Hellespont see also Talbert (1985: 27).

71. Munro (1926: 270) believed that the ships once used in the bridge could have been redeployed in the fleet afterwards, although this seem rather unlikely, but is sceptical of a storm having been the cause of the disappearance of the bridge. Cardia is said to have been the place where much of the equipment used for the bridge's construction was stored (Herodt. 9.115).
72. Barker (2005: 5) follows the suggestion of Burn (1984: 337).
73. Note the Greek spies caught by Xerxes but there will surely have been others who might report back what they saw or claimed to have seen (Herodt. 7.146–147).
74. Wallinga (2005: 39–42) argues that a significant number of the ships in the fleet were manned by 'skeleton' crews and that these ships were brought fully into service when the need arose and by crews coerced from various cities and islands along the invasion route. He mentions Carystus in this respect. However, undermanned ships will not have kept pace with the others so it is perhaps more likely that all ships were fully manned but that replacement rowers were always in high demand. And Herodotus indicates (7.122–123) that reinforcements were drawn from the Greek cities along the coast of southern Thrace, both for the army and fleet including Mende, Torone and Olynthus.
75. Among those listed with their preferred armour and dress are Persians, Medians, Assyrians, Bactrians, Indians, Arabs, Lydians, and Thracians. Homer was clearly in Herodotus' mind (7.20), during the composition of this section since he also refers to the participants in the Trojan War as being less than those under Xerxes' command. Homer (*Iliad*, 2.572–989) lists all the Greeks commanded by Agamemnon and all the Trojans and their allies. Thucydides (7.57–58), seemingly not to be outdone by Herodotus, gives precisely the same sort of information for all the cities and peoples involved in the siege at Syracuse in 413. Cataloguing the elements of these composite armies when marching or just prior to a climactic battle becomes something of a *topos* or topical element in ancient historical writing. Munro (1926: 271), noting the Homeric connection, considers also that Herodotus had access to some official documents for his list but that need not have been the case at all and an intermediate source is much more likely given that the date of composition of the history is perhaps as late as 430 BC.
76. Bubares was evidently the son of Darius' general Megabazus. Artachaees, a relative of Xerxes, died soon after the canal was completed (Herodt. 7.117). This must again be information Herodotus obtained from an earlier source.
77. However, Herodotus (7.122) notes that the fleet used the canal probably using an earlier and perhaps Ionian source for this information.
78. See some of the highly interesting points raised by Barker (2007: 1–13).
79. Markets were usually ad hoc affairs that sprang up wherever the army or navy halted or where for example (Herodt. 7.23), the workers – mainly infantry from the army – on the canal at Mount Athos had their encampments.
80. The fact that the Persians were not prepared to rely on local resources illustrates the lack of development on the European side of the Hellespont where the cities were small with a hostile hinterland. Although there were Hellenized towns and markets along the proposed route none were major urban centres while these proliferated in Asia Minor. Herodotus specifically states (7.23) that the grain was transported as flour for baking, although camels also carried flour for the troops when they were marching through Thrace (Herodt. 7.125).

81. Note that it is placed north of Perinthus by Greene (1987: 677), which is copied from the Loeb translation (Harvard 1920–1925) where Xerxes' bridging of the Hellespont is also incorrect.
82. The modern town has two harbours, one of these may have been described as Tyrodiza. If Tyrodiza was situated on the Melian Gulf it may have had the same relationship that Posidonia had to Sybaris. Tyrodiza on the Aegean may have been a useful harbour for the Perinthians to possess if they were ever in conflict with their neighbours who controlled the entrances to the Propontis, Byzantium to the north and Abydos or Lampsacus to the south. Munro (1926: 270) voices some scepticism of its location but that if it was near Perinthus it might suggest that some of Xerxes' army crossed at the Bosphorus and made for Doriscus from the north.
83. Herodotus' use of more than a single source seems likely since he enumerates a second time for Xerxes' army and naval arm as it marched through Thessaly (7.185–186), which is much the same but an embellishment on the first notice which actually appears twice for the army.
84. The Rhodians are probably meant by this phrase.
85. For the variant numbers given in the sources see Wallinga (2005: 32 n.1). The number of triremes is also given by Aeschylus in his tragedy *The Persians* (340–343), and is chronologically the closest extant evidence. Aeschylus claims that the Persians at the battle of Salamis possessed a thousand plus twice one hundred and seven, a total of 1207. See also Wallinga (2005: 34 n. 7). Herodotus must have used Aeschylus for the total figure and an intermediate source for the composition of the fleet. But the figures for Salamis and for the review at Doriscus and Cape Sepias (7.184) are extremely problematic since by the time the Persians reached Phaleron in late August 480 they had suffered heavy losses from storms along the coast of Magnesia (7.190: 400 ships of various sorts), and during the battle at Artemisium (8.6, two hundred ships sent around Euboea, 8.11, thirty warships on the first day of action, 8.16–17, heavy losses on the second day). Herodotus does not reiterate the total of 1207 for Salamis so may have considered Aeschylus' figure incorrect for that battle and referred to the crossing of the Hellespont. There is certainly some confusion between the two sources, which is not easily explained. Herodotus' figures include 3000 pentekonters compared with Diodorus' triaconters, which inflates the overall manpower involved whereas at 7.97 he claims a mixture of vessel types and includes the horse transports and other boats in his total number.
86. Doriscus remained a Persian outpost in Europe long after the Greek victory over Xerxes and only fell into Macedonian hands after Alexander's invasion of Asia in 334 BC. Its presence in Thrace throughout the Classical period fully exposes the close proximity of Persian rule and culture to the Greeks.
87. The frequent use of the lion in monuments or artworks, for example the tomb of 'Philip II' at Vergina contained the image of a lion hunt worked in ivory, shows that it was not unfamiliar to the communities of the time. And lion hunts were a common enough pasttime of the elite.
88. Pydna may have been given to Alexander at this time by Xerxes since it was evidently under Macedonian rule by the end of the 470s when Themistocles passed through on his way into exile to Asia Minor (Thuc. 1.137). Methone, however, remained independent until it was captured and added to the kingdom by Philip II in 354 BC.
89. Therme was renamed Thessalonica in 315 BC by Cassander, one of the successors of Alexander the Great. Cassander, son of Antipater, who made himself king in Macedonia

named the city after his wife who was also a sister of Alexander. Thessalonica became the main urban centre of that entire region to be eclipsed only after the foundation of Constantinople in the fourth century AD.

90. The sea has retreated a considerable distance in the Thermaic Gulf so the distance was further than it is today but also provided sufficient beaching area for the vast fleet.

91. Herodotus (7.130) gives this retort as another instance of the pride of the king since to dam the Pineus would have been an immense project. There was a belief that Thessaly had originally been a lake until an earthquake allowed it to drain to the sea (Herodt. 7.129).

92. Except for Thespiae and Plataea in Boeotia, Athens, Sparta and its Peloponnesian allies, most of the Greeks were prepared to Medize seeing no successful outcome from sustained hostilities even with the victory at Marathon ten years before to take comfort from. Argos is omitted from Herodotus' list here but its neutrality in the war was virtually the same as those states that chose Persian suzerainty. No heralds had been sent to Athens and Sparta since previous envoys sent by Darius had been killed (Herodt. 7.133). Those Greek states that chose to fight on made a pledge – at a meeting of allies which was convened at Corinth – that if they were successful in their war they would dedicate to Apollo at Delphi an offering that would be made up of a fine levied on 10 per cent of the wealth from all those Greeks who had submitted to the Persians (Diod. 11.3.3).

93. The Thessalians were known for their strength and excellence in cavalry.

94. Herodotus claims that the Greeks withdrew while Xerxes was at Abydos (7.174), that the Thessalians felt deserted and so surrendered to the Persians. This appears to be from a Thessalian source. Yet that would also mean that Thessaly had deserted to the king by May not when Xerxes was in Therme in June.

95. As indeed seems to be the case in Diodorus' account (11.2.5–6), and that the Greek army arrived only after the Thessalians had offered to submit to Persian rule.

96. Note that Herodotus (Herodt. 7.55–56) also says that Xerxes witnessed the crossing of his army, which took seven days and nights without interruption. However, in this passage Xerxes appears to have crossed twice or that Herodotus had access to two different sources, which disagreed about the order of events and which he reproduces without deciding which was the more likely. Salamis is always dated to late September, which meant that it was a battle that the Persians could not lose for if they did, as it turned out, the invaders would have to retreat from Attica. Xerxes was in Athens for about a month before the battle took place, hence from late August. He arrived in Athens about ten days after Thermopylae.

97. Eurybiades appears to have been the senior commander with Leonidas assigned to the land forces and Themistocles as adviser is matter dealing with the fleet, Diod. 11.4.2.

98. Thermopylae today is a little underwhelming since the sea has retreated about five kilometres (three miles) and the land has encroached on the Gulf of Lamia so that the modern road is several kilometres inland. At the same time the overhanging cliffs are less obvious and the main and busy national highway from Athens to Thessaloniki, which continues to use this route hardly contributes to the atmosphere. A little further to the south near the modern village of Molos there is more of a sense of what it must have appeared like in antiquity since here the sea remains close to the high ground which is still an imposing sight.

99. Diodorus (11.4.4–5) notes that there were another seven hundred probably Helot light armed troops with the Spartiates.

100. Herodotus does not mention the Melians (cf. Diod. 11.4.4–5), but notes that the Thebans served under compulsion since Thebes wished to Medize. Further troops especially from the Peloponnese were promised although events overtook this plan if it was ever seriously considered.

101. This suggests that both *poleis* had already taken the decision to abandon their cities and that plans for an evacuation were already underway, although it was usually claimed that the Athenians only shipped their citizens across to Salamis and Troezen after Thermopylae had fallen. There would have been insufficient time to put a full evacuation into effect in such short notice. Xerxes arrived in Attica just ten days after the Persian victory.

102. Note that Herodotus (7.222) claims that Leonidas kept the Theban troops as hostages so that their cities would not Medize; cf. Diodorus (11.4.7) who states that these hoplites were not Persian sympathizers. See Marincola (1996: 593) for a discussion of Herodotus' evidence.

103. Two of the three hundred Spartiates are said to have been absent because of illness, one of whom returned in time to die at Thermopylae the other died at Plataea (Herodt. 7.229–231).

104. Just a few weeks later in September the Greeks gathered three hundred and seventy-eight triremes at Salamis (Herodt. 8.48). Two late arrivals, deserters from the Persian fleet, gave a final total of three hundred and eighty at the battle with the Persian fleet (8.82). But note the apparent existence of another tradition, perhaps from Ephorus, which accounts for the discrepancy in Diodorus' account (11.12.4), and a total of 280 with 140 provided by the Athenians at Artemisium.

105. The tale is suspect, the ship which is said to have beached was Athenian but had fled north not south from Sciathos (Herodt. 7.181–182), which is unlikely seeing that it would have sailed in the direction from which the Persians had arrived.

106. The Hellespont is northeast of Cape Sepias so this storm was actually another example of the severe etesian winds blowing in from a northerly or northeasterly direction during the summer months. And this was July the height of the etesian winds' season.

107. The treasures lost from these ships made the local wealthy for many years afterwards (Herodt. 7.190).

108. The problem of the number of Persian ships at Salamis must be left for a later discussion but is fraught with difficulties and seemingly irreconcilable data provided by Aeschylus, Herodotus and later sources. Wallinga (2005) has tackled this issue to some extent. Note that beside 400 triremes lost at Cape Sepias a further 15 were captured by the Greek ships that had remained stationed at Artemisium (Herodt. 7.194).

109. Diodorus (11.14.2) records merely that the order was to pillage the site.

110. See Marincola (1996: 595) for some indication of the debate about the Delphic oracle's political sentiments and that this tale was invented much later. Both Athens and Sparta were members of the Amphictionic council and were staunch opponents of a compromise with Persia, so the real political position of Delphi is therefore much more complex.

111. On a recent visit to Delphi entrance to the stadium is no longer allowed because of falling rocks and (see plate) a large fissure has opened up in the rock face probably because of earth movement or a severe winter. A similar fissure further along above the sanctuary of Athena Pronaia coupled with a timely earth tremor will have accounted for the scattering of the Persian attackers. Still Apollo did look after his oldest home!

112. Glorious defeats are often as celebrated as famous victories: for example, Gordon of Khartoum, the Charge of the Light Brigade; Custer's Last Stand; Siege of the Alamo.
113. See Van Wees (2004: 311 n. 14) who cites Plutarch, *Camillus* (19.3.6) for 1 September = 6 Boedromion, but that arguments have been advanced – Lazenby (1993: 118–119) claims that the date was actually 11 September; cf. Munro (1926: 145), who argues improbably for September or October of the previous year. I suggest here an earlier date because of the synchronization with the festival of Apollo Carneus and that the Persians would probably not have left this invasion until the onset of autumn, and that a mid-August attack would have been in keeping with the meticulous preparations adopted by Datis. There seems little to doubt in Herodotus' mind of when the battle occurred, and that it was August rather than September. The battle at Salamis in 480, however, almost certainly happened in late September.

Chapter 3

1. In fact, late in November 50 BC, see Evans (2013: 160–161).
2. Peskett (1914: ix–x).
3. Afranius had served with Pompey in the East and had obtained the consulship in 60 through the latter's support. Petreius had been praetor in 64, and Varro a praetor in 74. Varro is better remembered as a literary figure but he was also a politician and general of considerable experience.
4. At this stage Spain was divided into the two provinces – Near and Far Spain. Under Augustus, however, Lusitania became a separate provincial entity while *Hispania Ulterior* was renamed Baetica, and northwest Iberia conquered only at this time was then added to the largest Iberian province of *Tarraconensis*.
5. Caesar, *BC* 1.39, claims that his opponents had at their disposal eighty cohorts of mixed infantry and 5000 cavalry. The problem of numbers in detachments described as cohorts in this period of the Roman republic has been discussed (Evans 2013: 172 n. 41). The cohort was clearly of variable size but with less than a half of what came to be the average cohort during the Early Empire, so probably between 200 and 250 soldiers. The lowest figure of 200 still gives a total of 16,000, which seems a realistic number and reflects an army of roughly half citizen troops and half allies, which was often to be seen in the field at this time.
6. From this point the solar calendar date, which was between six and eight weeks out of synchronization with the Roman civic calendar, and which was corrected by Caesar only in 45, will also be indicated.
7. Plutarch (*Caes.* 35.2) claims that Metellus actually barred Caesar from entering the Treasury in person and was hustled away and imprisoned, although later released, after which he left Rome and joined Pompey (Evans 2003: 74–77). The tribunes elected for 49 included Caesar's allies such as C. Scribonius Curio and Marcus Antonius, but there were obviously as many hostile to him among the college of ten.
8. Caesar uses the term *Gallia Ulterior*, which ought to indicate that down to his day the later Roman province of *Gallia Narbonensis* had this other name and that the chief city was Arelate (Arles) not as later Narbo Martius (Narbonne).
9. For the arrangement at Luca see Evans (2003: 87 n. 82).
10. Atia, previously married to C. Octavius, was the mother of Caesar's heir, the emperor Augustus. See Caesar's family tree at end of this chapter.

11. One major absentee was Cicero who considered himself a friend of Caesar but whose political connection with Pompey caused him to join the majority of senators in Greece. Cicero actually distrusted Pompey but also found Caesar's actions unwarranted. Atticus, who was close to both Caesar and Cicero, stayed in Rome but he was not a senator and was evidently wealthy enough to remain above the conflict throughout this period and remain on good terms with all major players.

12. Cato had been made proconsul of Sicily but vacated Syracuse when Caesar occupied southern Italy and went instead to Greece. L. Cornelius Lentulus Crus was one of the consuls in 49 and after Pharsalus fled to Egypt where, like Pompey, he was assassinated.

13. The Via Domitia named after Cn. Domitius Ahenobarbus (cos. 122) initially joined Narbo to Italy, but was extended soon after 100 BC into Iberia to Tarraco and eventually Valentia and the south.

14. The identity of this Fabius, perhaps a Fabius Hadrianus, is a little problematic since more than one senator with this name is active in the 50s. C. Fabius Hadrianus was a praetor in 58 and was probably the son of the praetor of 85/4 who had been an opponent of Sulla in the civil war in 83/2. His political connections made him a likely enough supporter of Caesar and the Fabius in Caesar's account (*BC* 1.37-40) was clearly in a position of some authority being sent first in command of three legions and then evidently assuming charge of three further legions sent by Caesar. An experienced ex-praetor, Hadrianus had been proconsul of Asia in 57 (Evans 2012: 155), would seem to be indicated from the position of seniority and responsibility this person held in the command structure. Moreover, he clearly appears to outrank L. Munatius Plancus (cos. 42) who is described as being in command of two of the legions which were later active around Ilerda (*BC* 1.40). However, a second C. Fabius is attested at this time who was a tribune of the plebs in 55. This Fabius has the same praenomen but can hardly have been the son of a public figure who held the praetorship just three years earlier and so if they are related, and the tribune does not appear in any source with the cognomen 'Hadrianus', then he was perhaps a younger cousin. A Gaius Fabius appears as one of Caesar's legates in the invasion of southern Britain in 54 (*BG.* 5.24) and is usually identified as the tribune of 55 and he reappears frequently in the text. However, it should be noted that the first mention of this Fabius has him in command of a legion and apparently senior in the command structure to Q. Tullius Cicero praetor in 62 and L. Roscius Fabatus, praetor in 49 which probably points to the older of the two Fabii. Fabius the ex-tribune even if a close political ally of Caesar and one with military experience would by then have been only in his early to mid-thirties and would not have been appointed to such a position above other more senior senators. Note that at *BG* 8.54, at the end of Caesar's account this Fabius is in command of four legions about to spend the winter among the Aedui in southern Gaul and he must be the same Fabius who was active in command at Ilerda. Whatever the identity of Gaius Fabius, he is not attested after this campaign and probably died during the course of the civil wars. See Evans (2003: 69 n. 20) where I followed Broughton's identification (1984: 86), but now think that this was probably incorrect and that the Fabius in the campaign to Ilerda was actually the former praetor of 58.

15. L. Cornelius Balbus, consul in 40, was one such friend from Gades who was rewarded for his financial support with Roman citizenship and the consulship. For Balbus' connection with Caesar see Syme (1939: 72). Caesar had also been with the staff of the proconsul C. Antistius Vetus (praetor 70) as his quaestor a posting that was also in *Hispania Ulterior* in about 69 (Syme 1939: 64 n. 5; Broughton 1984: 105–106). Caesar clearly had allies in

the south of Iberia. Caesar will also have inherited ties of patronage from earlier family members such as Gaius and Marcus Marius his uncles (Evans 2008: 77–90).

16. Caesar states that in addition to the numbers he gives (*BC* 1.39) there were also an unspecified number of auxiliary troops from the Aquitani and from other tribes who lived in the Pyrenees.

17. Caesar had been in Rome at the end of January and from there came directly to Arelate. The initial moves around Ilerda would have been in February perhaps early March but not later.

18. A Roman mile is 1500 metres, 1600 yards, hence the bridges were 6 kilometres or 3.7 miles apart.

19. The bridge closest to Ilerda (*BC* 1.40: '*propiore ponte*') seems to be the one that was destroyed by the storm and the enemy commanders became aware that this had happened when the debris came floating past their camp, although this bridge would have been easily in sight from the heights of Ilerda and observable by scouts.

20. Even without a baggage train and enforcing a rigorous daily timetable this distance could not have been covered in much more than forty kilometres a day or roughly two weeks. From Narbonne to Ilerda via Prades is still 370 kilometres (approximately 230 miles) and well over a week's march. Caesar's lightning movements should be seen in the context of the ancient world where movement over long distance tended to be slow and unpredictable.

21. One has to bear in mind that Caesar's own literary works are often the sole evidence for his actions but he certainly appears to have been quite a livewire both in his personal affairs and in his military commands. Everything he did appears to have been rapidly thought out yet usually highly competent and efficient.

22. Afranius would either have taken the auspices, which was an observation of the flight of birds such as eagles, or he could have offered a sacrifice to the gods – cattle or sheep – and then priests known as the *haruspices* would examine the state of the liver of the animal. A deformed or diseased organ would have been pronounced an ill omen and battle delayed until favourable omens were observed.

23. Excavation of a ditch necessarily means that earth must have been piled up unless it was spread out by those troops on duty. This would still have mean that the whole area within the ditch was probably elevated by the material dug out. Caesar unfortunately does not explain how his instructions were carried out.

24. Without a rampart those inside the camp would have been easy target for archers but Afranius again missed an opportunity of making life difficult for Caesar.

25. Caesar uses the Latin *antesignanus* to describe these troops, which would usually mean light armed troops such as archers or slingers and usually allied rather than citizen heavy infantry but here the meaning is more likely to be one or more cohorts of legionaries.

26. Caesar perhaps makes the specific reference to the Lusitani of *Hispania Ulterior* because he was acquainted with them from earlier in his career, but his battle-hardened veterans of the Gallic campaigns, including invasions across the Rhine into Germany and the Channel into Britain could hardly have found such tactics so intimidating. It is probably more likely that the opposition was either too strong or that it was unexpectedly tougher than Caesar had believed it would be.

27. It is worth noting that grain, of any origin, quality or quantity, was the primary foodstuff of armies in antiquity and that the consumption of meat was regarded as being at best

a second rate option. Livestock was, however, used in sacrificial rites which were also a fundamental part of any military engagement.

28. Caesar would surely have been alerted to the movement of perhaps as many as ten thousand men moving from his enemy's camp across the river even if they went under the cover of darkness. Clearly he felt that he was not in a sufficiently strong position to either attack or even impede their progress.

29. The victory may have been rather more dramatic than Caesar recorded since it prompted Afranius, the legate Petreius and other members of their command to send despatches to Rome (*BC* 1.53), where the news was apparently greeted with much enthusiasm and from where the news was also conveyed to Pompey.

30. The *modius* was a measurement of about a peck or 8.8 dry litres. The lack of supply had caused the price of grain to be inflated by fifty times compared to when it was freely available. The time of year coupled with the adverse weather contributed to the extreme shortage.

31. On the use of the coracle by Caesar see Kamm (2006: 107).

32. Caesar uses the same verb for both the initial crossing by means of the newly made boats and later the cavalry (*BC* 1.54–155), but these vessels were simply not suitable for use by men and their horses.

33. Caesar reports an almost immediate engagement between the cavalry and the enemy foragers who were supported by some light armed troops. Caesar's men seized valuable goods and killed a number of the enemy before retreating to the camp 'by the same bridge' (*BC* 1.55). The text here implies that this episode either took place on the Ilerda bank of the Segre and perhaps in the vicinity of the valley of the Cinga or that the transmitted MS is incorrect since Caesar had already bridged the Segre and the camp lay on the opposite bank to Ilerda already.

34. Caesar also mentions that some of the local tribes changed allegiance to him: the Iacetani, Ausetani and Illurgavonenses, all of whom lived around the region drained by the Ebro and Cinga rivers (*BC* 1.60). The Illurgavonenses also provided troops.

35. The precise location of this harbour is disputed. See the map for Octogesa on the likely proposed route of the Pompeian army.

36. Caesar may indicate that the bridge out of Ilerda had also been damaged in the recent storms, although he has not mentioned this before.

37. How Caesar identified the more timid or less physically fit is not disclosed, but he presumably relied on reports from the centurions and military tribunes.

38. Caesar states about the 'ninth hour of the day', roughly late afternoon or early evening in that part of Iberia in early spring.

39. Caesar says '*media circiter nocte*' or about the middle of the night (*BC* 1.66), although probably later than midnight and perhaps close to 3.00 am to allow the troops two to three hours' rapid march before the dawn.

40. Caesar adds some interesting comments about the psychology of marching at night or during the day: that troops in the night were prone to irrational fears, while in the light their sense of duty was reinforced since they actions could be observed by fellow troops.

41. Caesar's *BC* 1.72 is a curious passage in which the writer reveals something perhaps of his inner feelings about war and the carnage this could cause and that it ought to be avoided by a good general. Caesar was not above the ruthless extermination of an enemy as his account of the wars in Gaul clearly indicate, but here his comment reflects a much softer side to his personality.

42. It seems extraordinary that both senior commanders should absent themselves from their camp to supervise construction of defences, but that is what Caesar claims (*BC* 1.73). It may be that one or other of the Pompeian generals actually made the supervision of the defences a pretence for testing the situation to see if a peaceful conclusion could be found.

43. Appian (*B.C.* 2.43) has a more dramatic version in which Petreius kills one of his own officers for fraternizing with the enemy and this may have derived from the account of Asinius Pollio or Livy since it is not in the text of Caesar.

44. Caesar uses the verb '*desero*' or in other words that Petreius did not desert or let go of himself perhaps here meaning that he refused to neglect his obligations as an appointee of Pompey.

45. Afranius won his consulship in 60 with Pompey's support. Pompey had recently returned from Asia where he had favourably concluded the war with Mithridates of Pontus. The popularity he had acquired by ending this long fought war inevitably rubbed off onto his political allies.

46. Caesar (*BC* 1.78) gives a rather curious reason for this paucity of supplies among the auxiliary troops: that they were not accustomed to carrying grain, hence presumably reliant on living off the land. He therefore emphasizes the professionalism of the Roman heavy infantry in comparison to native levies. As Peskett observed (1914: 106) the text at 1.78 has been corrupted since it appears to indicate that the legionaries were ordered to carry twenty-two days' ('*dierum* XXII') supply of grain, which is simply impossible. Half a kilo of grain per day would mean a sack of grain weighing eleven kilos plus equipment and other supplies producing an unlikely load for each soldier. Besides this, the march to Octogesa was not much more than a two–day march if unmolested. Peskett suggested VI, VIII or XII, but perhaps IIII (four) is more likely.

47. The text as it is transmitted at this point, Peskett (1914: 106) is uncertain and seems to suggest that the column was held up by the covering cohorts, which makes little sense and rather it was those in the very end of the column ('*novissimum agmen claudebant*'), invariably the sick and wounded, who were the cause of any delays in the forward movement. It is clear that there are problems with the *MSS* here caused possibly by copyist error and uncertainty about the military terminology.

48. There is probably a deliberate construction in the text here since this section bears a strong resemblance to the plight of the Athenian column, described by Thucydides, trying to find a way out from Syracuse in 413 BC and being forced to change direction by the pursing cavalry, which prevented their enemy from marching to Leontinoi, its preferred objective (Evans, 2013: 75–78).

49. The level space between the camps was therefore about three kilometres (3200 yards).

50. Afranius' son acted as the intermediary again and was retained by Caesar as a hostage to ensure the good behaviour of his enemy.

51. This speech is one of the longest in Caesar's extant corpus of literary composition and displays a certain attachment to philosophical ideas and a wish no doubt to be seen to have risen above the demands of just discussing conventional wisdom regarding warfare.

52. Caesar naturally enough avoids mentioning that the legions that he had been allowed to levy for his Gallic campaigns in 59/8 and later were the same as those that he employed against Pompey and the senate majority.

53. The Varus River or Var describes the lower stretches of the Ebro before it joins the sea.

54. His appointment as legate by Pompey was probably a deliberate move to assuage Caesar's fears of a hostile army on his left flank while campaigning in Gaul. Varro was by some years the eldest of the commanders in the field having been praetor in 74, and if born as early as 116, nearly seventy years of age by the time the Ilerda campaign was fought. He lived on in retirement and literary pursuit down to about 27. It is notable that Varro was assigned to *Hispania Ulterior* with Petreius as his senior officer, and who was probably regarded as more reliable. Meanwhile, Afranius, a close friend to Pompey, was given the more politically sensitive and strategic *Hispania Citerior*.

55. The citizens of Hispalis, modern Seville, clearly had access to a harbour where such construction might be undertaken using the plentiful supplies of local timber from the mountains in the region.

56. Gallonius is described as a Roman *eques* and a close friend of Domitius Ahenobarbus who was then in Massilia. The temple of Hercules was a short distance from the city (Strabo, 3.5.2–3).

57. This reference to a cavalry guard of six hundred appears to be almost the same force that accompanied Caesar from Arelate to Ilerda just five or six weeks earlier. Caesar does not signify which cities were represented but suggests that all sent delegates.

58. Modern Carmona is about thirty-three kilometres from Seville (Hispalis) on the road to Corduba another eighty kilometres north east. Caesar does not detail why the city was stronger than its more famous neighbours but today is situated in the centre of a wine growing area. In antiquity the valley or the Guadalquivir River and adjacent mountains were mined for silver and this must have contributed to the prosperity of the communities there and made them strategically important for the combatants in this latest series of internal wars in the Roman Empire.

59. Caesar says that this legion was raised from the local Roman communities, although he stated earlier that Varro had levied his legions in Iberia.

60. Caesar describes Varro as '*perterritus*' or badly scared even terrified, which is perhaps an exaggeration for the latter will surely have realized that after the surrender of the main army at Ilerda he could do little except for some delaying tactics.

61. Sextus Caesar was only a distant cousin and probably descended from the consuls of the same name of 157 and 91 BC.

62. Lucius Domitius Ahenobarbus had been consul in 54 when he was a vigorous opponent of both Pompey and Caesar. Since then he had made his peace with Pompey, perhaps viewing him as a less deadly threat to the traditional form of government than Caesar's more charismatic and popular political stance.

63. Igilium was close to Cosa in Etruria. Cosanum is perhaps meant to be Cosa itself rather than a town of this name, which was situated in Calabria and too far from the centre of the events.

64. The chronology of the text at 1.34–35 is confusing since Caesar includes both current and past events without linking these in any particular chronological order. The section looks hurried and a little random in the presentation of the material.

65. Massilia was a free city with the treaty of friendship with Rome and therefore lay outside the jurisdiction of the province and its proconsul. It does seem unlikely that the fifteen senior envoys summoned by Caesar at Arelate can have been completely unaware of the course of action about to be undertaken by their sons! The text here should strike the reader as a little forced.

66. The Greek city states of the western Mediterranean invariably occupied coastal land and functioned as harbours or ports through which goods passed from Greece and Ionia to native tribes who in returned exported surplus food. This traffic was the source of great wealth for the Greeks but they often relied on grain supplies from the interior as clearly was the case here.

67. Trebonius, a loyal partisan of Caesar, was rewarded with the consulship in 45 but joined the conspiracy against the dictator. He was assigned the proconsulship of Asia in 44 but was captured and murdered by Dolabella in early 43 BC. Decimus Iunius Brutus Albinus, praetor in 44, was a close friend of Caesar but he too joined the conspiracy against the dictator and was killed soon after the battle of Mutina in 43.

68. The Albici may have been archers but the text suggests that they possessed another skill, therefore perhaps javelin throwers or slingers but not heavy infantry. Caesar cannot, however, resist the temptation of making Domitius look a fool whom he states demanded ('*deposcit*') certain vessels for himself, which he crewed with his own followers including shepherds ('*pastores*') who were slaves. It must mean that Caesar wanted to give the impression that the opposition was really rather slipshod and amateurish.

69. Caesar had employed Brutus as a naval commander in the campaign in Gaul against the Veneti in 56 BC.

70. This probably means that although the ships had been treated with pitch to make them water tight the crews had not had the time to put them through their paces and lose their rough edges.

71. The famous *testudo* or tortoise is one famously pictured in most descriptions of Roman legionary warfare, but can simply mean a covering against missiles aimed from above.

72. The *testudo* is described, *BC* 2.2, as being sixty feet in height, which seems improbably high seeing that the walls were almost certainly less than half that so may indicate that some error has crept into the transmitted text.

73. It is quite possible of course that Trebonius was instructed to pursue the siege to a certain degree but to delay a final push until Caesar was again present in person.

74. Caesar refers, *BC* 2.3, to *naves aeratae* or ships with bronze (beaks) and as such probably describes the trireme rather than one of the larger decked warships. Caesar (*BC* 2.3) has L. but this may be an error in the transmitted text since there are denarii dated to ca. 38 BC with the legend 'Q. Nasidius' (Crawford, 1974: 1.495, no. 483; Broughton, 1984: 3.147), and this Q. Nasidius was a naval commander under Sextus Pompeius at Mylae and Naulochus in 36 (Broughton, 1952: 2.394), and again at Actium serving with Mark Antony. It is just possible, although it seems unlikely given the rarity of the name, that two Nasidii were active in naval commands at the same time.

75. Caesar's text at this point (*BC* 2.4–5) is a little repetitive as if he had used two sources for this information, the second perhaps directly from Trebonius.

76. For the size of Brutus' ship see Lucan (*Pharsalia*, 3.535–7).

77. The total lost or captured looks a little suspicious here since these are the same as in the previous sea battle. One warship is said to have joined Nasidius, another seems to have regained the harbour but where were the rest? This description is not fully satisfactory and again reveals the writer relying on incomplete source material.

78. Nasidius clearly managed to reach Pompey and his squadron either returned immediately to Greece or was later handed over to Caesar when the latter completed his conquest of the Iberian provinces. Caesar released the senior commanders of the armies there and so

very likely would also have allowed Nasidius to go free if he was still in the area at that time.

79. Such written material about military matters need not have circulated that widely but prominent public figures such as Caesar would have received copies. By including this material in his own composition he actually allowed a more widespread dissemination of the knowledge contained in such works.

80. *Musculus* is the word employed by Caesar, which means a 'shed', although there seems to be a great variety of sheds in use in a siege. It was rolled out from the siege tower to the city wall, but Caesar does not explain how a bridge of sixty feet (20 metres) was brought up from ground level unless manufactured in sections that were only joined together just like a pontoon bridge crossing a river.

81. This section could also easily be taken from a manual on sieges for it has all the appearance of advice to the besieged on what action to take, when best to take advantage of the situation when the enemy has relaxed its guard and attention.

82. A garrison of occupying forces numbering perhaps six to eight thousand will have had a crippling effect on the economy and recovery of the city and it was probably several years before it regained its former prosperity.

83. The text of Aeneas Tacticus springs to mind in this context but there were certainly later emulators of this early work on sieges and Vitruvius and others like him will have tackled similar problems in a Roman context.

Chapter 4

1. Sulla emerged victorious from the civil war at the end of 82. Thereafter there was some upheaval in the 40s after Caesar's death – the sieges of Perusia and Mutina – but for the most part Italy experienced nearly one hundred and fifty years of peace.

2. On Tacitus' perceived bias, see Syme (1958: 205). Tacitus is equally hostile to Otho and Vitellius, *Hist.* 1.50: 'Praying for the success of either would be hateful to the gods swearing allegiance to either of them something to hate and that you knew in the war between them he who was the victor would be the worse.' Tacitus' negative portrait of both is particularly emphasized when he claims that some of his sources (*Hist.* 2.37: *invenio apud quosdam auctores*) said that the troops of the opposing armies, so disgusted by the character and actions of Otho and Vitellius – *flagitia ac dedecus* – were tempted to come to some sort of armistice and either settle on one of the contenders or demand that the senate chose a ruler. While the historian considers that some soldiers believed that this could have been a sensible course of action to take, he believes that the troops on the whole were happy with an undisciplined situation that granted them the freedom to kill and plunder at will.

3. Suetonius, *Galba*, 23, states his age at seventy-three and his murder in the seventh month of his rule, Dio, 63.6.6, that he was seventy-two years and twenty-three days old and ruled for nine months.

4. For the date of completion being roughly AD 108 see Syme (1958: 2.465).

5. The number twenty-three is surely an invention since Julius Caesar was supposedly killed with twenty-three stab wounds (Suet. *Iul.* 82.2).

6. The temporal connection is remarkable and related in such a way as to be unique in ancient historical prose. As soon as Otho was hailed emperor in the camp mounted troops immediately set out for the Forum where these killed Galba, Titus Vinius and Cornelius Laco at the Lacus Curtius. Piso was killed at the temple of Vesta about fifty metres away.

It is interesting that Galba was killed at almost precisely the same spot where Otho a short time beforehand had revealed his plot to his few supporters. Galba died with an equally small number of attendants showing the dwindling of support for him.

7. Suetonius (*Vitellius*, 7) claims that his subject was so short of money that he had to leave his family behind in rented accommodation and rent out his own house in order to raise travelling funds and that he was pursued by creditors before he left Italy. This is partly a topical element and owes something to the situation in which Julius Caesar supposedly found himself before he left Rome for his province in Iberia in 61 BC, Suet. *Iul.* 18.1.

8. Hordeonius Flaccus, proconsul of *Germania Superior* appointed by Galba in late 68 is described by Tacitus as 'old and lame' (*Hist.* 1.9) and despised by the troops under his command. He had been consul under Claudius. His uninspiring leadership actually saved his life when his legions refused to swear allegiance to Galba on 1 January 69 since they quickly changed their loyalty to Vitellius who retained Flaccus in his position. He was later murdered at the start of the Batavian rebellion in the following year (*Hist.* 4.36).

9. Tacitus (*Hist.* 1.6) claims that Galba had ordered a massacre of unarmed soldiers and had executed a number of senior public figures associated with Nero's regime or whom he regarded as threats to his own position. He was also heavily influenced by his inner circle, which consisted of two individuals: Titus Vinius and Cornelius Laco according to Tacitus (*Hist.* 1.6), to whom Suetonius (*Galba*) 14.2, adds a third name that of the emperor's freedman Icelus.

10. Tacitus makes the observation at the start of this work (*Hist.* 1.4) and the place of the military in the state but was later to reflect on this at the beginning of his second history the *Annales* (1.1).

11. Cornelius Aquinus is not mentioned again by Tacitus and is not to be found in any of the other writers who cover these events. He may have been relieved of his duties or even died during the winter of AD 68/9.

12. This was an increase of five legions since the Roman defeat by the Germanic chief Arminius in AD 9 at the Teutoberg forest when three legions had been destroyed. Thereafter, Augustus and his immediate successors retained the army at twenty-five legions probably because of financial constraints.

13. Chilver (1979: 18–19). The Rhine and Danube armies were therefore in theory at least of equal strength, reflecting the threat to these regions from outside the empire. Vexilations or contingents from the British garrison were certainly ordered to participate in the invasion while Vitellius was also accompanied from Lugdunum by *Legio* I (*Italica*).

14. There has been much discussion about the numbers serving in the Praetorian Guard and Urban Cohorts at this time. The total is naturally speculative since no unit was ever up to full complement. Ten or twelve Praetorian units and four serving under the Prefect of the City is likely to have produced about 15,000 effective fighting men at any one time. Chilver (1979: 18) considers that Otho had about 31,000 troops stationed in Italy but, in fact, without the *Vigiles* and units assigned to the fleet and a remaining garrison for the city probably rather less than 20,000 overall.

15. It was during an attack by the fleet on Forum Julii (Fréjus) that the mother of Agricola, Tacitus' father-in-law, was killed (Tac. *Agr.* 7).

16. Suedius Clemens, a centurion in the Praetorian Guard (*Hist.* 1.87) may well have died during this campaign or in the course of the following year since he is not recorded again. The use of '*ambitiosus*' implicitly reveals a negative trait in Clemens' character.

17. Tacitus mentions Paulinus and Celsus by name in this respect, but the prominent role initially played by Gallus illustrates that all three were regarded as outstanding generals. The injury later sustained by Gallus prevented actual participation in the first battle at Bedriacum (*Hist.* 2.33).

18. For Paulinus in Britain see, for example, Tacitus (*Agr.* 14–16).

19. Tacitus has much praise for Celsus. There is some doubt about his *praenomen*, which is given as either Publius or Aulus. Tacitus is especially frustrating on the question of full nomenclature, which he often fails to provide. Indeed the historian's own *praenomen* is uncertain either Publius or Gaius. However, it is as well to remember that Tacitus reflects contemporary fashion, which was beginning to discard the limited number of traditional first names for men. It is also noteworthy that in his coverage of the senior figures in this conflict he seldom employs the first name, and where they are known they are found in other texts or on other forms of evidence such as inscriptions.

20. T. Vestricius Spurinna (cos. 73; Cos II 98) became a consular colleague of the emperor Nerva. His recollection of events has probably been incorporated into Tacitus' account and some indication that Tacitus did some groundwork before creating his narrative of the first battle at Bedriacum. For Vestricius Spurinna see Pliny, *Letters*, 3.1, 5.17.

21. This is duly noted by Tacitus (*Hist.* 1.46) concerning the career of Plotius Firmus who seems to have spent most of his career in Rome, and 1.87 specifically of Licinius Proculus who appears to have been essentially an administrator rather than general but a close friend of Otho.

22. Tacitus claims that the overall strategy to force a rapid engagement (*Hist.* 2.33) was supported only by Titianus and Proculus, 'out of ignorant eagerness'.

23. Vitellius also employed a large number of auxiliary troops, particularly cavalry from the Rhineland and Gaul.

24. Vitellius had been in his province barely a month before the troops of the legions stationed there refused to swear their annual oath of allegiance to Galba and acclaimed their commander as emperor.

25. Galba (cos. AD 33) had been proconsul of *Hispania Tarraconensis* since AD 61, but Otho had been the equestrian governor of *Hispania Baetica* for nearly a decade by AD 68, sent there by Nero who had forced him to divorce his wife Poppaea Sabina whom he had married after the murder of his wife Octavia.

26. Both were rewarded with consulships in 69. Valens' *praenomen* is unrecorded but his place of origin seems to have been Anagnia in Latium and hence he was from a family with long citizenship status but not it seems of senatorial background.

27. It is worth noting that the proconsuls of the provinces: Aulus Vitellius and Hordeonius Flaccus in Germany, Pompeius Silvanus in Dalmatia, Tampius Flavianus in Pannonia, Cluvius Rufus and also Galba in Iberia were considerably older and less active than their legionary commanders. These were often little more than thirty years of age and they dominate the account of the civil war in 69. In Germany Fabius Valens and Aulus Caecina, the commander of the Flavian forces, Antonius Primus, Annius Bassus commander of *Legio* XI in Dalmatia, Vipstanus Messalla, the Othonian commanders Annius Gallus, Marius Celsus, Vestricius Spurinna.

28. In AD 68–69 Primus must have been an ex-praetor and was granted consular dignity by the senate in December 69 but no official consulship is otherwise recorded and he was clearly mistrusted by the Flavian emperors, although he appears to have been alive in the 80s.

29. Suetonius (*Vitellius*, 3.2) gives his birthdate as AD 15 in the consulships of Drusus Caesar, son of the emperor Tiberius and C. Norbanus Flaccus. Hordeonius Flaccus was consul in 47, a year before Vitellius, but was probably born much earlier. Vitellius' powerful background would have made an early consulship predictable but Flaccus is not known to have belonged to a senatorial family and therefore is likely to have been closer to forty years of age as consul, and in his 60s at his appointment, which would also fit the description of this figure by Tacitus.

30. *Legio* XXI Rapax was stationed at Vindonissa and while Caecina's command is not recorded by Tacitus since this legion was later under Caecina's direct command in the advance from the Rhine, it does suggest that he had already been its legionary legate.

31. Vitellius' bid for power had already been reported to Galba by probably 10 January, which had forced on the emperor the choice of a successor, not a tried and tested military figure but the member of a longstanding senatorial family. Piso was an unrealistic choice in the circumstances and while his good moral stature clearly fitted with Galba's own outlook on public life, his lack of public visibility especially among the Praetorian Guard, which had been offended by the new emperor, quickly fanned the flame of conspiracy against him.

32. Tacitus is a little unfair here and his bias is rather obvious for Vitellius must already have been on the march in as little as two weeks after his acclamation as emperor.

33. The name is either connected with Peninus, a local deity coupled with Jupiter, or possibly with 'Punic' and the route taken by Hannibal in his invasion of Italy in 218 BC.

34. Vindonissa (Windisch) lay within the territory of the Helvetii and 400 kilometres from Cremona via the modern route through Lugano and Milan. It is 375 kilometres from Windisch to the Great St Bernard Pass not far from Aosta (Augusta Praetoria) in the Po Valley It is, however, possible that Caecina began his march much further north from Moguntiacum (Mainz), which is 660 kilometres from Aosta. Rather less than 400 kilometres would take an army with its supply train about two weeks to march in good weather conditions and more than three weeks for the longer distance from Mainz. Tacitus' terse coverage of Caecina's advance suggests the shorter route and fair weather.

35. If these auxiliary troops had marched west from Rhaetia then it may indicate that Caecina's advance was in a southeasterly direction.

36. Tacitus clearly exaggerates since the attack on the Helvetii may have been premeditated but was not drawn out over a long period of time. The tribal leaders would have needed several weeks to organize a full levy of their people and this clearly did not occur hence the battle was fought by a relatively small percentage of the total Helvetian population.

37. Auxiliary troops were often named after their place of origin but this seems an exception. See Chilver (1979: 132–133) for its name deriving from Gaius Silius, proconsul of Upper Germany between AD 14 and 21. See Damon (2003: 241) for a modern discussion of the ala's history. Silius committed suicide after being accused of corruption during his provincial command. That a cavalry unit should have been created by Silius and retained his name after his disgrace seems rather unlikely and so the name of the ala may, in fact, be associated with some tract of land near the Rhine if these cavalrymen were indeed of Germanic ethnicity as the epigraphic evidence might suggest.

38. Vitellius had been proconsul in Africa perhaps about 57 or 58, which was probably his sole duty in the provinces. That he had made such an impact on these professional soldiers sounds doubtful except that he seems to have been easygoing and affable. That these

soldiers remembered him with esteem takes some believing and that they were probably swayed more by the attractions of rewards if Vitellius was successful against Otho.

39. The Iberian troops are described as Lusitani from southern Spain, while the cavalry appears to have originated in Petra southern Jordan, although both units may well have served along the Rhine long enough to take in local recruits.

40. It should be noted that Caesar was not above employing violence in order to ensure good behaviour where needed.

41. From Metz to Nancy is just forty kilometres (25 miles) and probably two days' march for 40,000 men and supply train and in the winter.

42. Valens will have halted at the main urban centres of the Lingones at modern-day Langres and Dijon.

43. The Batavians rebelled against Roman rule just a year later.

44. Tacitus (*Hist*. 1.64) gives no indication of his fate and he figures nowhere else.

45. Tacitus (*Hist*. 1.66) notes that the Vocontian town of Lacus Augusti (Luc-en-Diois) only avoided sack by offering a bribe to Valens, The historian implies that this was a regular feature of the advance and that Valens made a fortune out of threatening communities along the way.

46. Tacitus is quite specific here: three cohorts of Praetorians and one thousand former rowers from the fleet in the newly enlisted legion. This must be information he acquired personally from Spurinna.

47. See Chilver (1979: 187–188) for the possible whereabouts of Gallus at this stage.

48. There has been some discussion of the actual whereabouts of Bedriacum and whether it is modern Calvatone or Tornata, which is 38 kilometres from Cremona and three kilometres further south (Chilver, 1979: 188). The identification does not affect the discussion of the battle itself and the two villages are so close together in more or less the same geographical setting.

49. The place named 'Castores' (Tac. *Hist*. 2.24). For the name see also Chilver (1979: 191; Irvine, 1952: 157).

50. Tacitus claims that there was also a reserve of a thousand infantry and cavalry that perhaps accompanied one or other of the senior officers.

51. Paulinus had clearly become more responsible with old age for his proconsulship in Britain is not remembered for its caution or inactivity.

52. Tacitus (*Hist*. 2.25) provides the interesting information that a son of Antiochus, the client king of Commagene, was wounded in this encounter and was probably in command of a troop of cavalry.

53. Tacitus may have obtained this opinion from someone who had fought in either of the invading armies. Neither Valens nor Caecina can have been the historian's source since the former died later in 69 and the latter about a decade later. On the face of it, it would appear to be rivalry between armies composed of separate commands drawn from different regions: Caecina's army from Upper Germany, Valens' army from Lower Germany.

54. Tacitus must have seen Caecina in the 70s for he gives or just conceivably was provided with these details, which allow something of the personality of this figure to emerge, but there is only vague denigration reserved for Valens and as a result his character is less well formed in the text.

55. Tacitus believed that Otho was south of the Po and therefore at or near Brixellum, but Gallus had been in Bedriacum and although he was present with the emperor it is not clear if some of his force had remained north of the river.

56. Suetonius (*Vesp.* 6) has the Fourteenth Legion not yet at Aquileia a distance of nearly three hundred kilometres (180 miles).

57. The sources for Otho's death refer to him being alone in his room except for Plutarch who mentions tents, although this is perhaps because he associates the emperor as being a Hellenistic monarch on campaign. Alexander the Great, for example, is often described as occupying his tent.

58. Tacitus was probably acquainted with Celsus but there may have been others at this meeting, including the historian's friend Vestricius Spurinna who would have remembered the reservations expressed or opinion only voiced later by certain participants.

59. However, Otho for all his popularity had no military experience and those of his troops who considered him a worthy general were surely deluded.

60. The rapid fashion in which the generals of Otho sought terms after the defeat surely indicates some prior intrigue and that Vitellius took no action against any of the major players except for Martius Macer who was denied the consulship (*Hist.* 2.71).

61. Tacitus (*Hist.* 2.34) seems to be suggesting that at the time the level of the river was rising – '*augescente flumine*' – possibly an indication of the spring melt or some recent heavy rain.

62. Otho's army was mainly on the north bank of the Po already so cannot have witnessed the episode from the south bank.

63. A small garrison remained to guard the town.

64. However, Paulinus' argument for delaying battle, discussed earlier, made good logistical and tactical sense but Tacitus seems prepared to ignore this.

65. The point is made by Tacitus but difficult to believe since at that time of the year there was not yet great heat in the sun and the historian has already mentioned that the Po was flowing at high levels. The question of supplies may be one invented to illustrate incompetence by the command.

66. For the Arda as the destination of Otho's army see Irvine (1952: 162).

67. Compare Caesar's use of camps for precisely this reason in his constant harassment of the Pompeian army at Ilerda, above Chapter 3.

68. He is described as a 'Numidian' and such cavalry were apparently either employed in such duties (Irvine, 1952: 163), or it was a technical term for official despatch riders (Chilver, 1979: 205).

69. This may not be entirely accurate. Compare the presence of a senior commander on what seem to be routine duties to that of Afranius and Petreius – above Chapter 3 – in their ill-fated march from Ilerda.

70. Tacitus is plainly reporting from a source that provided no precise information such as that of the elder Pliny or recollections by one of the participants in the battle.

71. Drawing lots for their order in the line was probably not a regular military process and again may be an indication of the chaos of civil war. Tacitus makes no comment but a strong and popular general such as Caesar would have wanted his troops to be in the order he wanted not left to the chances of a lottery.

72. '*Rapax*' is Latin for furious, which sums up this unit's reputation, while '*Adiutrix*' or the 'reserve legion' was also an apt description.

73. The *Alaudae* or 'Larks' was another legion with a fierce reputation. Chilver (1979: 207) considers that *Legio* XIII was by then at full strength or about four thousand infantry, the vexillation from *Legio* XIV, if this is accurate information, can only have just arrived in the area.

74. Paulinus, Proculus, Titianus and Celsus all made their escape in different directions. Unfortunately, Tacitus gives no indication of where these senior figures were at the start of the engagement. It is possible that Paulinus and Proculus were together in the centre and Titianus and Celsus on the right wing, both of which suffered fewer casualties than the left wing.

75. Sabinus, nephew of the Prefect of the City, received the consulship later in the year from Vitellius so some understanding between the two may be assumed.

76. Plutarch states that the Praetorian Guard, with no battle experience, were the first to break (*Otho*, 12.9).

77. See Chilver (1979: 208) who found this figure impossible but forgot about the baggage train.

78. Plutarch (*Otho*, 13.6–12) claims that Gallus and Celsus were sent to Valens and Caecina and that Caecina at least returned with them. Celsus played a prominent role in the new peace and like Flavius Sabinus was made consul by Vitellius. Suetonius and Proculus were at some other place of refuge since they met Vitellius separately later in the month. Titianus was at the camp near Bedriacum but played no role in the negotiations but was also treated well by Vitellius.

79. Some of these were witnessed by Plutarch in his visit there several years later (*Otho*, 14.2).

80. For Otho's heroic suicide see, for example, Ash (1999: 90): 'Tacitus' characterization of Otho is usually called inconsistent because the emperor's noble suicide seems too sudden a reversal of his previous personality. Yet from an early point, Tacitus foreshadows Otho's glorious death'. Cf. *Hist.* 1.21: 'a spirited man should die for a reason.' 'Tacitus somehow saw the noble suicide as an isolated event that was inexplicable in the light of Otho's past conduct,' (Ash 1999: 94); cf. 96: 'heroic suicide.'

81. Plutarch (*Otho*, 4.5–6) describes him the equal of Vitellius in vice and misconduct, which might suggest intelligence; Suetonius (*Otho*, 12.2) also considered him hardly a paragon of virtue but that does not preclude some medical know-how.

82. Vitellius carried a knife as one of his emblems of office, which he tried to surrender to the consul when he first thought of abdication.

83. The younger Cato had a reputation for heavy drinking and a foul temper, and Plutarch also he claims he was partly deaf (*Cat. Min.* 63.5).

84. The biography of the younger Cato is divided into eighty-three sections while the life of Otho, an earlier composition, amounts to just eighteen. The main source is likely to have been Livy and possibly Asinius Pollio who was no admirer of Caesar.

85. Suetonius (*Nero*, 67.3) adds the detail that the poison Nero had earlier obtained in the event of precisely such an eventuality was stolen when his palace was ransacked by its servants just before he quit the city.

86. The history of Byzantine John Zonaras written in the 12 century AD reproduces Dio's composition for Roman history down to the death of Alexander Severus in 235. John Xiphilinus wrote his epitome of Roman history covering the late Roman Republic down to AD 235 with some breaks and also used Dio's work about a century earlier than Zonaras.

87. Murison (1999: 65) considers that Martial viewed 'Otho's suicide admiringly and from a solidly Roman perspective', whatever that may mean. Ash (1999: 85) sees a stronger link between Otho and Cato and that in death the former 'aligns ... with the Stoic hero'. On the whole Ash (88–89) considers Tacitus' treatment of Otho rather more sympathetic than hostile.

88. No source except Martial links Otho with Cato. Tacitus had the opportunity but uses the comparison elsewhere (*Hist*. 4.8) in a reported speech by Eprius Marcellus who accused Helvidius Priscus of trying to emulate Cato and Brutus. Helvidius did indeed commit suicide and so Tacitus' comments reflect something of hindsight. Suetonius refers to Cato only in the lives of Caesar and Augustus. Neither Plutarch nor Dio mentions Cato in this context. Plutarch's lack of interest considering his detailed coverage of Cato's death is suggestive.

89. Tacitus (*Hist* 2.57) claims that Vitellius had been marching only for a few days when he was informed of the victory over Otho. This would have placed him in mid-April still in Lower Germany or possibly in the Upper Saône Valley, down which he afterwards sailed probably by barge (*Hist*. 2.59).

90. The new Praetorian Prefects were Publilius Sabinus and Julius Priscus, both experienced military men. The former was the nominee of Caecina, the latter of Valens (*Hist*. 2.92). Valens and Caecina retained the real power in the city.

91. Marius Celsus was consul later in 69.

92. *Legio* VII and *Legio* VIII reached only Aquileia before being ordered to return to their former camps in Moesia (Tac. *Hist*. 2.85).

93. Other troops are said to have been encouraged to retire or resign from the legions

94. There is no mention of the rebuilding of the burned amphitheatre at Placentia. Perhaps its support for Otho's cause meant that it was penalized by being denied access to state funds. Vitellius' generosity was certainly partial and granted on a whim.

95. Martius Macer was not allowed to take up the consulship designated for him later in 69 since he had been prominent in his support of Otho, but he may have died in the recent battle. Two other senators were also affected by the changes to the consulships of 69 made by Vitellius: Valerius Marinus and Pedanius Costa. Tacitus (*Hist*. 2.71) states that the former had his consulship delayed, while the latter was penalized for his friendship with Verginius Rufus.

96. Vespasian was acclaimed emperor by the legions of Egypt on 1 July, the legions of Judaea and Syria on 3 July and most the eastern provinces by 15 July, while Vespasian's accession was dated from 1 July 69. Vitellius had barely arrived in Rome but he had been recognized as emperor by delegates from the East after Bedriacum. Vitellius reappointed Flavius Sabinus who had been Prefect of the City under Nero between 56 and 68 and again under Otho. Sabinus had been proconsul of Moesia, between 49 and 56. He was some years older than his brother Vespasian and although well respected Tacitus clearly regarded him as ineffectual especially in any crisis (*Hist*. 3.73).

97. Cluvius Rufus was appointed by Galba in 68 and switched his allegiance to Vitellius rather than Otho since he was isolated from Italy and the forces at his disposal were far less than those in the Rhine army. Besides, he had been consul before AD 41, and like Hordeonius Flaccus in Germany, was elderly with little or no military experience.

98. Tacitus states that the legions that accompanied Vitellius to Rome had enjoyed a lengthy break in their duties but that the delights of the city had softened them physically and the lack of discipline since Bedriacum had made them difficult to command effectively. Tacitus (*Hist*. 2.94–97) writes of four months of inactivity from May to September during which time Vitellius had indulged every whim of his troops and condoned or ignored corrupt government by his inner circle of advisers.

99. Born perhaps as early as AD 20 and evidently a former praetor but who had been fined for forging wills (*de falsis*) and debarred from the senate. Tacitus (*Hist*. 2.86) states that he

had regained his place and seniority under Galba, and as a result was ignored by Otho, but used the unstable environment of mid-69 to again achieve prominence.

100. Cornelius Fuscus procurator of either Pannonia or Dalmatia, Tacitus is unclear on this issue (*Hist* 2.86). Although his office is not attested he must have served under Vespasian in some equestrian capacity, and eventually became Prefect of the Praetorian Guard between 81 and 86 under Domitian. One of the earliest and most active of the Flavian supporters, he worked alongside Antonius Primus. Unlike Primus who never obtained a position of trust under those whom he had championed, Fuscus was clearly close to the new imperial dynasty.

101. Tacitus gives the legionary legate of the 13th Legion as Vedius Aquila, the commander of the 7th Legion was Primus. This legion was perhaps under the command of Minicius Justus who was relieved of his duties for being too strict and his replacement is not named (Tac. *Hist.* 3.7). Primus by general consent was now acting as the senior general for the campaign.

102. Among the subordinate commanders Tacitus draws attention to one in particular as not only energetic and competent but who was also honourable, indeed just about the only person of any dignity in the campaign leading to the second battle at Bedriacum. This was Lucius Vipstanus Messalla, a tribune or junior officer in *Legio* VII (Claudia), which was stationed in Moesia, and which he commanded at Hostilia. He later achieved some fame as an orator and although he seems to have died young and perhaps did not achieve high office was known to the historian who may have remembered this figure's recollections about his own role in the Flavian invasion in 69.

103. The legion was usually accompanied by auxiliary forces and Tacitus states that some of the Danubian tribes had offered, or been bribed to give, assistance.

104. Both Flavianus and Saturninus had been consuls several years before probably during the rule of Claudius, 41–54, and hence would have expected to hold a more senior position than Primus who had yet to be consul. They were also likely to be more cautious in their attitude to the plans proposed by Primus who was undoubtedly the main beneficiary of their removal. He might well have argued that these older senators might not be as firm in their loyalty to Vespasian, but having broken with Vitellius they had actually committed themselves fully to the rebellion. Pompeius Silvanus, proconsul of Dalmatia, and Tampius Flavianus, proconsul of Pannonia, are both described as 'old and wealthy' by Tacitus (*Hist.* 2.86). Flavianus could not have been as inconsequential as is claimed, however, if he obtained a second consulship in 76 during Vespasian's rule. Aponius Saturninus was proconsul of Moesia.

105. Bassus later had the command of the fleets restored to him. Tacitus (*Hist.* 4.3) notes that Bassus was in command of a cavalry cohort at the end of 69 in Rome.

106. Tacitus (*Hist.* 3.14) mentions just one legion by name but later (3.21) notes that detachments from five other legions had been present at Hostilia, and there must also have been auxiliary troops.

107. Wellesley (1972: 97; 1975: 140) and Murison (1999: 100–101) note that there was a lunar eclipse on the night of 18 October, probably as the Vitellian forces at Hostilia were about to leave their camp or preparing to do so and which could have been construed an ill omen. Tacitus makes no comment about this celestial event, which appears in Dio's history (Book 65/4.11.1). It was either noted by the historian accessing a different source to Tacitus or the latter's source or just possibly was noted by Xiphilinus who preserved Dio's narrative in his epitome. Lunar eclipses were quite common events but generally

caused greater anxiety than solar eclipses since they were not understood. For the lunar eclipse of 413 BC, which delayed the withdrawal of the Athenians from Syracuse with disastrous effect on the besieging army, see Evans (2013).

108. Tacitus (*Hist.* 3.15) suggests that there were also rumours of substantial reinforcements from Germany. These were more probably rumours than fact since the Rhine army had been drained of manpower and Vitellius had taken no action to recruit any of the Germanic tribes. Still, such tales would have been useful to restore discipline in Primus' legions which had only recently mutinied.

109. It is also possible that this fight continued for some time or indeed is overplayed in Tacitus' narrative, which is vague and almost rhetorical.

110. This can only mean that the troops at Hostilia had abandoned much of their equipment and baggage train, and probably left wounded and sick comrades behind. To cover so much in so little time suggests a flight rather than a measured advance.

111. In passing, Tacitus (*Hist.* 3.21) notes that some of Otho's Praetorian Guard were positioned next to Legion III and had probably recently re-joined the Flavian ranks. How many is not specified and it is likely that these numbered only a few hundred former imperial guardsmen.

112. Messalla is mentioned by name later in the narrative (*Hist.* 3.28), but also the history of the elder Pliny.

113. Sunset in Rome on 24 October is approximately 18.15, Cremona some five hundred and twenty kilometres (320 miles) north would have seen the dusk at about 18.00, assuming that it was a clear evening.

114. A source celebrating the achievements of Varus can been assumed here, either in an earlier history consulted by Tacitus or one of the legate's fellow commanders, again perhaps Messalla.

115. It should be noted that the description of this night battle is very similar in its detail to that given by Thucydides to the fight on Epipolai at Syracuse in August 413 BC where the Athenian attackers led by Demosthenes were routed for almost exactly the same impact of the moonlight on proceedings. Tacitus almost certainly reworked some of these elements into his text for Bedriacum.

116. Sunrise would have been a little before 7.00 am.

117. Mucianus was expected, although in fact he was delayed by hostilities along the Danube frontier, which he dealt with first before continuing on to Italy arriving in December.

118. Tacitus (*Hist.* 3.26) gives an account of a son killing his father in this battle and states that families and friends were pitted against each in other in these two armies. The account is most likely fanciful, although said to have been told by Vipstanus Messalla since the two armies had quite different origins and few of the legions drew their recruits from the same source. This is actually a topical element that is used to dramatize the effects of civil war or *stasis* in a body of citizens; it has a long pedigree in historical writing and is meant to invoke pathos among its audience or readers.

119. There was some uncertainty about who suggested the sack of Cremona; Messalla claimed it was the imperial freedman Hormus, whereas in Pliny's history it was Antonius Primus. It was common practice to blame freedmen for excesses in public life and so the promise probably emanated originally from Primus, as Pliny is said to have written.

120. Caecina was immediately sent under guard to Vespasian who treated him with courtesy but, like Primus, he was never trusted by the new regime.

121. There were plainly two versions of Valens' attitude and movements after the departure of Caecina. The first, *Hist*. 2.100, has a much more concerned Valens writing to his officers and instructing them to await his arrival, the second, 3.36 and 3.40, and the one that is the dominant feature in the narrative is far more negative. Tacitus' use of two sources again here seems to be indicated.

122. These cohorts were perhaps drawn from Rome's urban units, which were less loyal to Vitellius (Wellesley, 1964: 170; 1972) 133), but then from what did Flavius Sabinus draw his support when he rebelled from Vitellius in December? It is therefore more likely that all these units were auxiliary troops.

123. These troops were quickly besieged by Cornelius Fuscus and the Ravenna fleet and probably surrendered very soon, although Tacitus is not specific (*Hist*. 3.42).

124. Marius Maturus is said to have taken the oath of loyalty of Vespasian shortly afterwards (*Hist*. 3.43).

125. Valens was murdered in early December (Tac. *Hist*. 3.62), at Urvinum, close to where the Vitellian troops had been kept under guard since their defeat at Cremona.

126. Both Tacitus (*Hist*. 2.86) and Suetonius (*Vitellius*, 18) give Vitellius' age as fifty-seven, although he was probably born in AD 15, hence fifty-four at his death.

Bibliography

The ancient sources

Ammianus Marcellinus, *The Later Roman Empire (AD 354–378)*, trans. W. Hamilton, Harmondsworth 1986.

Appian, *Roman History*, 4 volumes, trans. H. White, Harvard 1913.

Aristotle, *Politics*, trans. B. Jowett, New York 1943.

Caesar, *The Gallic War*, trans. H.J. Edwards, Harvard 1917.

Caesar, *The Gallic War*, trans. C. Hammond, Oxford 1996.

Caesar, *The Civil Wars*, trans. A.G. Peskett, Harvard 1914.

Caesar, *The Civil War*, trans. J.F. Gardner, Harmondsworth 1967.

Cassius Dio, *Dio's Roman History*, 9 volumes, trans. E. Cary, Harvard 1925.

Diodorus, *Diodorus of Sicily*, 12 volumes, trans. C.H. Oldfather, Harvard 1946–52.

Herodotus, *Herodoti Historiae*, 2 volumes, ed. C. Hude, Oxford 1927.

Herodotus, *The Histories*, trans. A. De Sélincourt, notes by J. Marincola, Harmondsworth 1996.

Herodotus, *The History*, trans. D. Greene, Chicago 1987.

Homer, *The Iliad*, trans. R. Fagles, New York 1990.

Lucan, *Pharsalia*, trans. R. Graves, Harmondsworth 1956.

Plutarch, *Plutarch's Lives*, 11 volumes, trans. B. Perrin, Harvard 1914.

Plutarch, *Fall of the Roman Republic*, trans. R. Warner, Harmondsworth 1958.

Polybius, *The Histories*, 6 volumes, trans. W.R. Paton, Harvard 1922–1926.

Sallust, Sallust, trans. J.C. Rolfe, Harvard 1921.

Strabo, The Geography of Strabo, 3 volumes, trans. H.C. Hamilton and W. Falconer, London 1889.

Strabo, The Geography of Strabo, 8 volumes, trans. H.L. Jones, Harvard 1917–28.

Suetonius, *Suetonius*, 2 volumes, trans. J.C. Rolfe, Harvard 1913–1914.

Tacitus, *Cornelii Taciti Historiarum Libri*, ed. C.D. Fisher, Oxford 1911.

Tacitus, *Tacitus in Five Volumes*, trans. C.H. Moore, Harvard 1925.

Tacitus, *The Agricola and the Germania*, trans. H. Mattingly, Harmondsworth 1948.

Tacitus, *Histories Books I & II*, ed. A.L. Irvine, London 1952.

Tacitus, *The Histories*, trans. K. Wellesley, Harmondsworth 1964.

Tacitus, *The Annals of Imperial Rome*, trans. M. Grant, Harmondsworth 1996.

Tacitus, *Histories Book I*, ed. C. Damon, Cambridge 2003.

Tacitus, *Histories Book II*, ed. R. Ash, Cambridge 2007.

Tacitus, *The Histories Book III*, ed. K. Wellesley, Sydney 1972.

Xenophon, *A History of My Times (Hellenica)*, trans. R. Warner, Harmondsworth 1966.

Modern works

Akurgal, E., *Ancient Civilisations and Ruins of Turkey*, Istanbul 1978.

Ash, R., *Ordering Anarchy: Armies and Leaders in Tacitus' Histories*, London 1999.

Austin, M.M., 'Greek Tyrants and the Persians, 546–479 B.C.', *Classical Quarterly* 40 (1990) 289–306.

Barker, P.F., *From the Scamander to Syracuse: Studies in Ancient Logistics*, MA dissertation, University of South Africa, Pretoria 2005.

Barker, P.F., 'Where was *Leuce Acte*?', (unpublished paper), University of South Africa, Pretoria 2007.

Bingham, S., *The Praetorian Guard: A History of Rome's Elite Special Forces*, London 2013.

Brogan, O., *Roman Gaul*, London 1953.

Broughton, T.R.S., *The Magistrates of the Roman Republic*, Volumes 1–2, New York 1951–52; Volume 3, Atlanta 1984.

Brown, T.S., *Timaeus of Tauromenium*, Berkeley 1958.

Brunt, P.A., 'The Revolt of Vindex and the fall of Nero', *Latomus* 18 (1959) 531–559.

Brunt, P.A., 'Tacitus on the Batavian Revolt', *Latomus* 19 (1960) 494–517.

Burn, A.R., *Persia and the Greeks*, London 1984.

Cairns, F. and E. Fantham (ed.), *Caesar against Liberty: Perspectives on his Autocracy*, Cambridge 2003.

Chilver, G.E.F., *A Historical Commentary on Tacitus' 'Histories' I and II*, Oxford 1979.

Chilver, G.E.F., *A Historical Commentary on Tacitus' 'Histories' IV and V*, revised, G.B. Townend, Oxford 1985.

Crawford, M.H., *Roman Republican Coinage*, 2 volumes, Cambridge 1974.

Durrell, L., *Caesar's Vast Ghost: Aspects of Provence*, London 1990.

Evans, R., *Questioning Reputations*, Pretoria 2003.

Evans, R., 'Gaius and Marcus Marius in Iberia and Gaul: Family Affairs and Provincial Clients', *Acta Classica*, 50 (2008) 77–90.

Evans, R., *Pergamum: Beyond Hellenistic Kingship*, London 2012.

Evans, R., *Fields of Death: Retracing Ancient Battlefields*, Barnsley 2013.

Fisher, N.R.E., *Hybris: A Study in the Values of Honour and Shame in Ancient Greece*, Warminster 1992.

Gelzer, M., *Caesar: Politician and Statesman*, trans. P. Needham, Oxford 1969.

Gottschalk, H.B., *Heraclides of Pontus*, Oxford 1980.

Gray, G.B., and M. Cary, 'The Reign of Darius' in, *The Cambridge Ancient History*, Volume 4, 1st edition, Cambridge 1926, pp.173–228.

Hammond, N.G.L., *A History of Greece to 322 B.C.*, Oxford 1959.

Hammond, N.G.L. and L.J. Roseman, 'The Construction of Xerxes' Bridge over the Hellespont'. *JHS* 116 (1996) 88–107.

Hornblower, S., *Thucydides and Pindar: Historical Narrative and the World of Epinikian Poetry*, Oxford 2004.

Hornblower, S., *A Commentary on Thucydides, Volume III: Books 5.25–8.109*, Oxford 2008.

How, W.W. and J. Wells, *A Commentary on Herodotus*, Oxford 1912.

Johnston, S.I., *Ancient Greek Divination*, Oxford 2008.

Jones, A.H.M., *The Cities of the Eastern Roman Provinces*, Oxford 1937.

Joseph, T., 'Review of F.S. L'Hoir, *Tragedy, Rhetoric and the Historiography of Tacitus' Annales*, Ann Arbor 2006' in *Bryn Mawr Classical Review* 2006.12.27.

Kamm, A., *Julius Caesar: A Life*, Abingdon 2006.

Lazenby, J.F., *The Defence of Greece: 490–479 B.C.*, Warminster 1993.

MacKendrick, P., *Roman France*, London 1971.

Meiggs, R., *The Athenian Empire*, Oxford 1972.

Meiggs, R. and D. Lewis, *A Selection of Greek Historical Inscriptions to the End of the Fifth Century B.C.*, Oxford 1969.

Munro, J.A.R., 'Marathon' in *The Cambridge Ancient History*, Volume 4, 1st edition, Cambridge 1926, pp.229–252.

Murison, C.L., *Rebellion and Reconstruction: Galba to Domitian. An Historical Commentary on Cassius Dio's 'Roman History', Books 64–67 (A.D. 68–96)*, Atlanta 1999.

Neils, J., *The Parthenon Frieze*, Cambridge 2001.

Pearson, L., *The Greek Historians of the West: Timaeus and His Predecessors*, Atlanta 1987.

Pelling, C., *Literary Texts and the Greek Historian*, London 2000.

Ramsey, J.T., 'Review of S. Bartsch, *Actors in the Audience*, Harvard 1994' in *Bryn Mawr Classical Review* 95.03.02.

Richardson, J.S., *Appian: Wars of the Romans in Iberia*, Warminster 2000.

Rivet, A.L.F., *Gallia Narbonensis: Southern Gaul in Roman Times*, London 1988.

Robinson, E.W., *The First Democracies: Early Popular Government outside Athens, Historia Einzelschriften –107*, Stuttgart 1997.

Sabin, P., 'The Mechanics of Battle in the Second Punic War', in *The Second Punic War: A Reappraisal*, eds. T. Cornell, B. Rankov and P. Sabin, London 1996, pp.59–79.

Sacks, K.S., *Diodorus Siculus and the First Century*, Princeton 1990.

Shochat, Y., 'Tacitus' Attitude to Otho', *Latomus* 40 (1981) 365–377.

Syme, R., *The Roman Revolution*, Oxford 1939.

Syme, R., *Tacitus*, 2 volumes, Oxford 1958.

Talbert, R.J.A., *Atlas of Classical History*, London 1985.

Tarn, W.W., *Alexander the Great: Volume II Sources and Studies*, Cambridge 1948.

Thompson, W.E., 'The Stasis at Corinth', *Studi Italiani di Filologia Classica* 79 (1986) 155–171.

Tod, M.N., *Greek Historical Inscriptions*, Volume I, Oxford 1946.

Trundle, M., *Greek Mercenaries: From the Late Archaic Period to Alexander*, Abingdon 2004.

Van Wees, H., *Greek Warfare: Myths and Realities*, London 2004.

Wallinga, H.T., *Xerxes' Greek Adventure: The Naval Perspective*, Leiden 2005.

Wellesley, K., *The Long Year A.D. 69*, London 1975.

Wyke M. (ed.), *Julius Caesar in Western Culture*, Oxford 2006.

Index